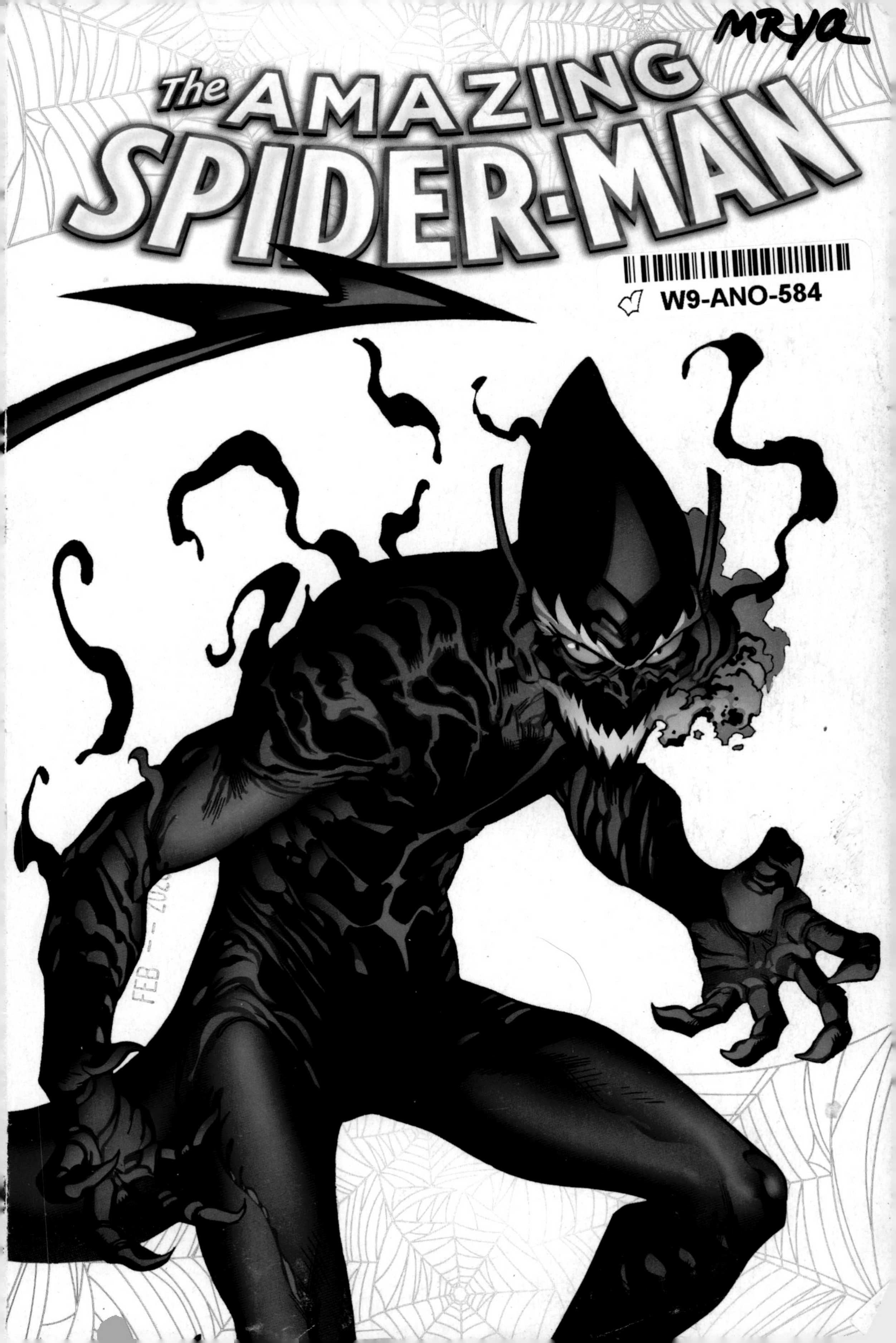
The AMAZING
SPIDER-MAN

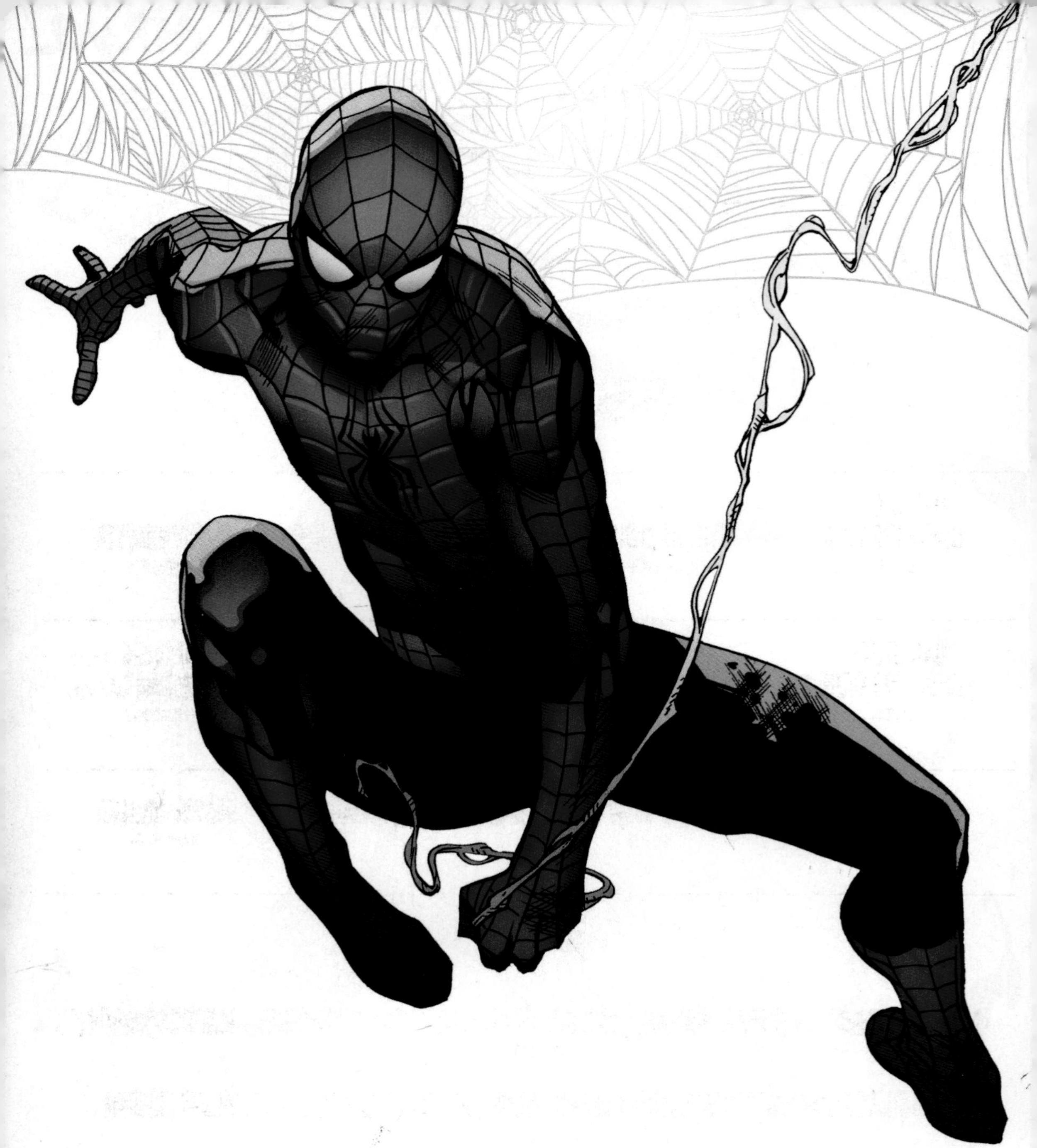

COLLECTION EDITOR **JENNIFER GRÜNWALD**
ASSISTANT EDITOR **CAITLIN O'CONNELL**
ASSOCIATE MANAGING EDITOR **KATERI WOODY**
EDITOR, SPECIAL PROJECTS **MARK D. BEAZLEY**

VP PRODUCTION & SPECIAL PROJECTS **JEFF YOUNGQUIST**
SVP PRINT, SALES & MARKETING **DAVID GABRIEL**
BOOK DESIGNER **ADAM DEL RE**

EDITOR IN CHIEF **C.B. CEBULSKI**
CHIEF CREATIVE OFFICER **JOE QUESADA**
PRESIDENT **DAN BUCKLEY**
EXECUTIVE PRODUCER **ALAN FINE**

AMAZING SPIDER-MAN: RED GOBLIN. Contains material originally published in magazine form as AMAZING SPIDER-MAN #794-801. First printing 2019. ISBN 978-1-302-92042-5. Published by MARVEL WORLDWIDE, INC., a subsidiary of MARVEL ENTERTAINMENT, LLC. OFFICE OF PUBLICATION: 135 West 50th Street, New York, NY 10020. **Printed in the U.S.A.** DAN BUCKLEY, President, Marvel Entertainment; JOHN NEE, Publisher; JOE QUESADA, Chief Creative Officer; TOM BREVOORT, SVP of Publishing; DAVID BOGART, Associate Publisher & SVP of Talent Affairs; DAVID GABRIEL, SVP of Sales & Marketing, Publishing; JEFF YOUNGQUIST, VP of Production & Special Projects; DAN CARR, Executive Director of Publishing Technology; ALEX MORALES, Director of Publishing Operations; DAN EDINGTON, Managing Editor; SUSAN CRESPI, Production Manager; STAN LEE, Chairman Emeritus. For information regarding advertising in Marvel Comics or on Marvel.com, please contact Vit DeBellis, Custom Solutions & Integrated Advertising Manager, at vdebellis@marvel.com. For Marvel subscription inquiries, please call 888-511-5480. **Manufactured between 9/6/2019 and 10/8/2019 by LSC COMMUNICATIONS INC., KENDALLVILLE, IN, USA.**

10 9 8 7 6 5 4 3 2 1

The AMAZING SPIDER-MAN

RED GOBLIN

--- ISSUE #794 ---

**DAN SLOTT &
CHRISTOS GAGE**
WRITERS

STUART IMMONEN
PENCILER

WADE VON GRAWBADGER
INKER

MARTE GRACIA
COLOR ARTIST

--- ISSUES #795-796 ---

**DAN SLOTT &
CHRISTOS GAGE**
WRITERS

MIKE HAWTHORNE
PENCILER

TERRY PALLOT WITH
CAM SMITH (#796)
INKERS

MARTE GRACIA (#795) &
ERICK ARCINIEGA (#796)
COLOR ARTISTS

--- ISSUES #797-799 ---

DAN SLOTT
WRITER

STUART IMMONEN
PENCILER

WADE VON GRAWBADGER
INKER

MARTE GRACIA
COLOR ARTIST

--- ISSUE #800 ---

DAN SLOTT
WRITER

NICK BRADSHAW, HUMBERTO RAMOS, GIUSEPPE CAMUNCOLI, STUART IMMONEN & MARCOS MARTIN
PENCILERS

NICK BRADSHAW, VICTOR OLAZABA, CAM SMITH, WADE VON GRAWBADGER & MARCOS MARTIN
INKERS

EDGAR DELGADO, JAVA TARTAGLIA, MARTE GRACIA & MUNTSA VICENTE
COLOR ARTISTS

--- ISSUE #801 ---

DAN SLOTT
WRITER

MARCOS MARTIN
ARTIST

MUNTSA VICENTE
COLOR ARTIST

VC's JOE CARAMAGNA
LETTERER

ALEX ROSS
COVER ART

ALLISON STOCK, TOM GRONEMAN & KATHLEEN WISNESKI
ASSISTANT EDITORS

NICK LOWE WITH **DEVIN LEWIS**
EDITORS

SPIDER-MAN CREATED BY
STAN LEE & STEVE DITKO

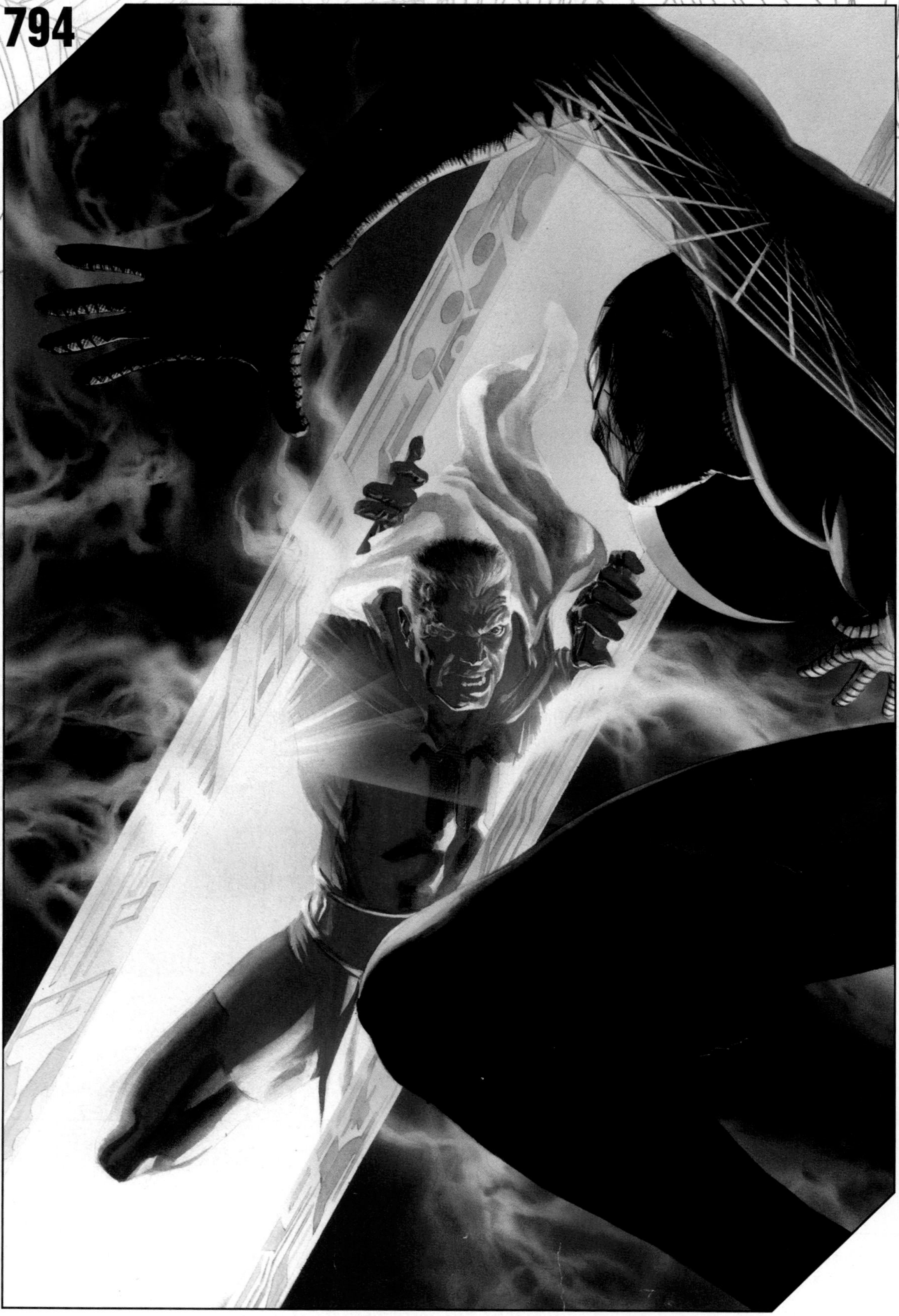

THREAT LEVEL: RED PART ONE "LAST CHANCE"

WHEN PETER PARKER WAS BITTEN BY A RADIOACTIVE SPIDER, HE GAINED THE PROPORTIONAL SPEED, STRENGTH AND AGILITY OF A SPIDER; ADHESIVE FINGERTIPS AND TOES; AND THE UNIQUE PRECOGNITIVE AWARENESS OF DANGER CALLED "SPIDER-SENSE"! AFTER LEARNING THAT WITH GREAT POWER THERE MUST ALSO COME GREAT RESPONSIBILITY, HE BECAME THE CRIME-FIGHTING SUPER HERO CALLED...

the AMAZING SPIDER-MAN

Since the downfall of Parker Industries, dejected and penniless former C.E.O. *PETER PARKER* has been crashing on the couch of *BOBBI MORSE* A.K.A. *MOCKINGBIRD*, with little to keep him happy save for his patrols as *THE AMAZING SPIDER-MAN*.

Almost exactly one year has passed since Spider-Man battled the Zodiac terrorist organization and its leader, *SCORPIO*. After obtaining the *ZODIAC KEY, Scorpio* used its power to unlock a gateway into the Zodiac Dimension, which granted him all knowledge of everything that would occur within the next year.

Spider-Man foiled the villain's plans to use this knowledge for evil and sealed Scorpio inside the mysterious dimension itself, buying the world precious time before the gateway would open once more 365 days later...TODAY!

PETER PARKER, A.K.A. THE AMAZING SPIDER-MAN

MOCKINGBIRD

MAX MODELL

SCORPIO

ANNA MARIA MARCONI

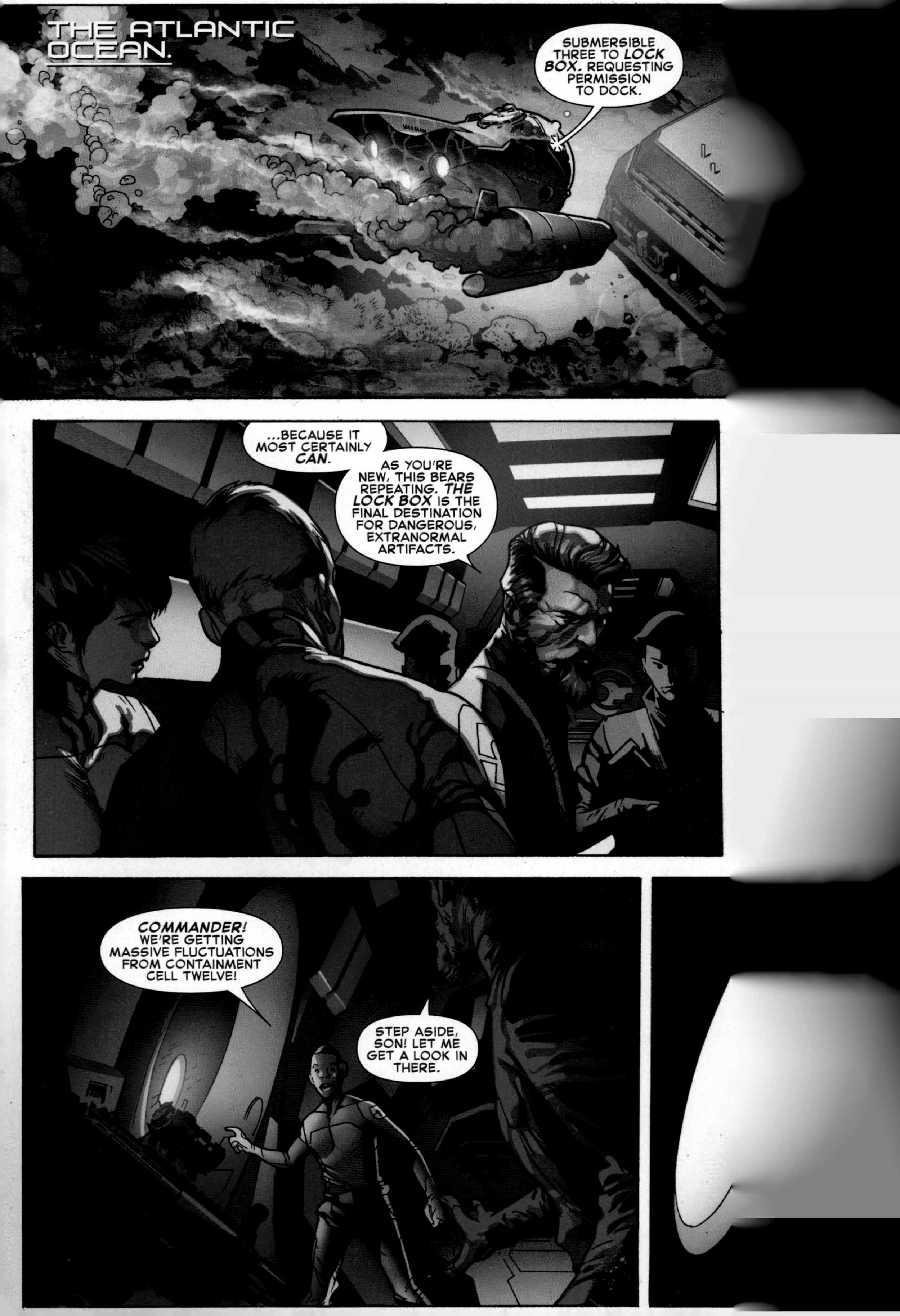
THE ATLANTIC OCEAN.
SUBMERSIBLE THREE TO LOCK BOX. REQUESTING PERMISSION TO DOCK.
...BECAUSE IT MOST CERTAINLY CAN.
AS YOU'RE NEW, THIS BEARS REPEATING. THE LOCK BOX IS THE FINAL DESTINATION FOR DANGEROUS, EXTRANORMAL ARTIFACTS.
COMMANDER! WE'RE GETTING MASSIVE FLUCTUATIONS FROM CONTAINMENT CELL TWELVE!
STEP ASIDE, SON! LET ME GET A LOOK IN THERE.

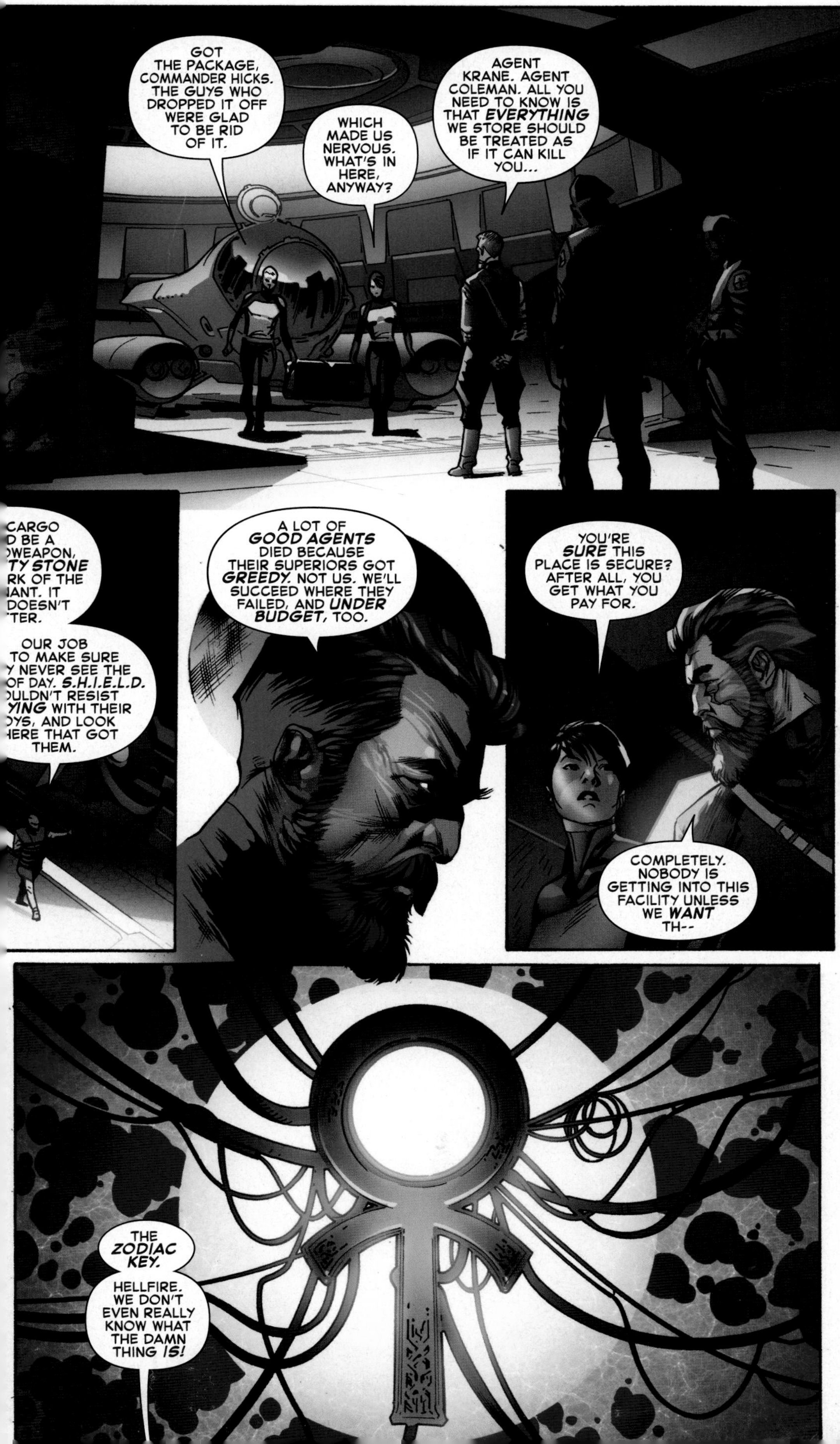
GOT THE PACKAGE, COMMANDER HICKS. THE GUYS WHO DROPPED IT OFF WERE GLAD TO BE RID OF IT.
WHICH MADE US NERVOUS. WHAT'S IN HERE, ANYWAY?
AGENT KRANE. AGENT COLEMAN. ALL YOU NEED TO KNOW IS THAT EVERYTHING WE STORE SHOULD BE TREATED AS IF IT CAN KILL YOU...
CARGO D BE A OWEAPON, TY STONE RK OF THE NANT. IT DOESN'T TTER.
OUR JOB TO MAKE SURE Y NEVER SEE THE OF DAY. S.H.I.E.L.D. OULDN'T RESIST YING WITH THEIR OYS, AND LOOK HERE THAT GOT THEM.
A LOT OF GOOD AGENTS DIED BECAUSE THEIR SUPERIORS GOT GREEDY. NOT US. WE'LL SUCCEED WHERE THEY FAILED, AND UNDER BUDGET, TOO.
YOU'RE SURE THIS PLACE IS SECURE? AFTER ALL, YOU GET WHAT YOU PAY FOR.
COMPLETELY. NOBODY IS GETTING INTO THIS FACILITY UNLESS WE WANT TH--
THE ZODIAC KEY.
HELLFIRE. WE DON'T EVEN REALLY KNOW WHAT THE DAMN THING IS!

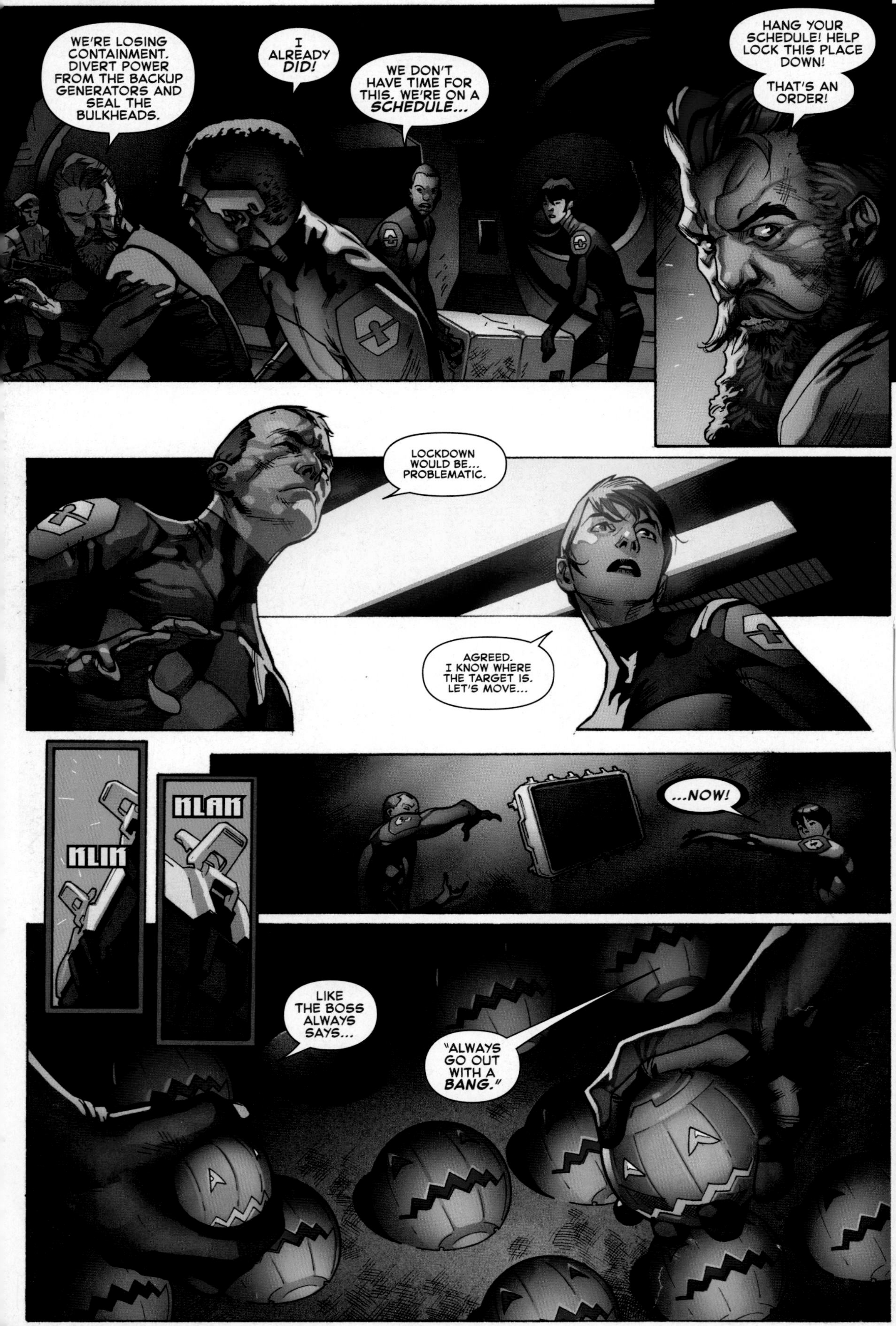
WE'RE LOSING CONTAINMENT. DIVERT POWER FROM THE BACKUP GENERATORS AND SEAL THE BULKHEADS.
I ALREADY DID!
WE DON'T HAVE TIME FOR THIS. WE'RE ON A SCHEDULE...
HANG YOUR SCHEDULE! HELP LOCK THIS PLACE DOWN!
THAT'S AN ORDER!
LOCKDOWN WOULD BE... PROBLEMATIC.
AGREED. I KNOW WHERE THE TARGET IS. LET'S MOVE...
KLIK
KLAK
...NOW!
LIKE THE BOSS ALWAYS SAYS...
"ALWAYS GO OUT WITH A BANG."

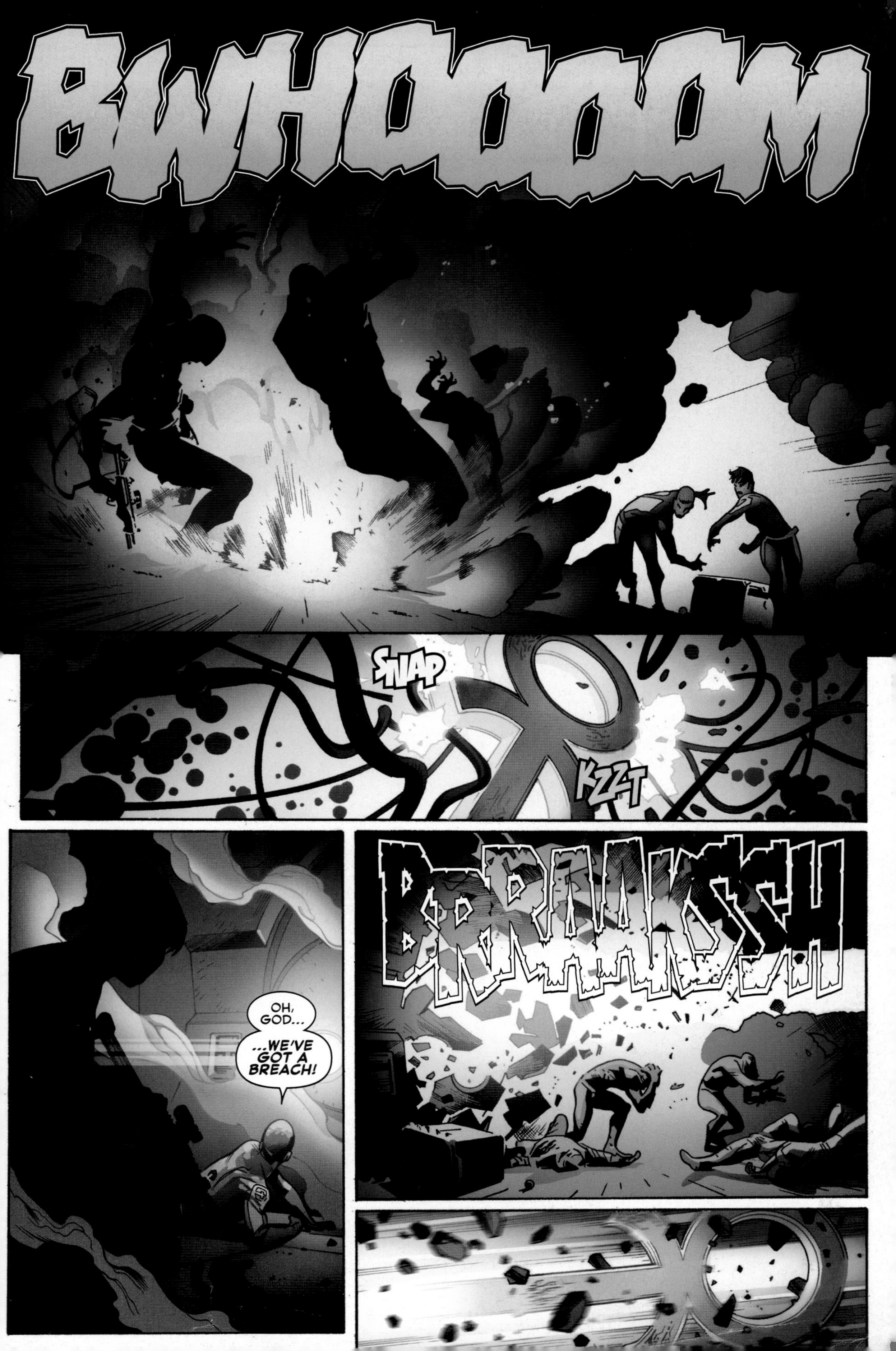
BWHOOOOM
SNAP
KZZT
OH, GOD...
...WE'VE GOT A BREACH!
BRRAAKSSH

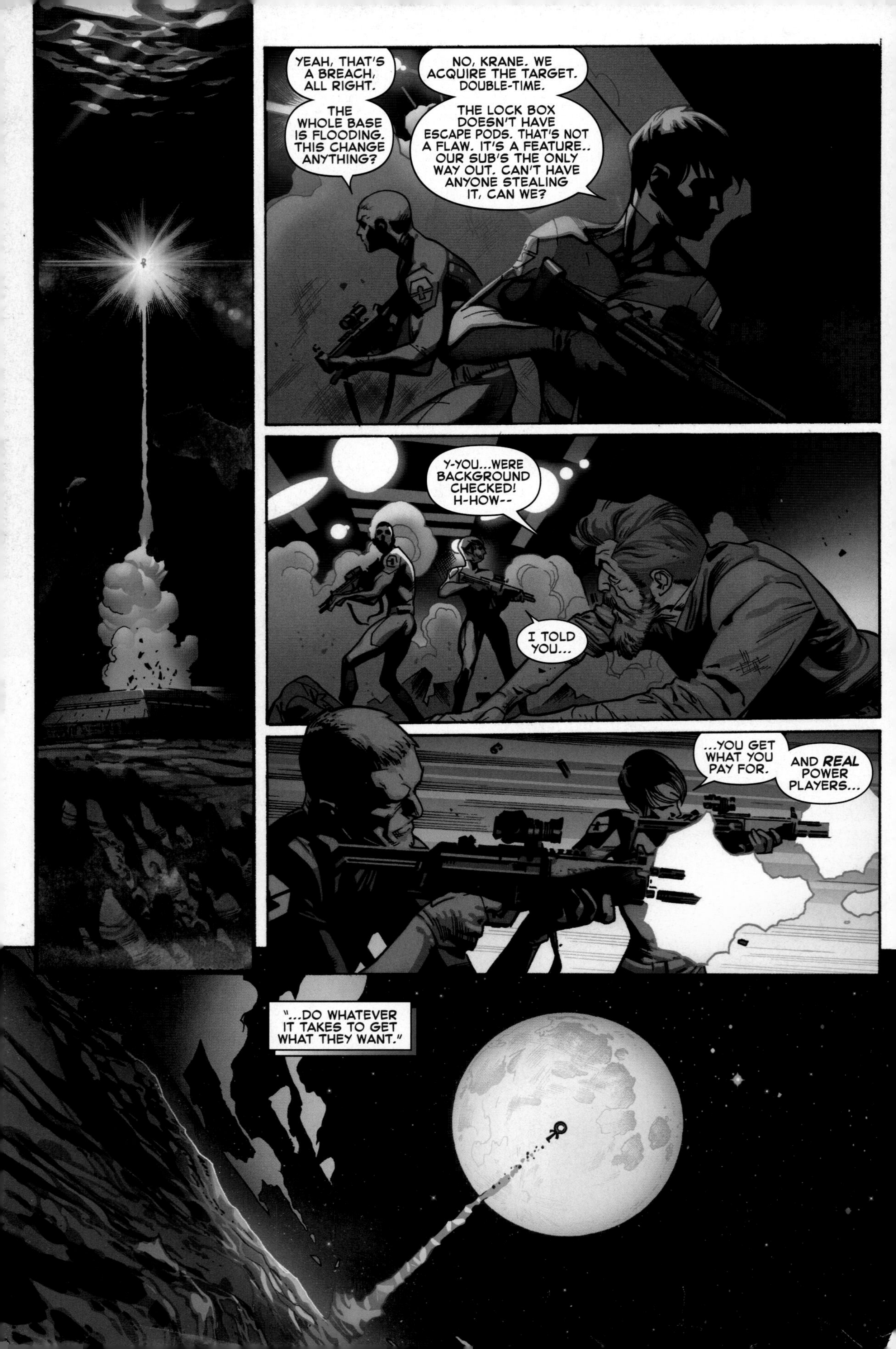
YEAH, THAT'S A BREACH, ALL RIGHT.
THE WHOLE BASE IS FLOODING. THIS CHANGE ANYTHING?
NO, KRANE. WE ACQUIRE THE TARGET. DOUBLE-TIME.
THE LOCK BOX DOESN'T HAVE ESCAPE PODS. THAT'S NOT A FLAW. IT'S A FEATURE.. OUR SUB'S THE ONLY WAY OUT. CAN'T HAVE ANYONE STEALING IT, CAN WE?
Y-YOU...WERE BACKGROUND CHECKED! H-HOW--
I TOLD YOU...
...YOU GET WHAT YOU PAY FOR.
AND REAL POWER PLAYERS...
"...DO WHATEVER IT TAKES TO GET WHAT THEY WANT."

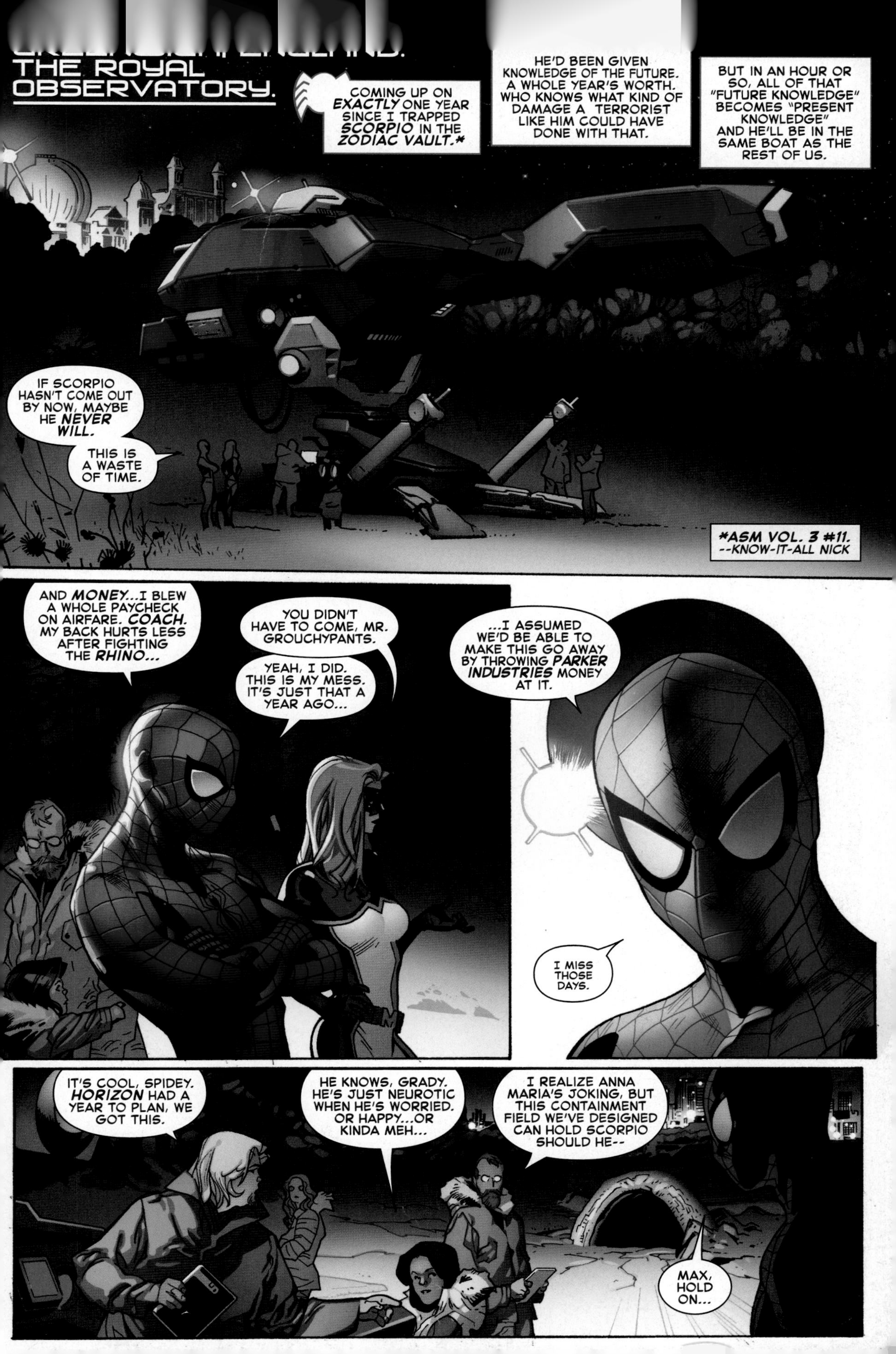
THE ROYAL OBSERVATORY.
COMING UP ON EXACTLY ONE YEAR SINCE I TRAPPED SCORPIO IN THE ZODIAC VAULT.*
HE'D BEEN GIVEN KNOWLEDGE OF THE FUTURE. A WHOLE YEAR'S WORTH. WHO KNOWS WHAT KIND OF DAMAGE A TERRORIST LIKE HIM COULD HAVE DONE WITH THAT.
BUT IN AN HOUR OR SO, ALL OF THAT "FUTURE KNOWLEDGE" BECOMES "PRESENT KNOWLEDGE" AND HE'LL BE IN THE SAME BOAT AS THE REST OF US.
IF SCORPIO HASN'T COME OUT BY NOW, MAYBE HE NEVER WILL.
THIS IS A WASTE OF TIME.
*ASM VOL. 3 #11. --KNOW-IT-ALL NICK
AND MONEY...I BLEW A WHOLE PAYCHECK ON AIRFARE. COACH. MY BACK HURTS LESS AFTER FIGHTING THE RHINO...
YOU DIDN'T HAVE TO COME, MR. GROUCHYPANTS.
YEAH, I DID. THIS IS MY MESS. IT'S JUST THAT A YEAR AGO...
...I ASSUMED WE'D BE ABLE TO MAKE THIS GO AWAY BY THROWING PARKER INDUSTRIES MONEY AT IT.
I MISS THOSE DAYS.
IT'S COOL, SPIDEY. HORIZON HAD A YEAR TO PLAN, WE GOT THIS.
HE KNOWS, GRADY. HE'S JUST NEUROTIC WHEN HE'S WORRIED. OR HAPPY...OR KINDA MEH...
I REALIZE ANNA MARIA'S JOKING, BUT THIS CONTAINMENT FIELD WE'VE DESIGNED CAN HOLD SCORPIO SHOULD HE--
MAX, HOLD ON...

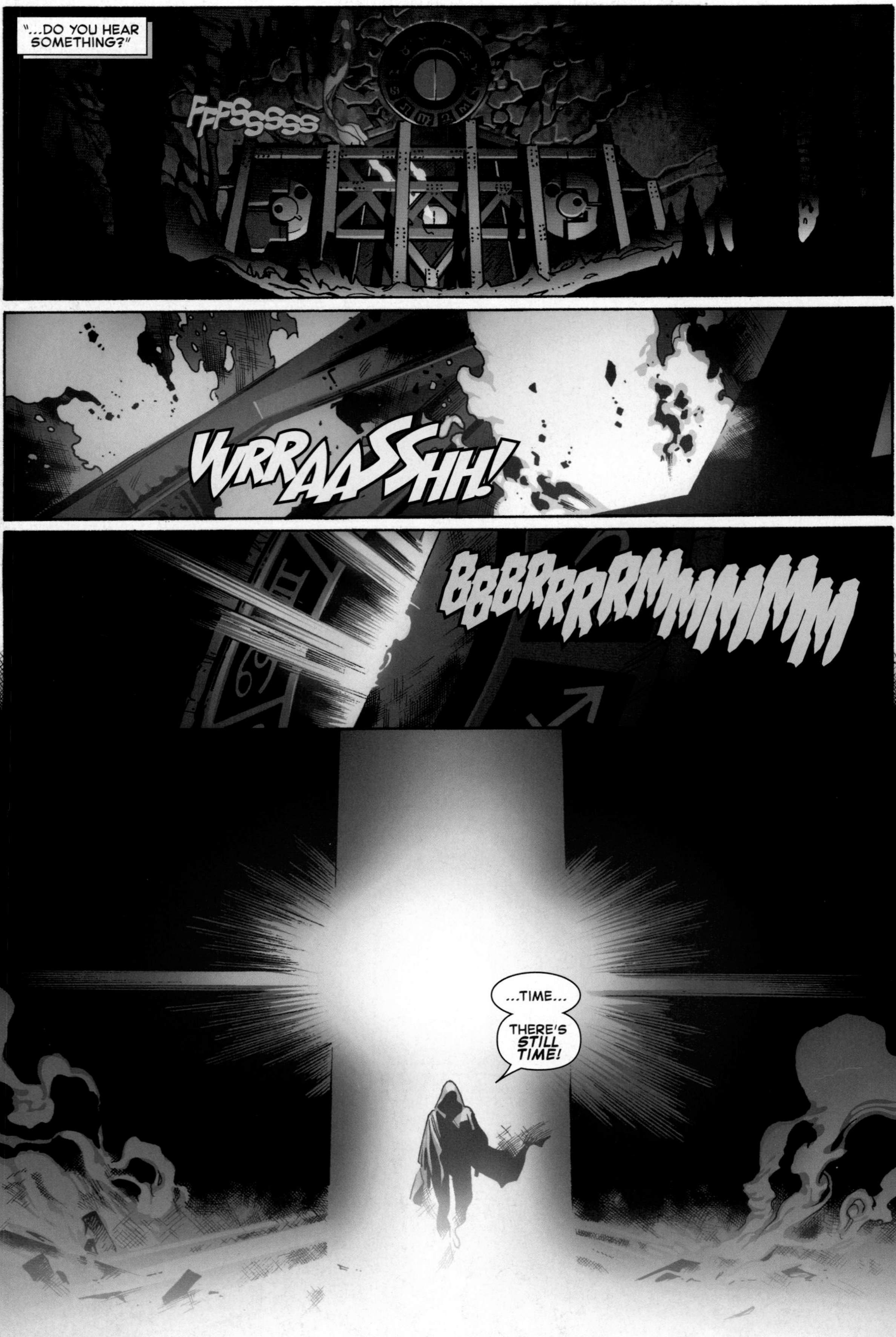
"...DO YOU HEAR SOMETHING?"
FFFSSSSSS
VURRAASSHH!
BBBRRRRMMMMMMM
...TIME...
THERE'S STILL TIME!

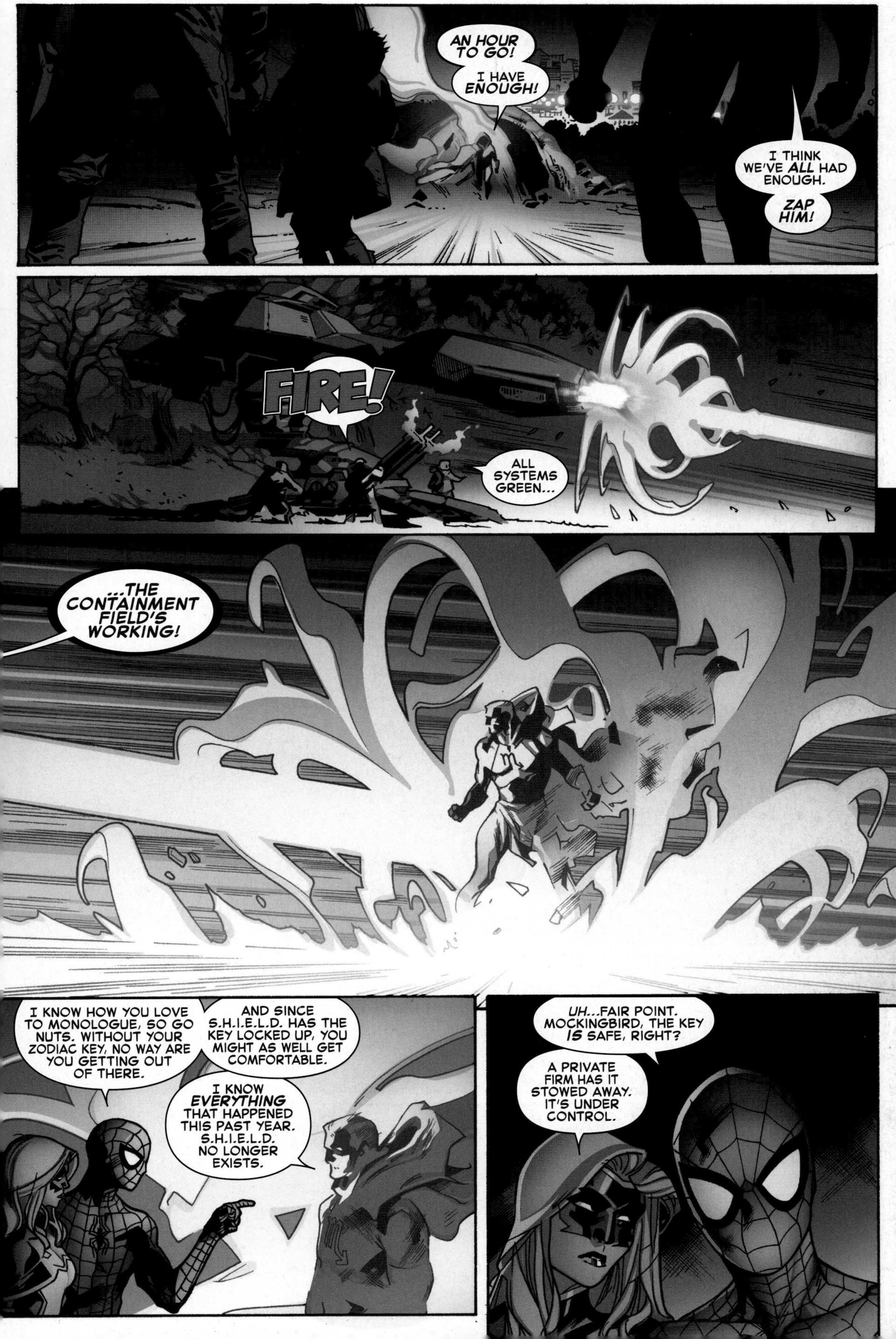
AN HOUR TO GO!
I HAVE ENOUGH!
I THINK WE'VE ALL HAD ENOUGH.
ZAP HIM!
FIRE!
ALL SYSTEMS GREEN...
...THE CONTAINMENT FIELD'S WORKING!
I KNOW HOW YOU LOVE TO MONOLOGUE, SO GO NUTS. WITHOUT YOUR ZODIAC KEY, NO WAY ARE YOU GETTING OUT OF THERE.
AND SINCE S.H.I.E.L.D. HAS THE KEY LOCKED UP, YOU MIGHT AS WELL GET COMFORTABLE.
I KNOW EVERYTHING THAT HAPPENED THIS PAST YEAR. S.H.I.E.L.D. NO LONGER EXISTS.
UH...FAIR POINT. MOCKINGBIRD, THE KEY IS SAFE, RIGHT?
A PRIVATE FIRM HAS IT STOWED AWAY. IT'S UNDER CONTROL.

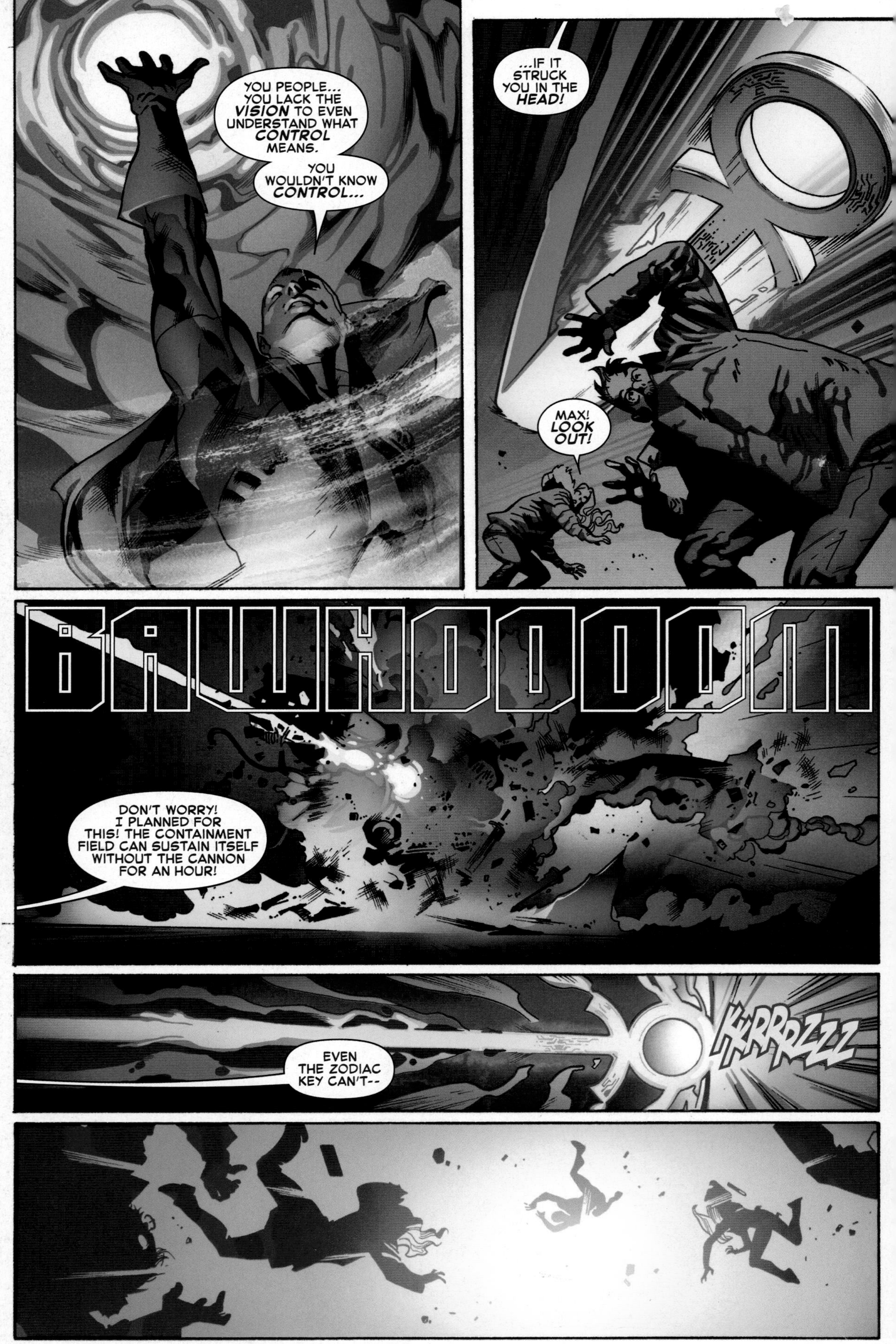
YOU PEOPLE... YOU LACK THE VISION TO EVEN UNDERSTAND WHAT CONTROL MEANS.
YOU WOULDN'T KNOW CONTROL...
...IF IT STRUCK YOU IN THE HEAD!
MAX! LOOK OUT!
BAWHOOOOM
DON'T WORRY! I PLANNED FOR THIS! THE CONTAINMENT FIELD CAN SUSTAIN ITSELF WITHOUT THE CANNON FOR AN HOUR!
KRRRZZZ
EVEN THE ZODIAC KEY CAN'T--

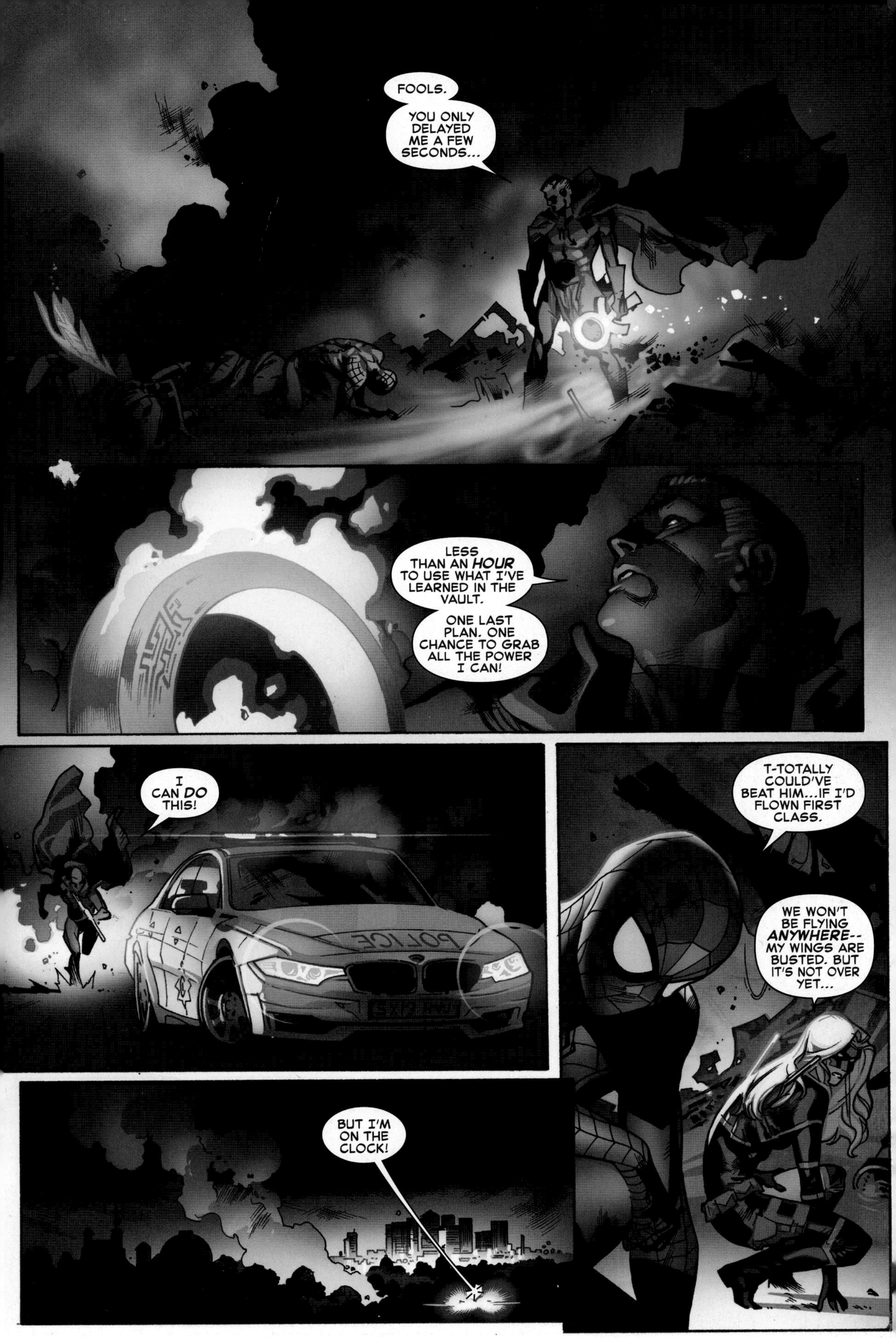

FOOLS.
YOU ONLY DELAYED ME A FEW SECONDS...
LESS THAN AN *HOUR* TO USE WHAT I'VE LEARNED IN THE VAULT.
ONE LAST PLAN. ONE CHANCE TO GRAB ALL THE POWER I CAN!
I CAN *DO* THIS!
POLICE
BUT I'M ON THE CLOCK!
T-TOTALLY COULD'VE BEAT HIM...IF I'D FLOWN FIRST CLASS.
WE WON'T BE FLYING *ANYWHERE*-- MY WINGS ARE BUSTED. BUT IT'S NOT OVER YET...

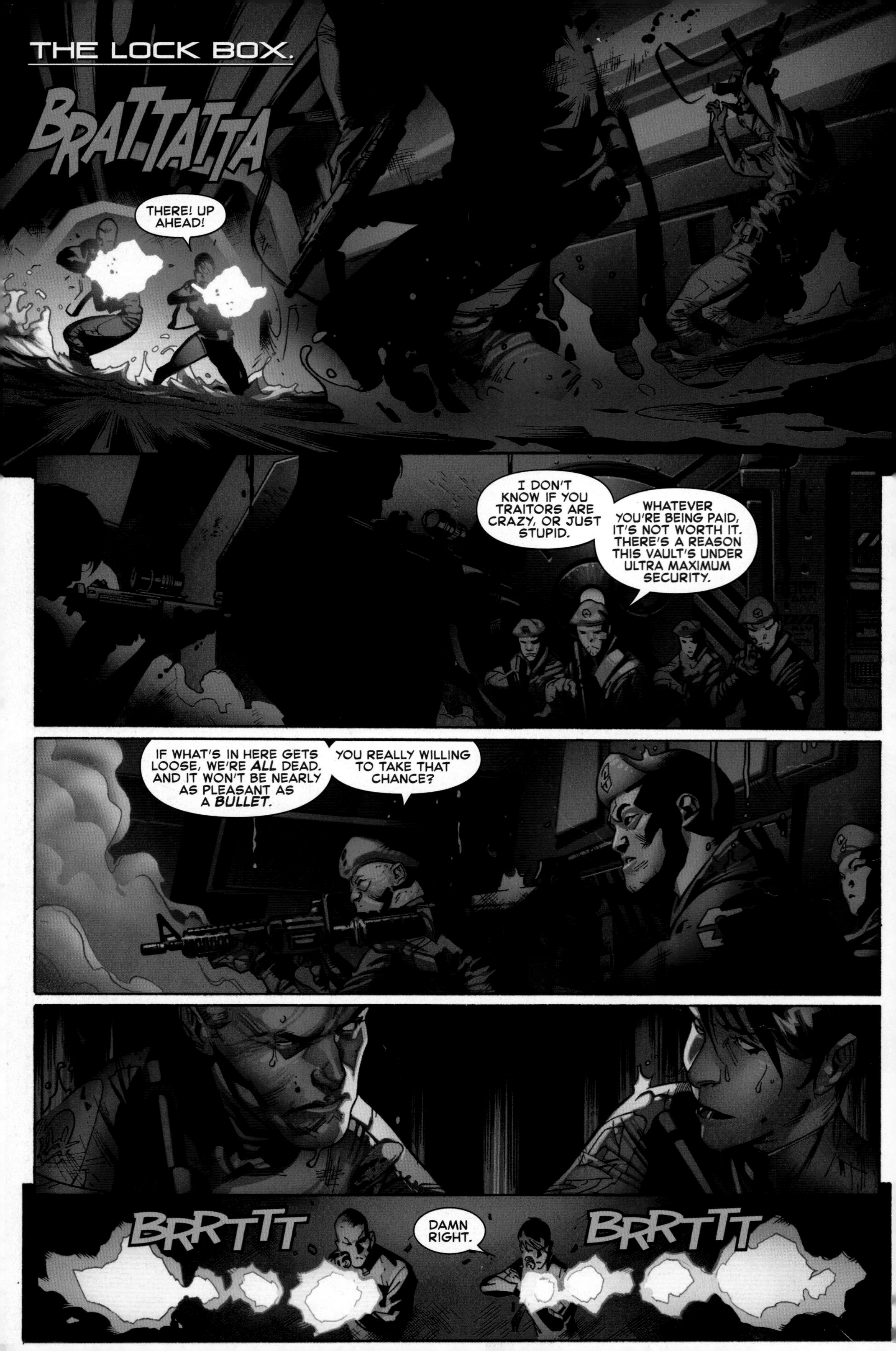
THE LOCK BOX.
BRATTATTA
THERE! UP AHEAD!
I DON'T KNOW IF YOU TRAITORS ARE CRAZY, OR JUST STUPID.
WHATEVER YOU'RE BEING PAID, IT'S NOT WORTH IT. THERE'S A REASON THIS VAULT'S UNDER ULTRA MAXIMUM SECURITY.
IF WHAT'S IN HERE GETS LOOSE, WE'RE ALL DEAD. AND IT WON'T BE NEARLY AS PLEASANT AS A BULLET.
YOU REALLY WILLING TO TAKE THAT CHANCE?
BRRTTT
DAMN RIGHT.
BRRTTT

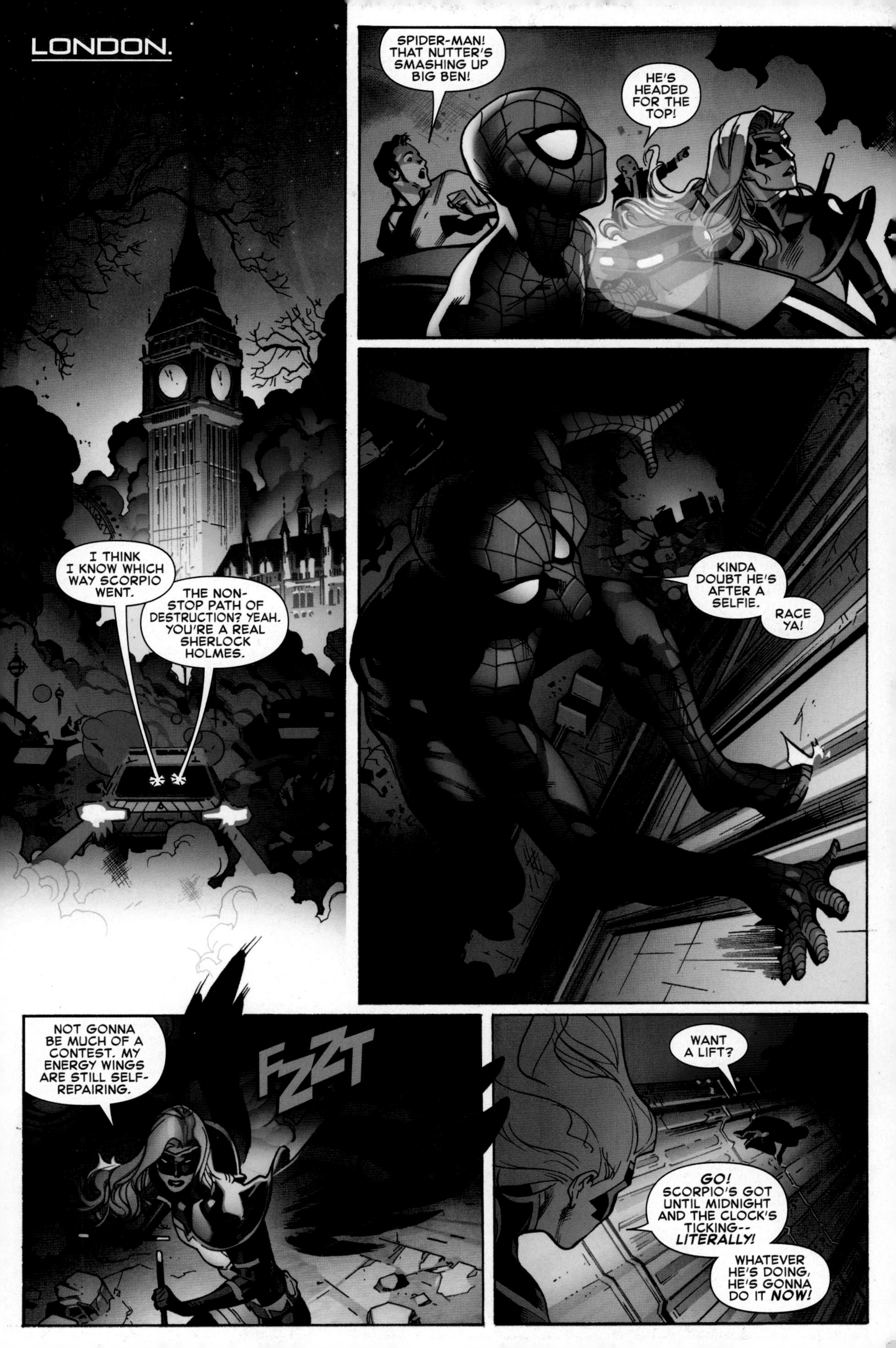
LONDON.
I THINK I KNOW WHICH WAY SCORPIO WENT.
THE NON-STOP PATH OF DESTRUCTION? YEAH. YOU'RE A REAL SHERLOCK HOLMES.
SPIDER-MAN! THAT NUTTER'S SMASHING UP BIG BEN!
HE'S HEADED FOR THE TOP!
KINDA DOUBT HE'S AFTER A SELFIE.
RACE YA!
NOT GONNA BE MUCH OF A CONTEST. MY ENERGY WINGS ARE STILL SELF-REPAIRING.
FZZZT
WANT A LIFT?
GO! SCORPIO'S GOT UNTIL MIDNIGHT AND THE CLOCK'S TICKING--LITERALLY!
WHATEVER HE'S DOING, HE'S GONNA DO IT NOW!

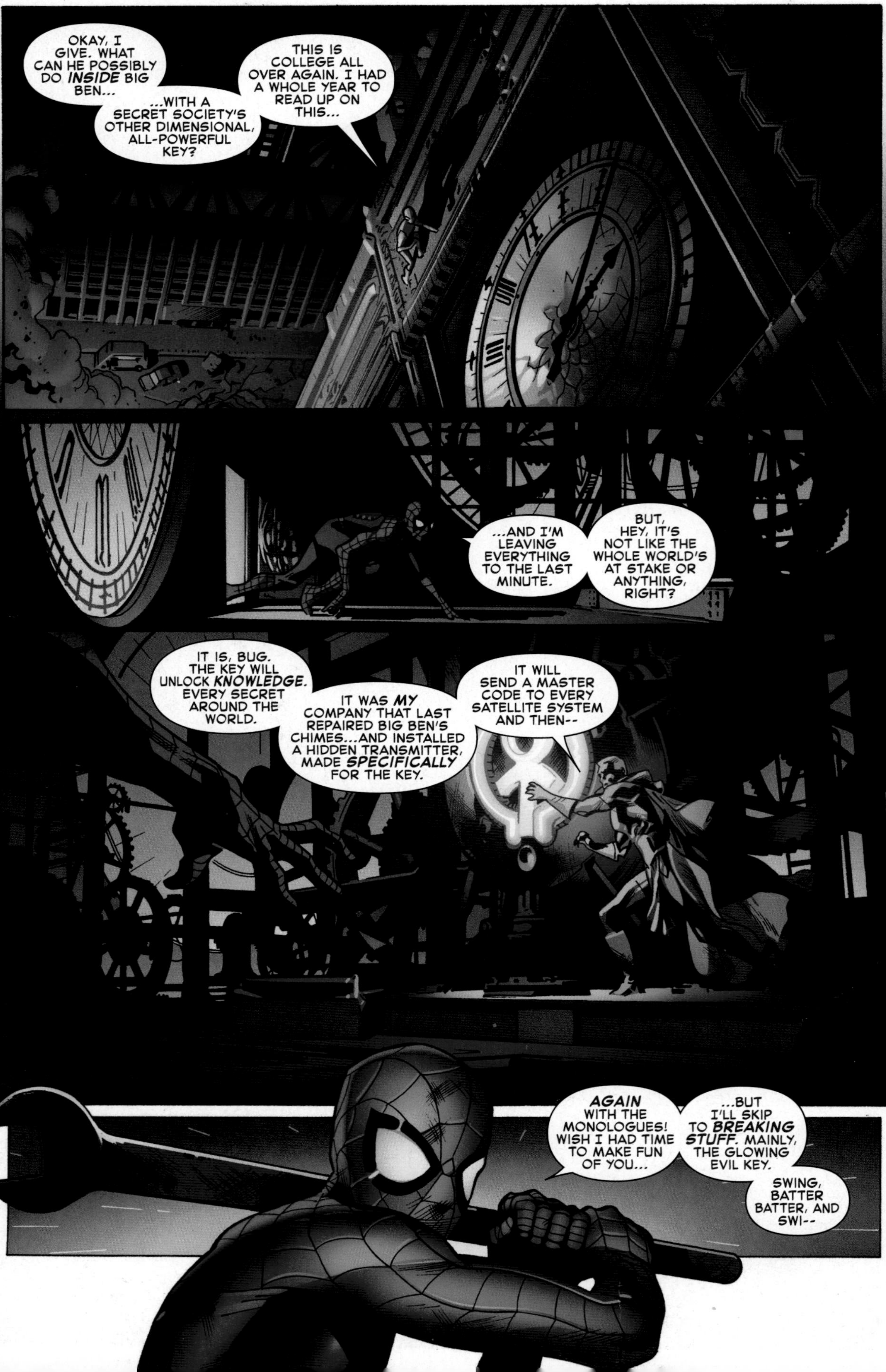
OKAY, I GIVE. WHAT CAN HE POSSIBLY DO INSIDE BIG BEN...
...WITH A SECRET SOCIETY'S OTHER DIMENSIONAL, ALL-POWERFUL KEY?
THIS IS COLLEGE ALL OVER AGAIN. I HAD A WHOLE YEAR TO READ UP ON THIS...
...AND I'M LEAVING EVERYTHING TO THE LAST MINUTE.
BUT, HEY, IT'S NOT LIKE THE WHOLE WORLD'S AT STAKE OR ANYTHING, RIGHT?
IT IS, BUG. THE KEY WILL UNLOCK KNOWLEDGE. EVERY SECRET AROUND THE WORLD.
IT WAS MY COMPANY THAT LAST REPAIRED BIG BEN'S CHIMES...AND INSTALLED A HIDDEN TRANSMITTER, MADE SPECIFICALLY FOR THE KEY.
IT WILL SEND A MASTER CODE TO EVERY SATELLITE SYSTEM AND THEN--
AGAIN WITH THE MONOLOGUES! WISH I HAD TIME TO MAKE FUN OF YOU...
...BUT I'LL SKIP TO BREAKING STUFF. MAINLY, THE GLOWING EVIL KEY.
SWING, BATTER BATTER, AND SWI--

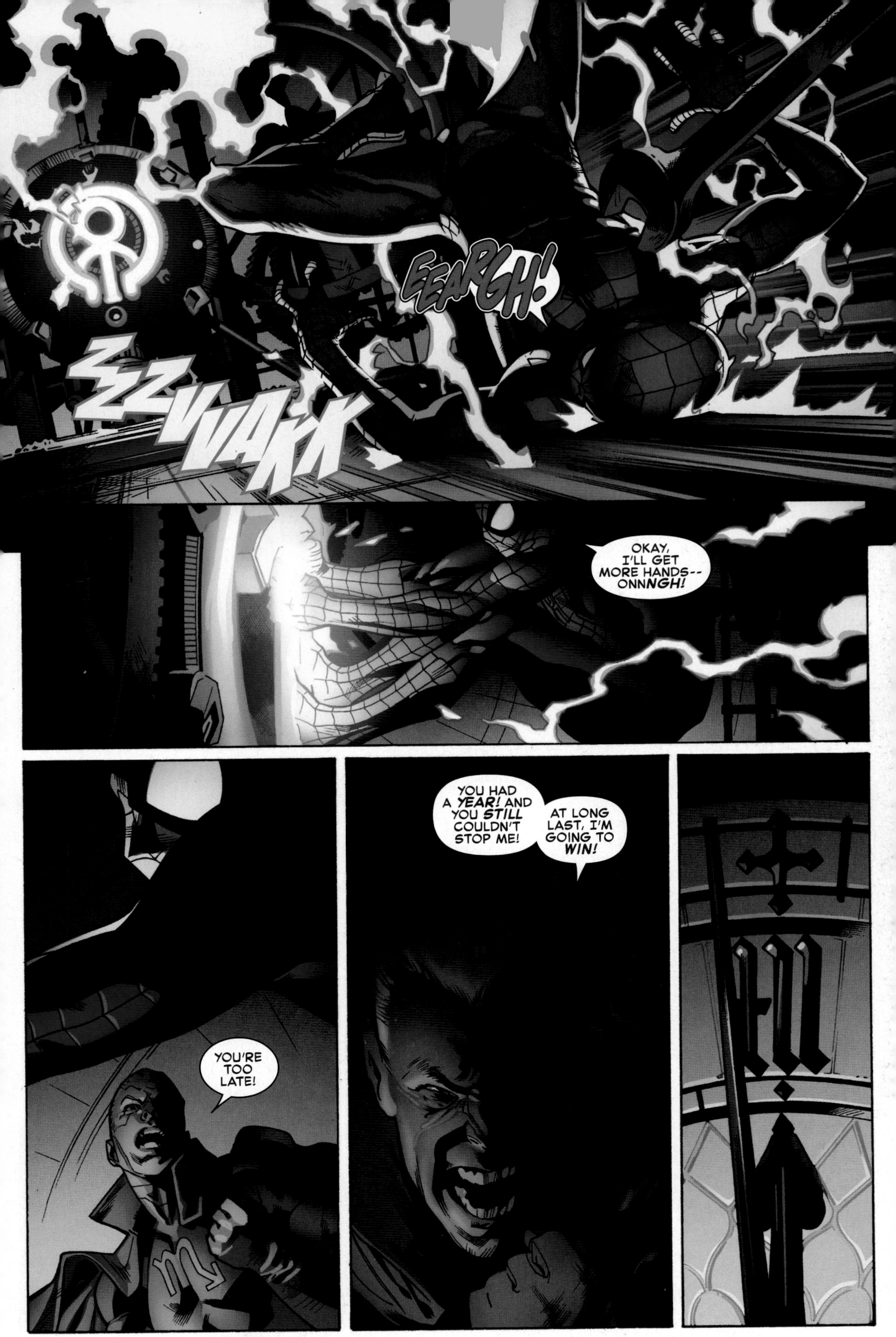
EEEARGH!
ZZZVVAKK
OKAY, I'LL GET MORE HANDS--ONNNGH!
YOU'RE TOO LATE!
YOU HAD A YEAR! AND YOU STILL COULDN'T STOP ME!
AT LONG LAST, I'M GOING TO WIN!

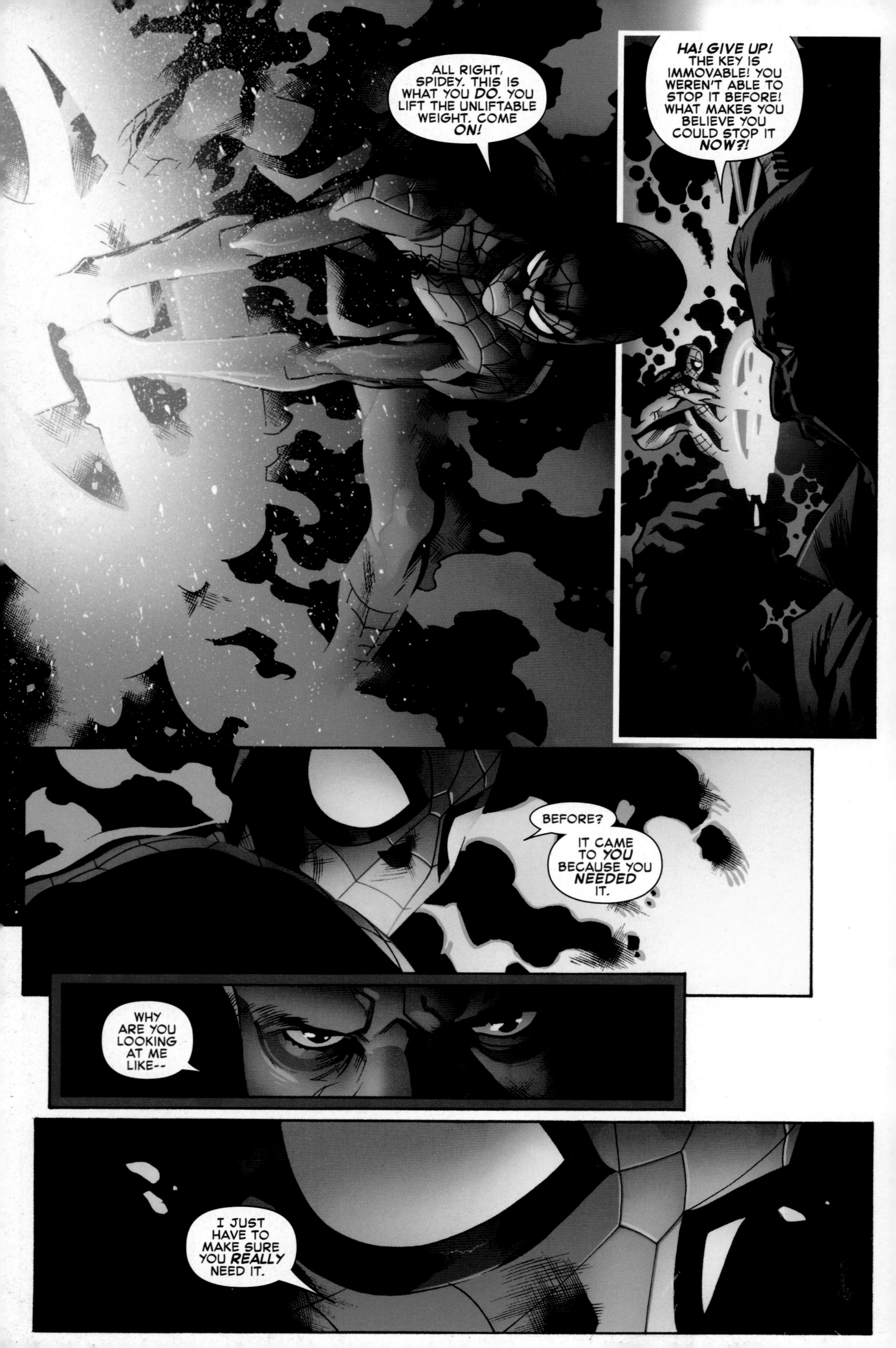
ALL RIGHT, SPIDEY. THIS IS WHAT YOU DO. YOU LIFT THE UNLIFTABLE WEIGHT. COME ON!
HA! GIVE UP! THE KEY IS IMMOVABLE! YOU WEREN'T ABLE TO STOP IT BEFORE! WHAT MAKES YOU BELIEVE YOU COULD STOP IT NOW?!
BEFORE?
IT CAME TO YOU BECAUSE YOU NEEDED IT.
WHY ARE YOU LOOKING AT ME LIKE--
I JUST HAVE TO MAKE SURE YOU REALLY NEED IT.

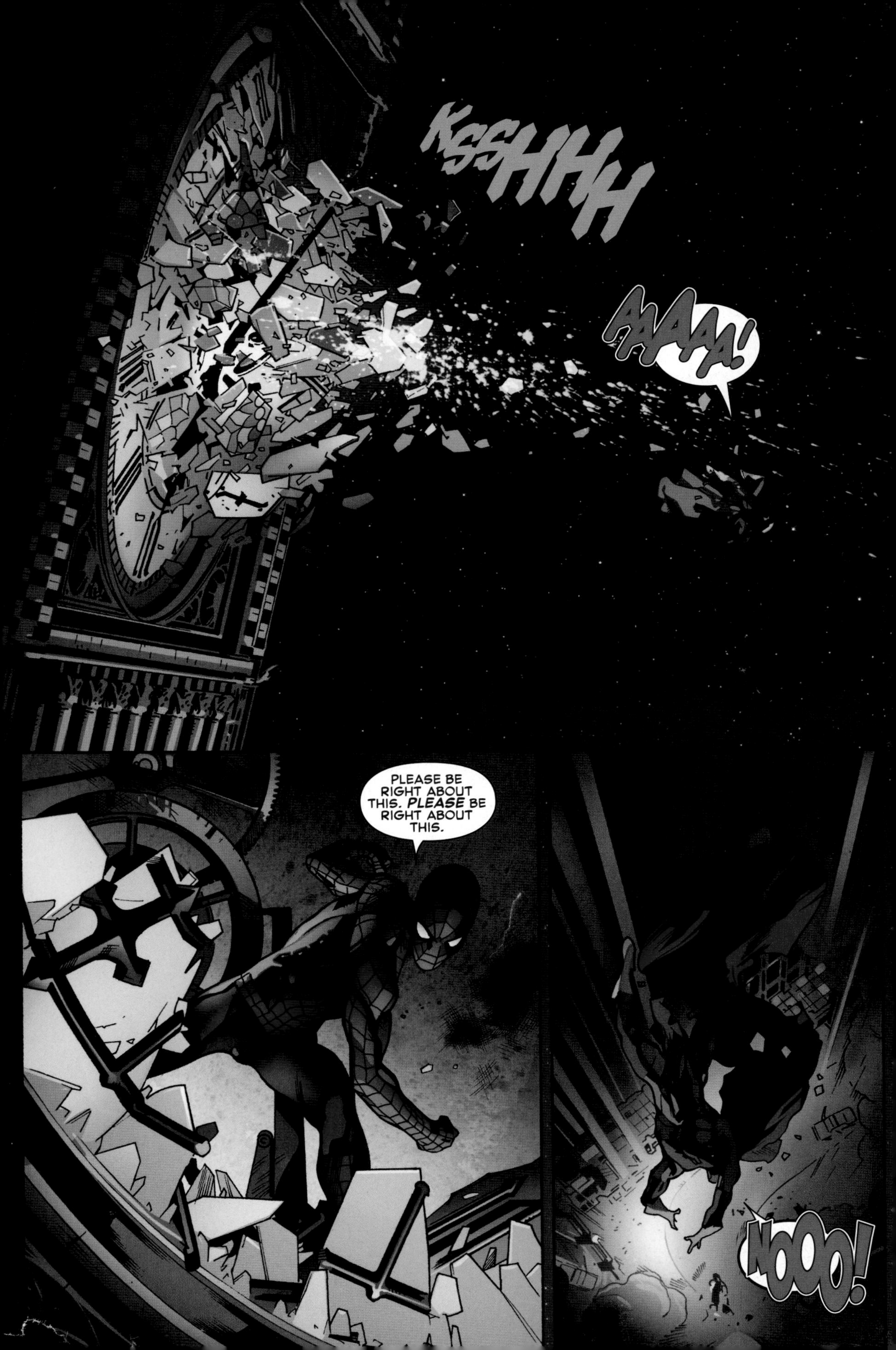
KSSHHH
AAAAA!
PLEASE BE RIGHT ABOUT THIS. PLEASE BE RIGHT ABOUT THIS.
NOOO!

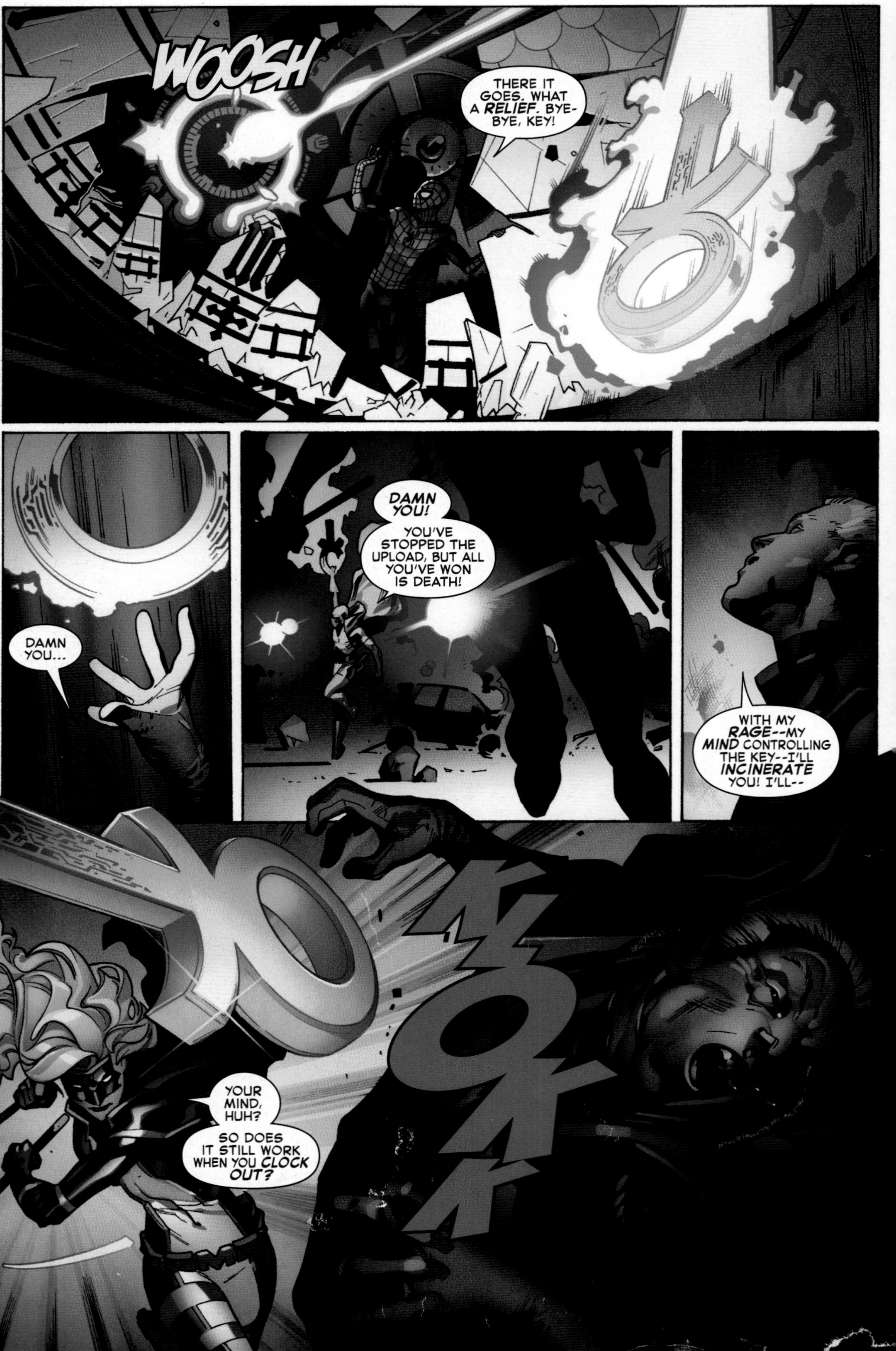
WOOSH
THERE IT GOES. WHAT A RELIEF. BYE-BYE, KEY!
DAMN YOU...
DAMN YOU!
YOU'VE STOPPED THE UPLOAD, BUT ALL YOU'VE WON IS DEATH!
WITH MY RAGE--MY MIND CONTROLLING THE KEY--I'LL INCINERATE YOU! I'LL--
YOUR MIND, HUH?
SO DOES IT STILL WORK WHEN YOU CLOCK OUT?

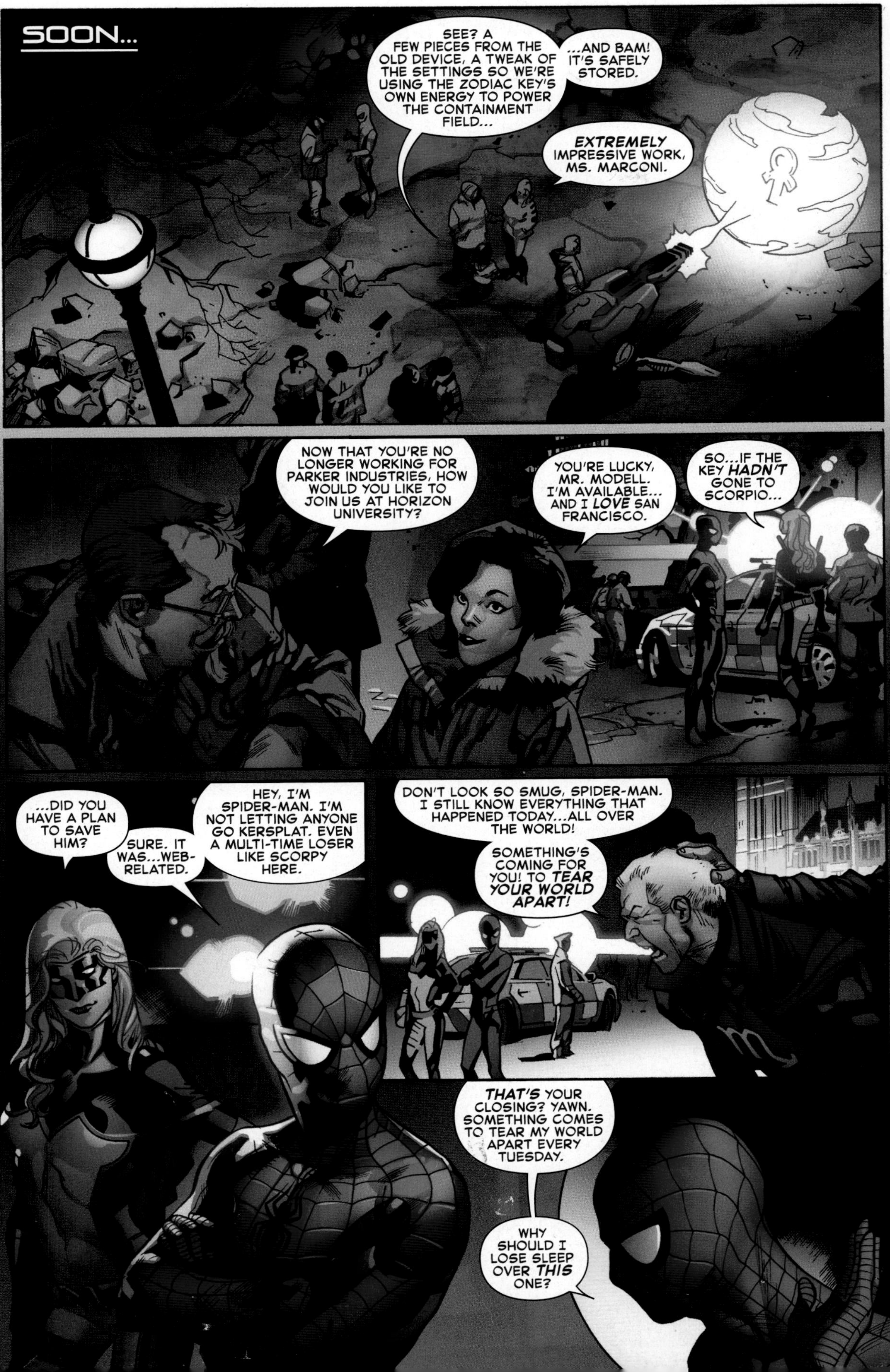
SOON...
SEE? A FEW PIECES FROM THE OLD DEVICE, A TWEAK OF THE SETTINGS SO WE'RE USING THE ZODIAC KEY'S OWN ENERGY TO POWER THE CONTAINMENT FIELD...
...AND BAM! IT'S SAFELY STORED.
EXTREMELY IMPRESSIVE WORK, MS. MARCONI.
NOW THAT YOU'RE NO LONGER WORKING FOR PARKER INDUSTRIES, HOW WOULD YOU LIKE TO JOIN US AT HORIZON UNIVERSITY?
YOU'RE LUCKY, MR. MODELL. I'M AVAILABLE... AND I LOVE SAN FRANCISCO.
SO...IF THE KEY HADN'T GONE TO SCORPIO...
...DID YOU HAVE A PLAN TO SAVE HIM?
SURE. IT WAS...WEB-RELATED.
HEY, I'M SPIDER-MAN. I'M NOT LETTING ANYONE GO KERSPLAT. EVEN A MULTI-TIME LOSER LIKE SCORPY HERE.
DON'T LOOK SO SMUG, SPIDER-MAN. I STILL KNOW EVERYTHING THAT HAPPENED TODAY...ALL OVER THE WORLD!
SOMETHING'S COMING FOR YOU! TO TEAR YOUR WORLD APART!
THAT'S YOUR CLOSING? YAWN. SOMETHING COMES TO TEAR MY WORLD APART EVERY TUESDAY.
WHY SHOULD I LOSE SLEEP OVER THIS ONE?

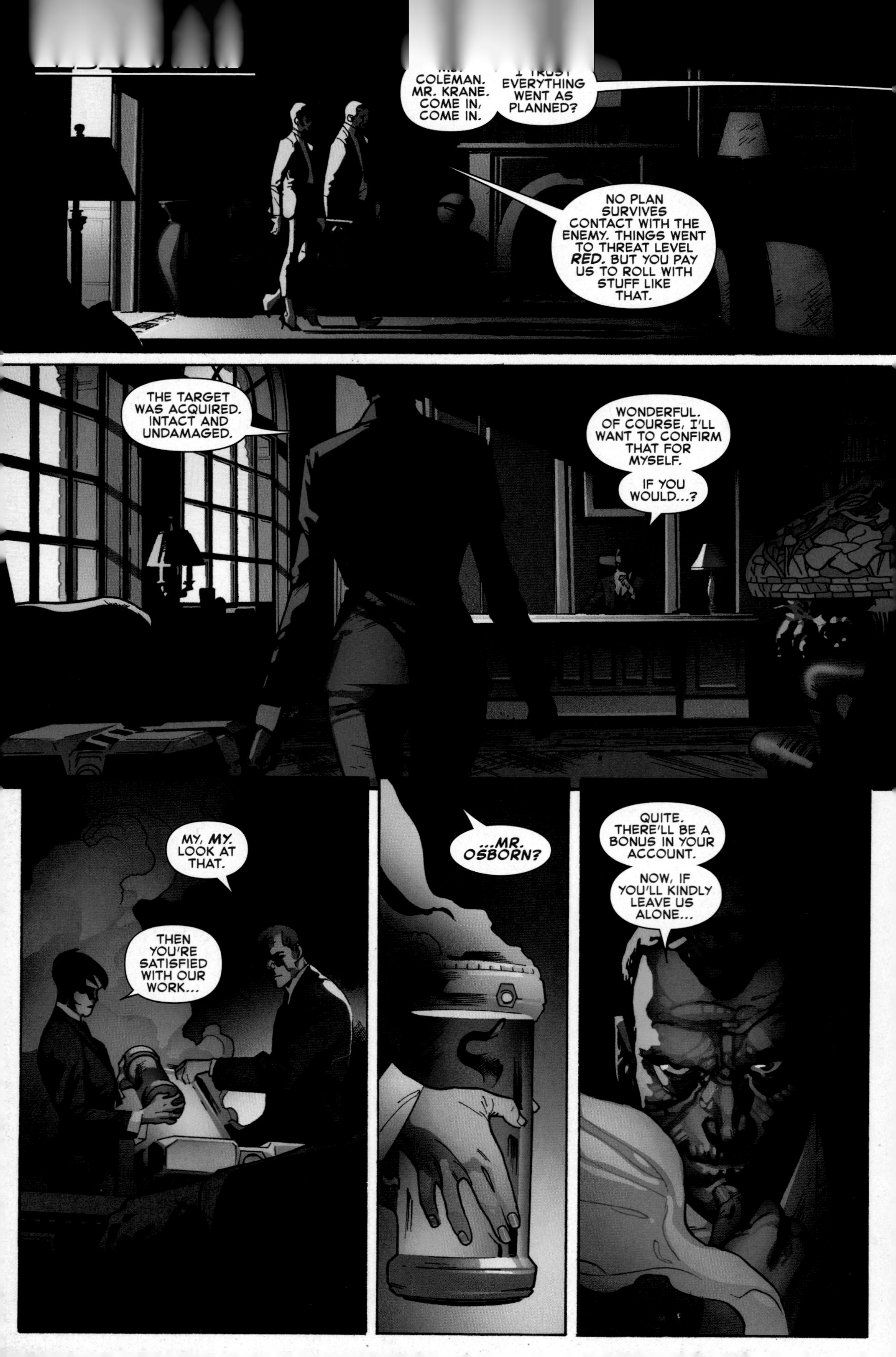
COLEMAN. MR. KRANE. COME IN, COME IN.
EVERYTHING WENT AS PLANNED?
NO PLAN SURVIVES CONTACT WITH THE ENEMY. THINGS WENT TO THREAT LEVEL RED. BUT YOU PAY US TO ROLL WITH STUFF LIKE THAT.
THE TARGET WAS ACQUIRED. INTACT AND UNDAMAGED.
WONDERFUL. OF COURSE, I'LL WANT TO CONFIRM THAT FOR MYSELF.
IF YOU WOULD...?
MY, MY. LOOK AT THAT.
THEN YOU'RE SATISFIED WITH OUR WORK...
...MR. OSBORN?
QUITE. THERE'LL BE A BONUS IN YOUR ACCOUNT.
NOW, IF YOU'LL KINDLY LEAVE US ALONE...

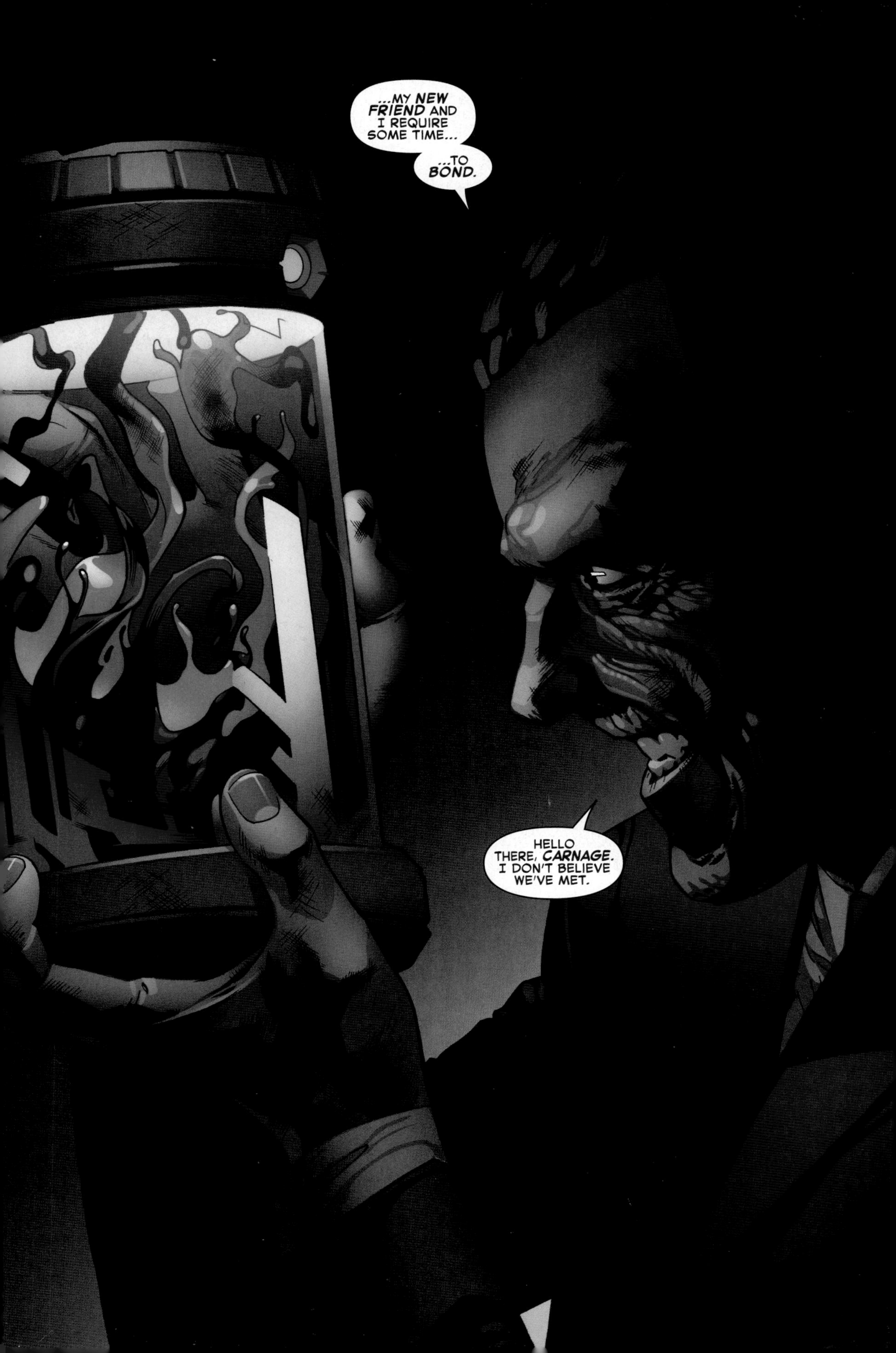

...MY NEW FRIEND AND I REQUIRE SOME TIME...
...TO BOND.
HELLO THERE, CARNAGE. I DON'T BELIEVE WE'VE MET.

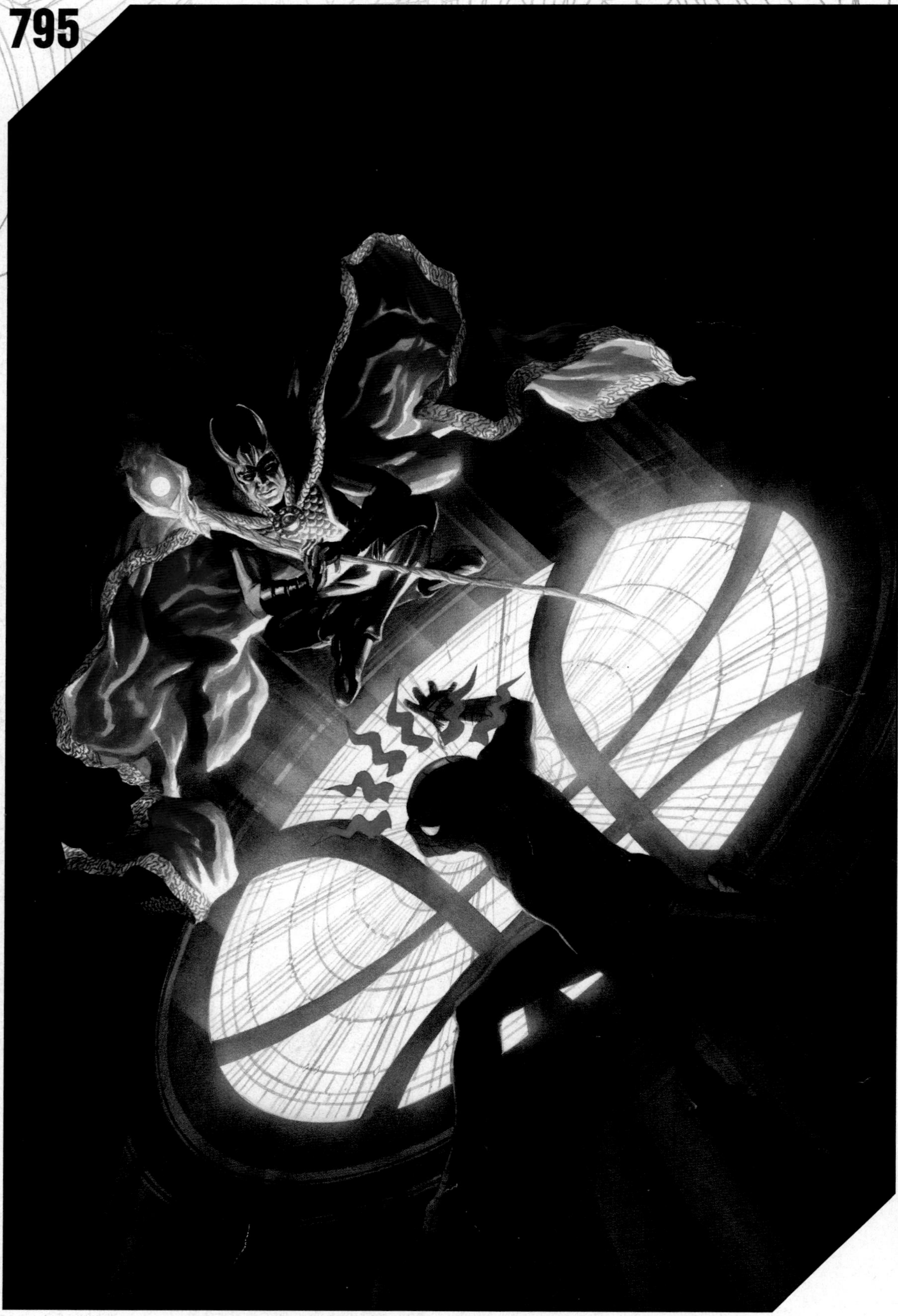

THREAT LEVEL: RED PART TWO "THE FAVOR"

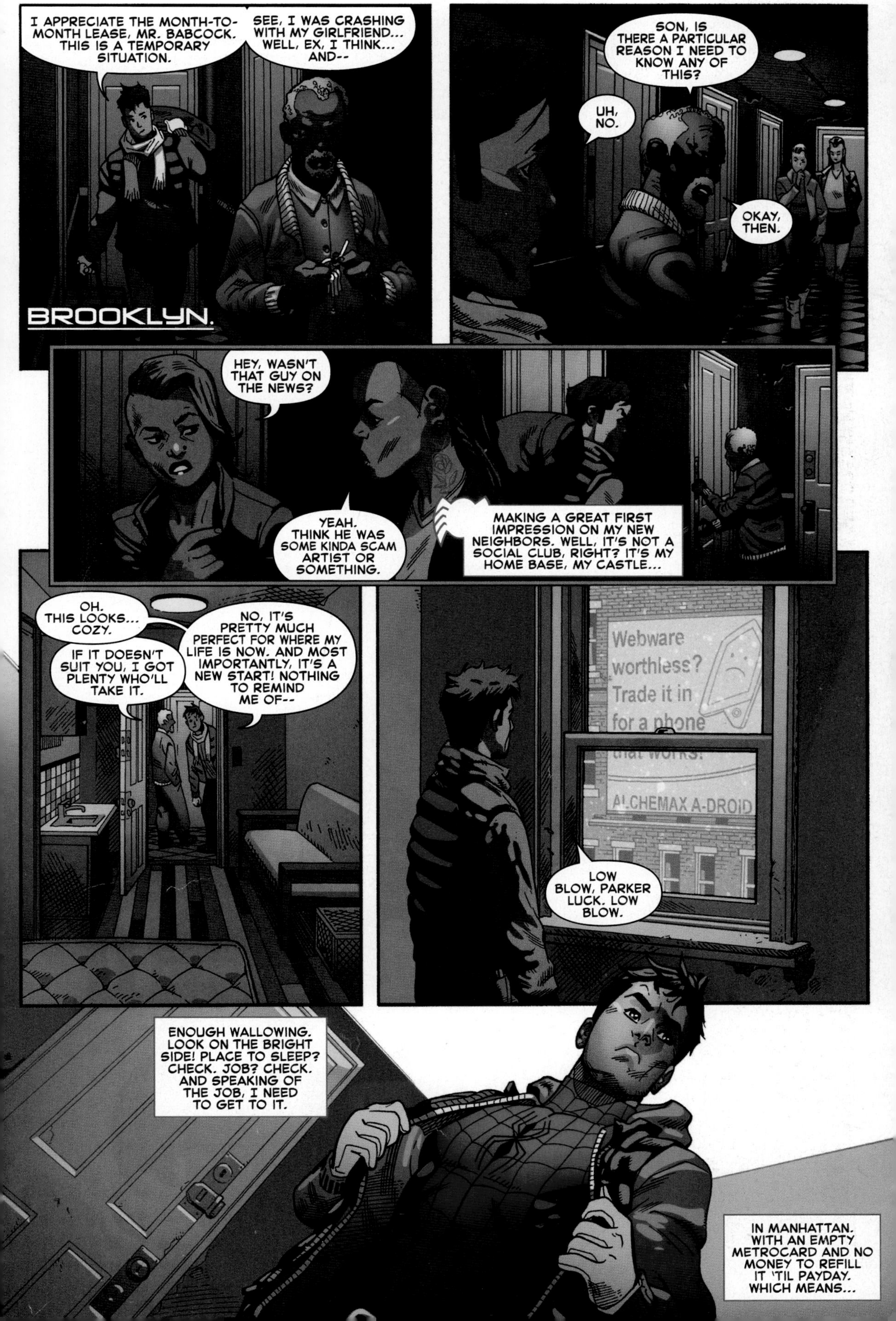
I APPRECIATE THE MONTH-TO-MONTH LEASE, MR. BABCOCK. THIS IS A TEMPORARY SITUATION.
SEE, I WAS CRASHING WITH MY GIRLFRIEND... WELL, EX, I THINK... AND--
BROOKLYN.
SON, IS THERE A PARTICULAR REASON I NEED TO KNOW ANY OF THIS?
UH, NO.
OKAY, THEN.
HEY, WASN'T THAT GUY ON THE NEWS?
YEAH. THINK HE WAS SOME KINDA SCAM ARTIST OR SOMETHING.
MAKING A GREAT FIRST IMPRESSION ON MY NEW NEIGHBORS. WELL, IT'S NOT A SOCIAL CLUB, RIGHT? IT'S MY HOME BASE, MY CASTLE...
OH. THIS LOOKS... COZY.
IF IT DOESN'T SUIT YOU, I GOT PLENTY WHO'LL TAKE IT.
NO, IT'S PRETTY MUCH PERFECT FOR WHERE MY LIFE IS NOW. AND MOST IMPORTANTLY, IT'S A NEW START! NOTHING TO REMIND ME OF--
Webware worthless? Trade it in for a phone
ALCHEMAX A-DROID
LOW BLOW, PARKER LUCK. LOW BLOW.
ENOUGH WALLOWING. LOOK ON THE BRIGHT SIDE! PLACE TO SLEEP? CHECK. JOB? CHECK. AND SPEAKING OF THE JOB, I NEED TO GET TO IT.
IN MANHATTAN. WITH AN EMPTY METROCARD AND NO MONEY TO REFILL IT 'TIL PAYDAY. WHICH MEANS...

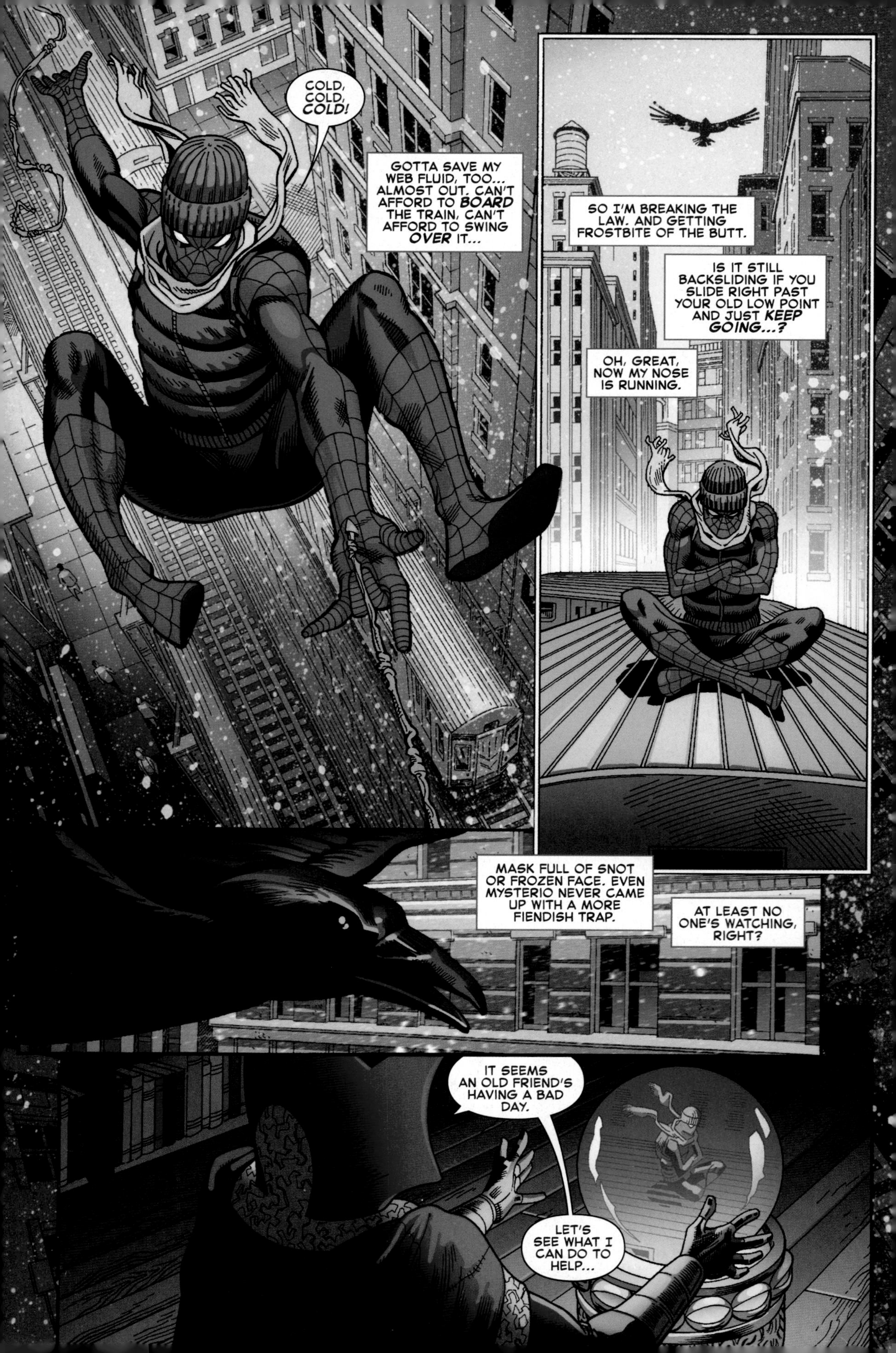
COLD, COLD, COLD!
GOTTA SAVE MY WEB FLUID, TOO... ALMOST OUT. CAN'T AFFORD TO BOARD THE TRAIN, CAN'T AFFORD TO SWING OVER IT...
SO I'M BREAKING THE LAW. AND GETTING FROSTBITE OF THE BUTT.
IS IT STILL BACKSLIDING IF YOU SLIDE RIGHT PAST YOUR OLD LOW POINT AND JUST KEEP GOING...?
OH, GREAT, NOW MY NOSE IS RUNNING.
MASK FULL OF SNOT OR FROZEN FACE. EVEN MYSTERIO NEVER CAME UP WITH A MORE FIENDISH TRAP.
AT LEAST NO ONE'S WATCHING, RIGHT?
IT SEEMS AN OLD FRIEND'S HAVING A BAD DAY.
LET'S SEE WHAT I CAN DO TO HELP...

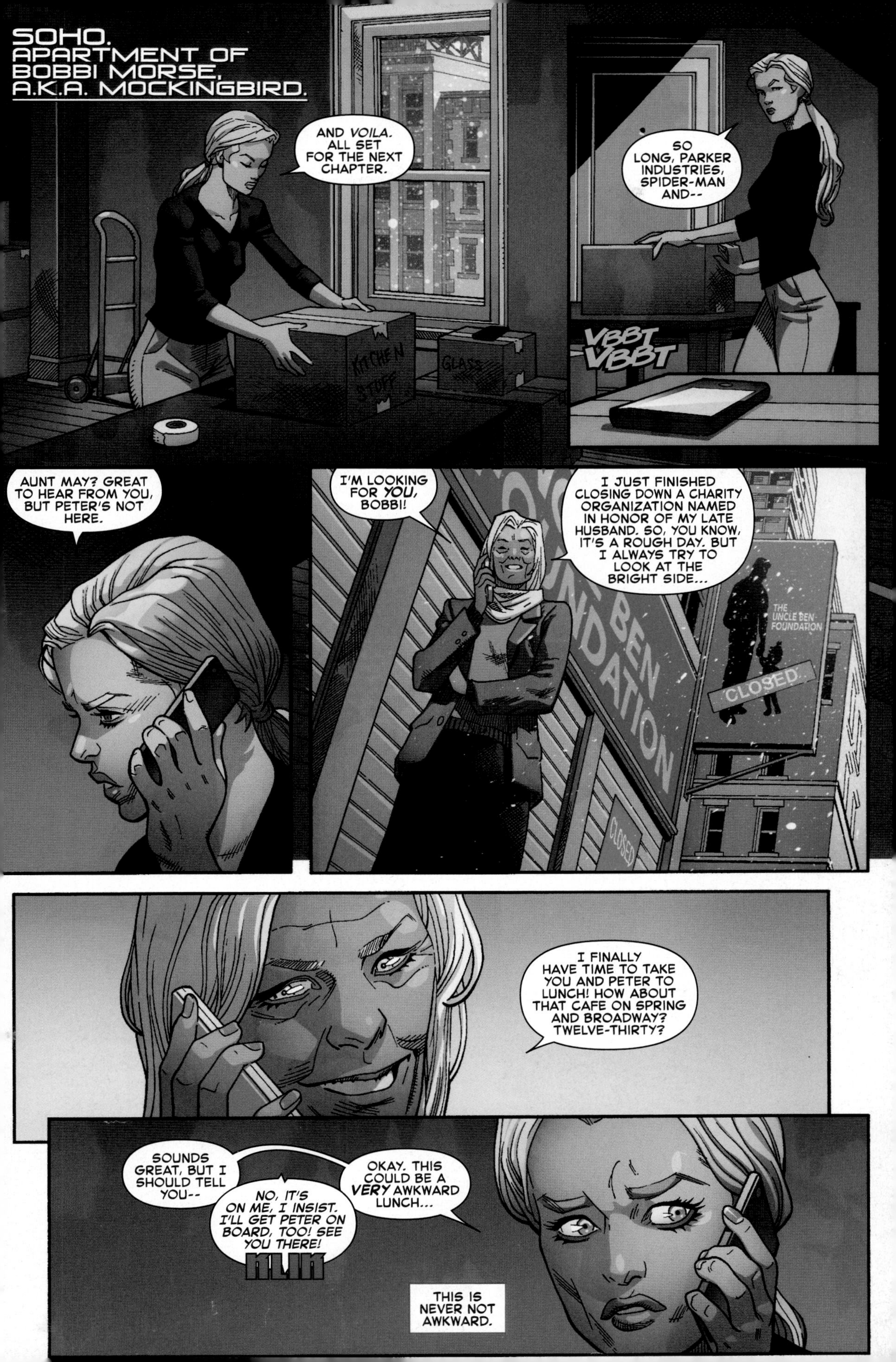
SOHO. APARTMENT OF BOBBI MORSE, A.K.A. MOCKINGBIRD.
AND VOILA. ALL SET FOR THE NEXT CHAPTER.
KITCHEN STUFF
GLASS
SO LONG, PARKER INDUSTRIES, SPIDER-MAN AND--
VBBT VBBT
AUNT MAY? GREAT TO HEAR FROM YOU, BUT PETER'S NOT HERE.
I'M LOOKING FOR YOU, BOBBI!
I JUST FINISHED CLOSING DOWN A CHARITY ORGANIZATION NAMED IN HONOR OF MY LATE HUSBAND. SO, YOU KNOW, IT'S A ROUGH DAY. BUT I ALWAYS TRY TO LOOK AT THE BRIGHT SIDE...
THE UNCLE BEN FOUNDATION
CLOSED
CLOSED
I FINALLY HAVE TIME TO TAKE YOU AND PETER TO LUNCH! HOW ABOUT THAT CAFE ON SPRING AND BROADWAY? TWELVE-THIRTY?
SOUNDS GREAT, BUT I SHOULD TELL YOU--
NO, IT'S ON ME, I INSIST. I'LL GET PETER ON BOARD, TOO! SEE YOU THERE!
KLIK
OKAY. THIS COULD BE A VERY AWKWARD LUNCH...
THIS IS NEVER NOT AWKWARD.

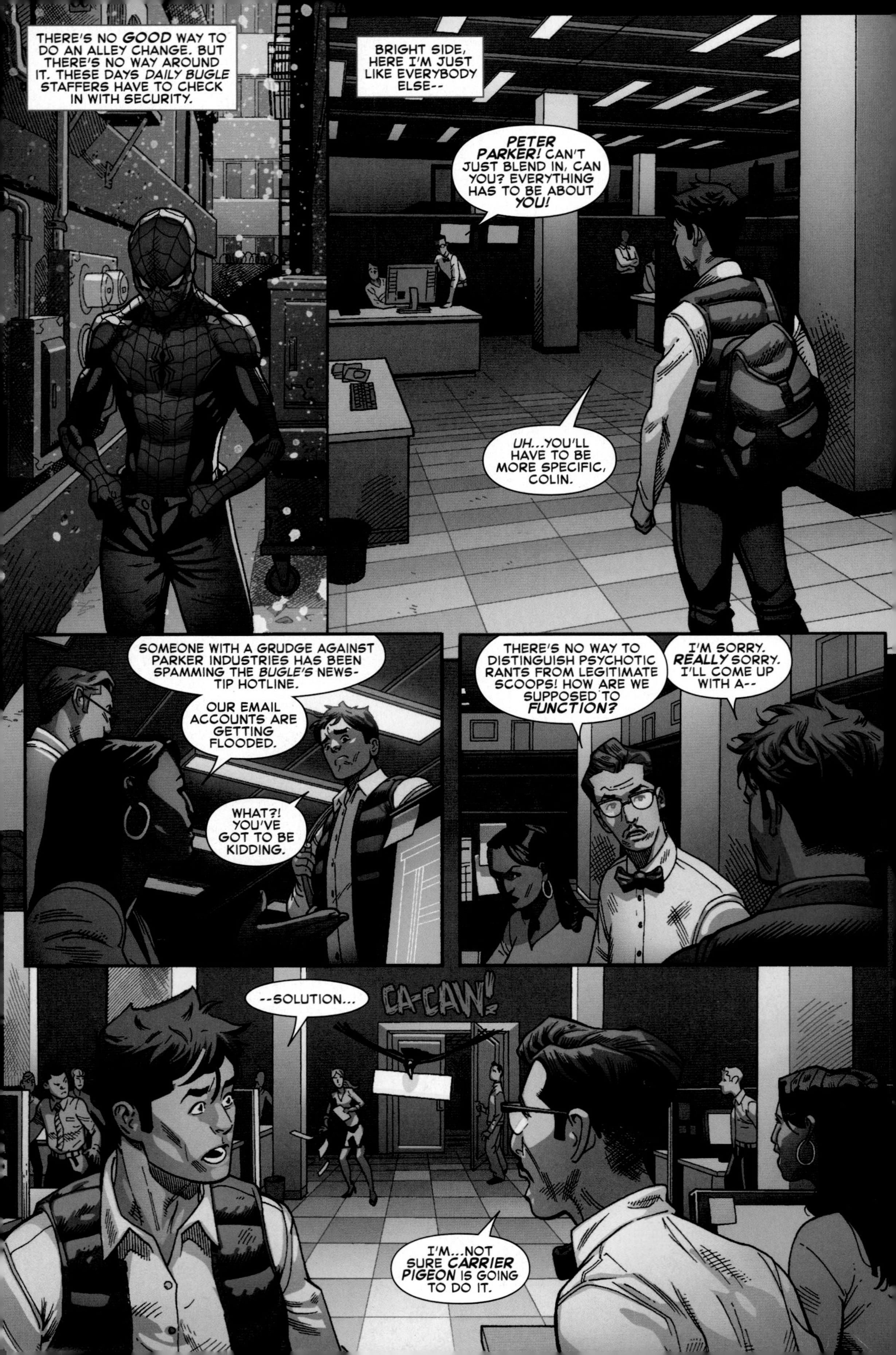
THERE'S NO GOOD WAY TO DO AN ALLEY CHANGE. BUT THERE'S NO WAY AROUND IT. THESE DAYS DAILY BUGLE STAFFERS HAVE TO CHECK IN WITH SECURITY.
BRIGHT SIDE, HERE I'M JUST LIKE EVERYBODY ELSE--
PETER PARKER! CAN'T JUST BLEND IN, CAN YOU? EVERYTHING HAS TO BE ABOUT YOU!
UH...YOU'LL HAVE TO BE MORE SPECIFIC, COLIN.
SOMEONE WITH A GRUDGE AGAINST PARKER INDUSTRIES HAS BEEN SPAMMING THE BUGLE'S NEWS-TIP HOTLINE.
OUR EMAIL ACCOUNTS ARE GETTING FLOODED.
WHAT?! YOU'VE GOT TO BE KIDDING.
THERE'S NO WAY TO DISTINGUISH PSYCHOTIC RANTS FROM LEGITIMATE SCOOPS! HOW ARE WE SUPPOSED TO FUNCTION?
I'M SORRY. REALLY SORRY. I'LL COME UP WITH A--
--SOLUTION...
CA-CAW!
I'M...NOT SURE CARRIER PIGEON IS GOING TO DO IT.

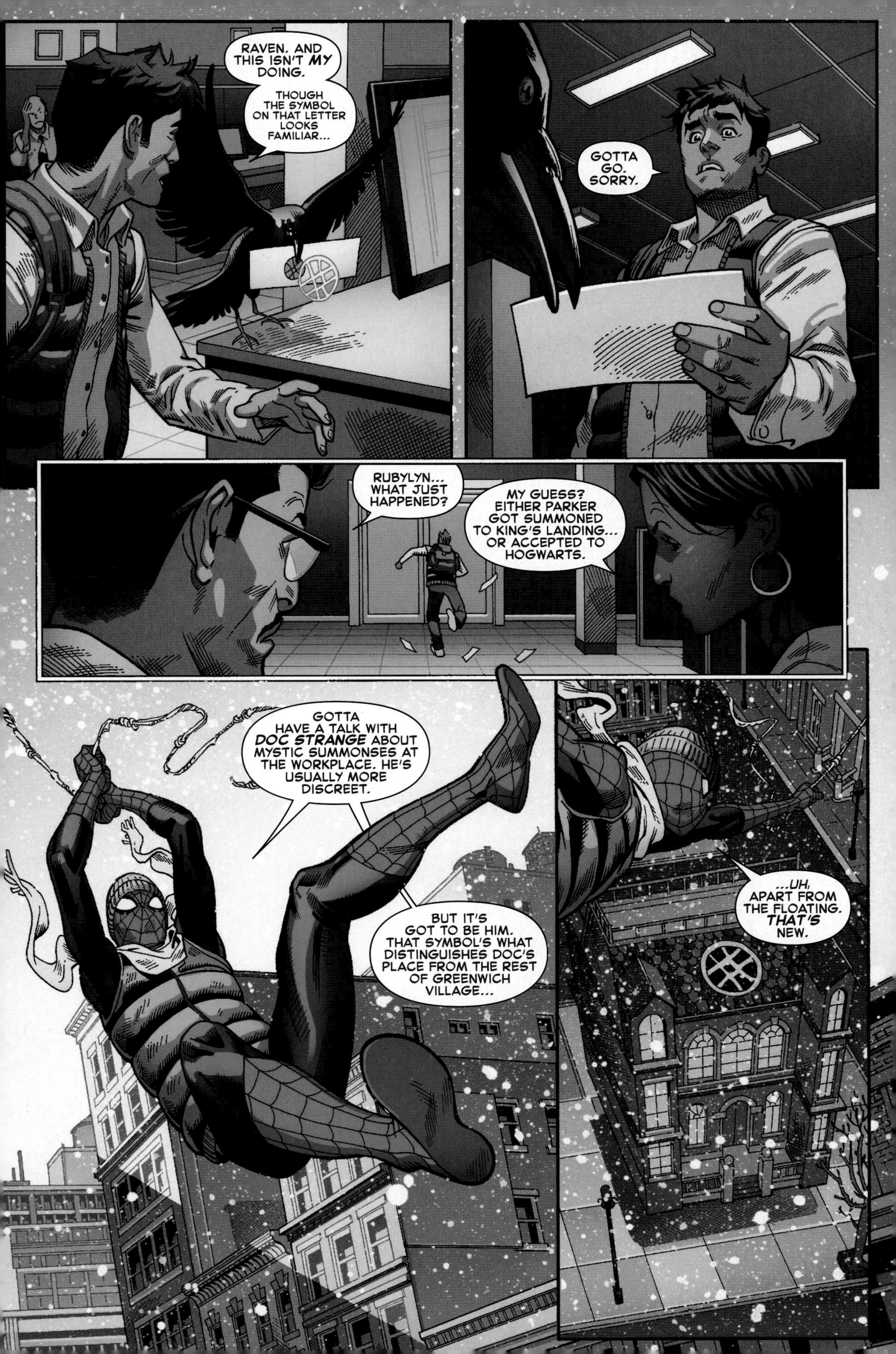
RAVEN. AND THIS ISN'T MY DOING.
THOUGH THE SYMBOL ON THAT LETTER LOOKS FAMILIAR...
GOTTA GO. SORRY.
RUBYLYN... WHAT JUST HAPPENED?
MY GUESS? EITHER PARKER GOT SUMMONED TO KING'S LANDING... OR ACCEPTED TO HOGWARTS.
GOTTA HAVE A TALK WITH DOC STRANGE ABOUT MYSTIC SUMMONSES AT THE WORKPLACE. HE'S USUALLY MORE DISCREET.
BUT IT'S GOT TO BE HIM. THAT SYMBOL'S WHAT DISTINGUISHES DOC'S PLACE FROM THE REST OF GREENWICH VILLAGE...
...UH, APART FROM THE FLOATING. THAT'S NEW.

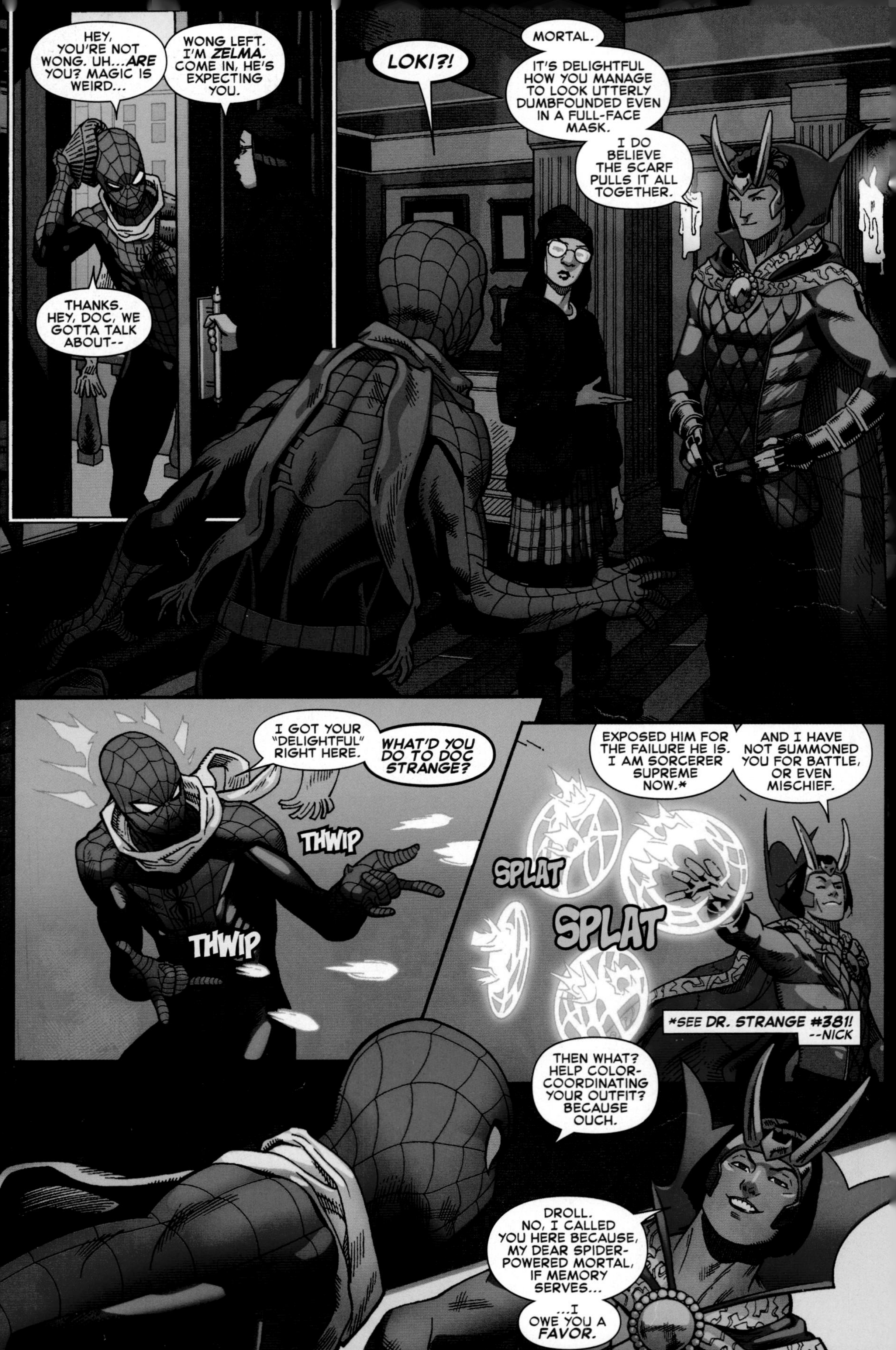

HEY, YOU'RE NOT WONG. UH...ARE YOU? MAGIC IS WEIRD...
WONG LEFT. I'M ZELMA. COME IN, HE'S EXPECTING YOU.
THANKS. HEY, DOC, WE GOTTA TALK ABOUT--
LOKI?!
MORTAL.
IT'S DELIGHTFUL HOW YOU MANAGE TO LOOK UTTERLY DUMBFOUNDED EVEN IN A FULL-FACE MASK.
I DO BELIEVE THE SCARF PULLS IT ALL TOGETHER.
I GOT YOUR "DELIGHTFUL" RIGHT HERE.
WHAT'D YOU DO TO DOC STRANGE?
THWIP
THWIP
EXPOSED HIM FOR THE FAILURE HE IS. I AM SORCERER SUPREME NOW.*
AND I HAVE NOT SUMMONED YOU FOR BATTLE, OR EVEN MISCHIEF.
SPLAT
SPLAT
*SEE DR. STRANGE #381! --NICK
THEN WHAT? HELP COLOR-COORDINATING YOUR OUTFIT? BECAUSE OUCH.
DROLL. NO, I CALLED YOU HERE BECAUSE, MY DEAR SPIDER-POWERED MORTAL, IF MEMORY SERVES...
...I OWE YOU A FAVOR.

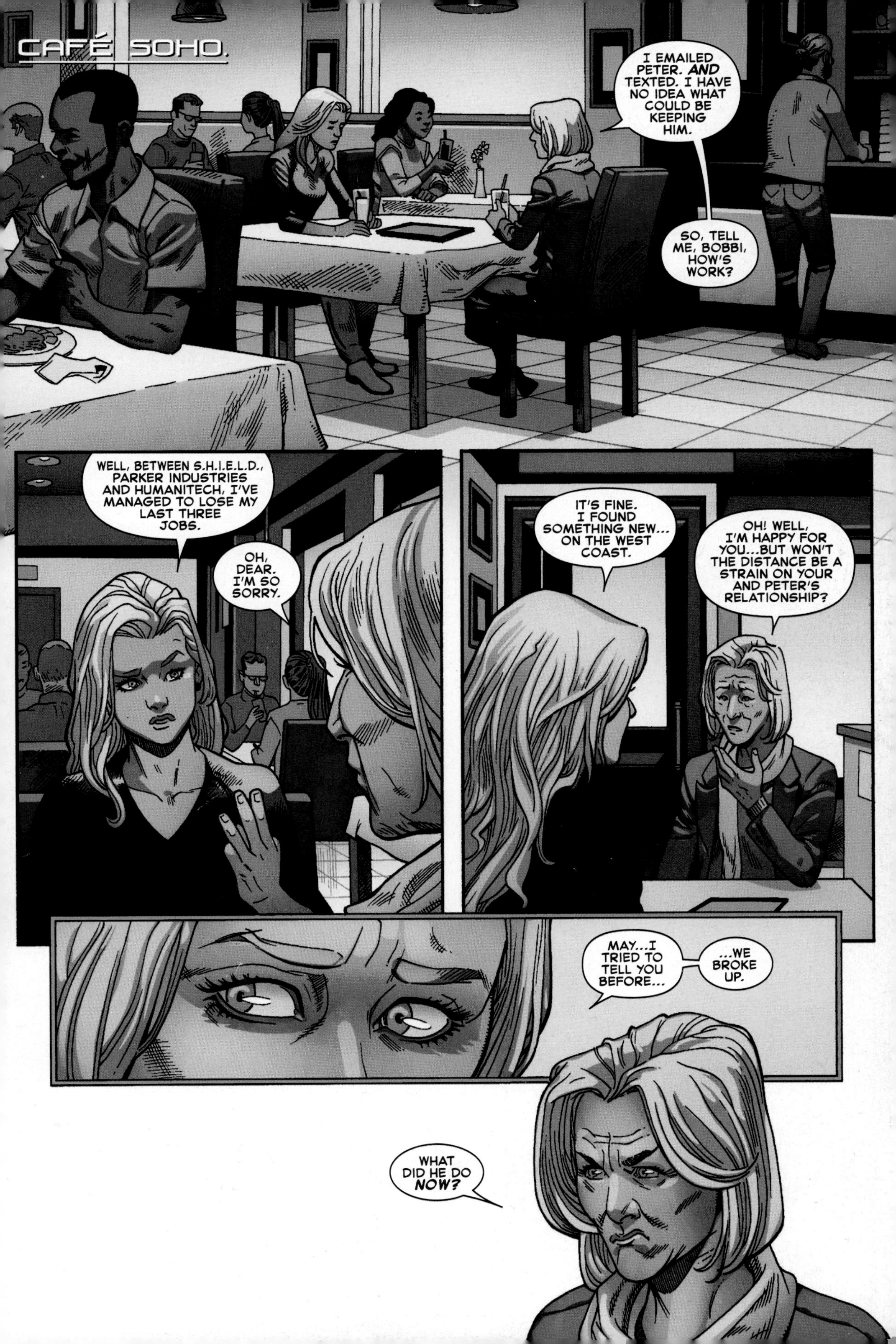

CAFÉ SOHO.
I EMAILED PETER. AND TEXTED. I HAVE NO IDEA WHAT COULD BE KEEPING HIM.
SO, TELL ME, BOBBI, HOW'S WORK?
WELL, BETWEEN S.H.I.E.L.D., PARKER INDUSTRIES AND HUMANITECH, I'VE MANAGED TO LOSE MY LAST THREE JOBS.
OH, DEAR. I'M SO SORRY.
IT'S FINE. I FOUND SOMETHING NEW... ON THE WEST COAST.
OH! WELL, I'M HAPPY FOR YOU...BUT WON'T THE DISTANCE BE A STRAIN ON YOUR AND PETER'S RELATIONSHIP?
MAY...I TRIED TO TELL YOU BEFORE...
...WE BROKE UP.
WHAT DID HE DO NOW?

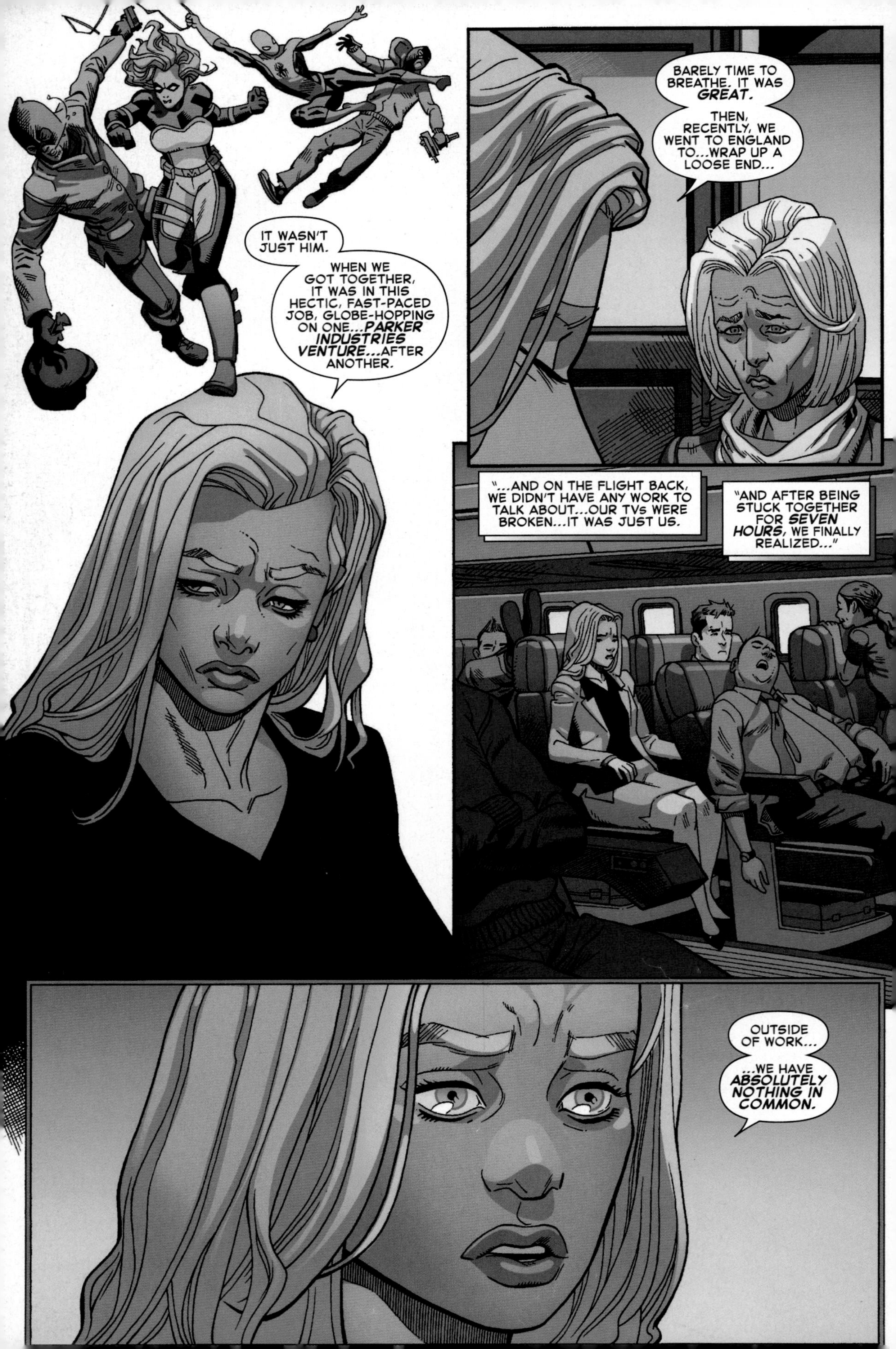
IT WASN'T JUST HIM.
WHEN WE GOT TOGETHER, IT WAS IN THIS HECTIC, FAST-PACED JOB, GLOBE-HOPPING ON ONE... PARKER INDUSTRIES VENTURE... AFTER ANOTHER.
BARELY TIME TO BREATHE. IT WAS GREAT.
THEN, RECENTLY, WE WENT TO ENGLAND TO... WRAP UP A LOOSE END...
"...AND ON THE FLIGHT BACK, WE DIDN'T HAVE ANY WORK TO TALK ABOUT... OUR TVs WERE BROKEN... IT WAS JUST US.
"AND AFTER BEING STUCK TOGETHER FOR SEVEN HOURS, WE FINALLY REALIZED..."
OUTSIDE OF WORK...
...WE HAVE ABSOLUTELY NOTHING IN COMMON.

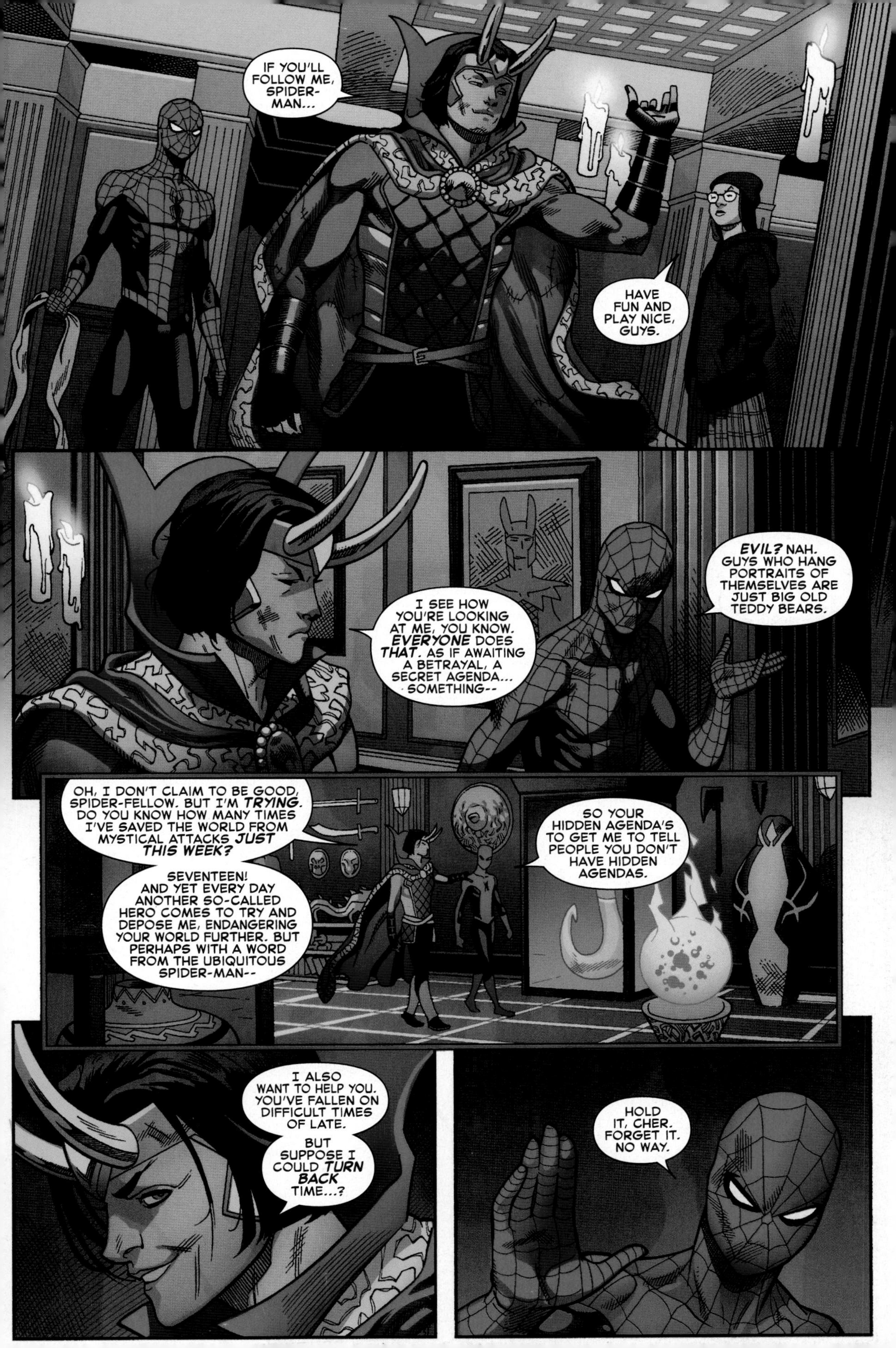

IF YOU'LL FOLLOW ME, SPIDER-MAN...
HAVE FUN AND PLAY NICE, GUYS.
I SEE HOW YOU'RE LOOKING AT ME, YOU KNOW. EVERYONE DOES THAT. AS IF AWAITING A BETRAYAL, A SECRET AGENDA... SOMETHING--
EVIL? NAH. GUYS WHO HANG PORTRAITS OF THEMSELVES ARE JUST BIG OLD TEDDY BEARS.
OH, I DON'T CLAIM TO BE GOOD, SPIDER-FELLOW. BUT I'M TRYING. DO YOU KNOW HOW MANY TIMES I'VE SAVED THE WORLD FROM MYSTICAL ATTACKS JUST THIS WEEK?
SEVENTEEN! AND YET EVERY DAY ANOTHER SO-CALLED HERO COMES TO TRY AND DEPOSE ME, ENDANGERING YOUR WORLD FURTHER. BUT PERHAPS WITH A WORD FROM THE UBIQUITOUS SPIDER-MAN--
SO YOUR HIDDEN AGENDA'S TO GET ME TO TELL PEOPLE YOU DON'T HAVE HIDDEN AGENDAS.
I ALSO WANT TO HELP YOU. YOU'VE FALLEN ON DIFFICULT TIMES OF LATE.
BUT SUPPOSE I COULD TURN BACK TIME...?
HOLD IT, CHER. FORGET IT. NO WAY.

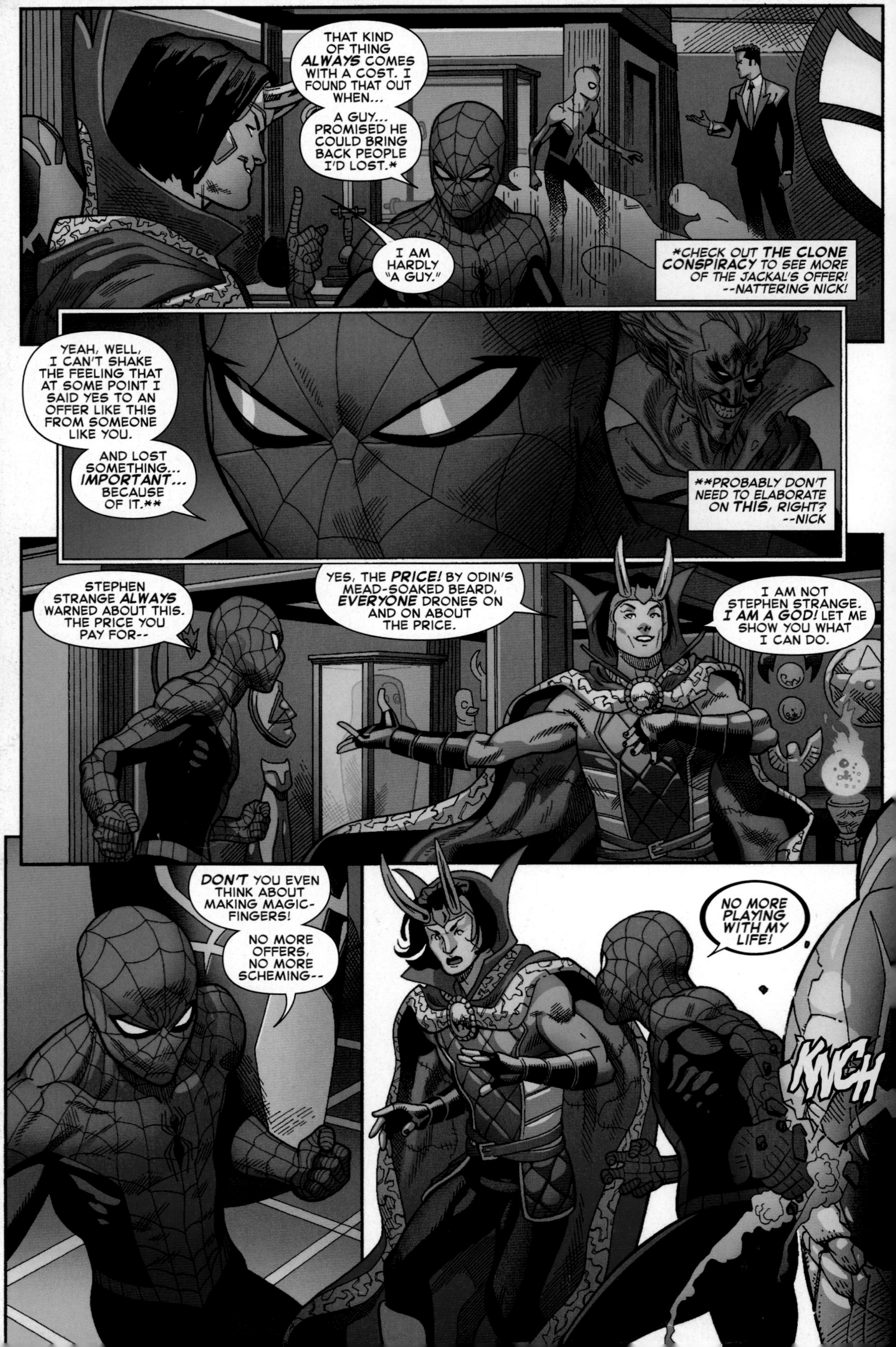
THAT KIND OF THING ALWAYS COMES WITH A COST. I FOUND THAT OUT WHEN...
A GUY... PROMISED HE COULD BRING BACK PEOPLE I'D LOST.*
I AM HARDLY "A GUY."
*CHECK OUT THE CLONE CONSPIRACY TO SEE MORE OF THE JACKAL'S OFFER! --NATTERING NICK!
YEAH, WELL, I CAN'T SHAKE THE FEELING THAT AT SOME POINT I SAID YES TO AN OFFER LIKE THIS FROM SOMEONE LIKE YOU.
AND LOST SOMETHING... IMPORTANT... BECAUSE OF IT.**
**PROBABLY DON'T NEED TO ELABORATE ON THIS, RIGHT? --NICK
STEPHEN STRANGE ALWAYS WARNED ABOUT THIS. THE PRICE YOU PAY FOR--
YES, THE PRICE! BY ODIN'S MEAD-SOAKED BEARD, EVERYONE DRONES ON AND ON ABOUT THE PRICE.
I AM NOT STEPHEN STRANGE. I AM A GOD! LET ME SHOW YOU WHAT I CAN DO.
DON'T YOU EVEN THINK ABOUT MAKING MAGIC-FINGERS!
NO MORE OFFERS, NO MORE SCHEMING--
NO MORE PLAYING WITH MY LIFE!
KNCH

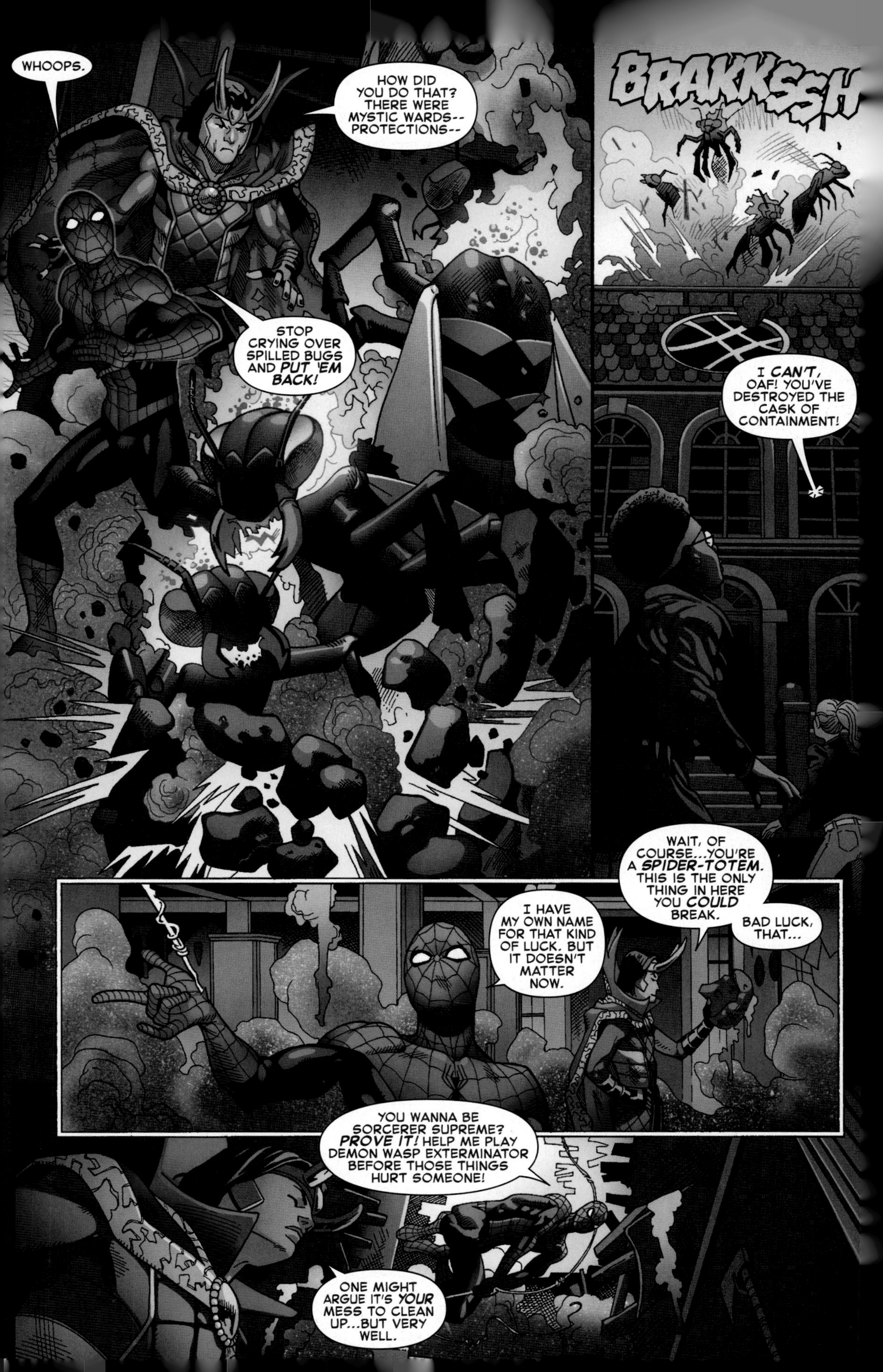
WHOOPS.
HOW DID YOU DO THAT? THERE WERE MYSTIC WARDS-- PROTECTIONS--
STOP CRYING OVER SPILLED BUGS AND PUT 'EM BACK!
BRAKKSSH
I CAN'T, OAF! YOU'VE DESTROYED THE CASK OF CONTAINMENT!
WAIT, OF COURSE...YOU'RE A SPIDER-TOTEM. THIS IS THE ONLY THING IN HERE YOU COULD BREAK.
BAD LUCK, THAT...
I HAVE MY OWN NAME FOR THAT KIND OF LUCK. BUT IT DOESN'T MATTER NOW.
YOU WANNA BE SORCERER SUPREME? PROVE IT! HELP ME PLAY DEMON WASP EXTERMINATOR BEFORE THOSE THINGS HURT SOMEONE!
ONE MIGHT ARGUE IT'S YOUR MESS TO CLEAN UP...BUT VERY WELL.

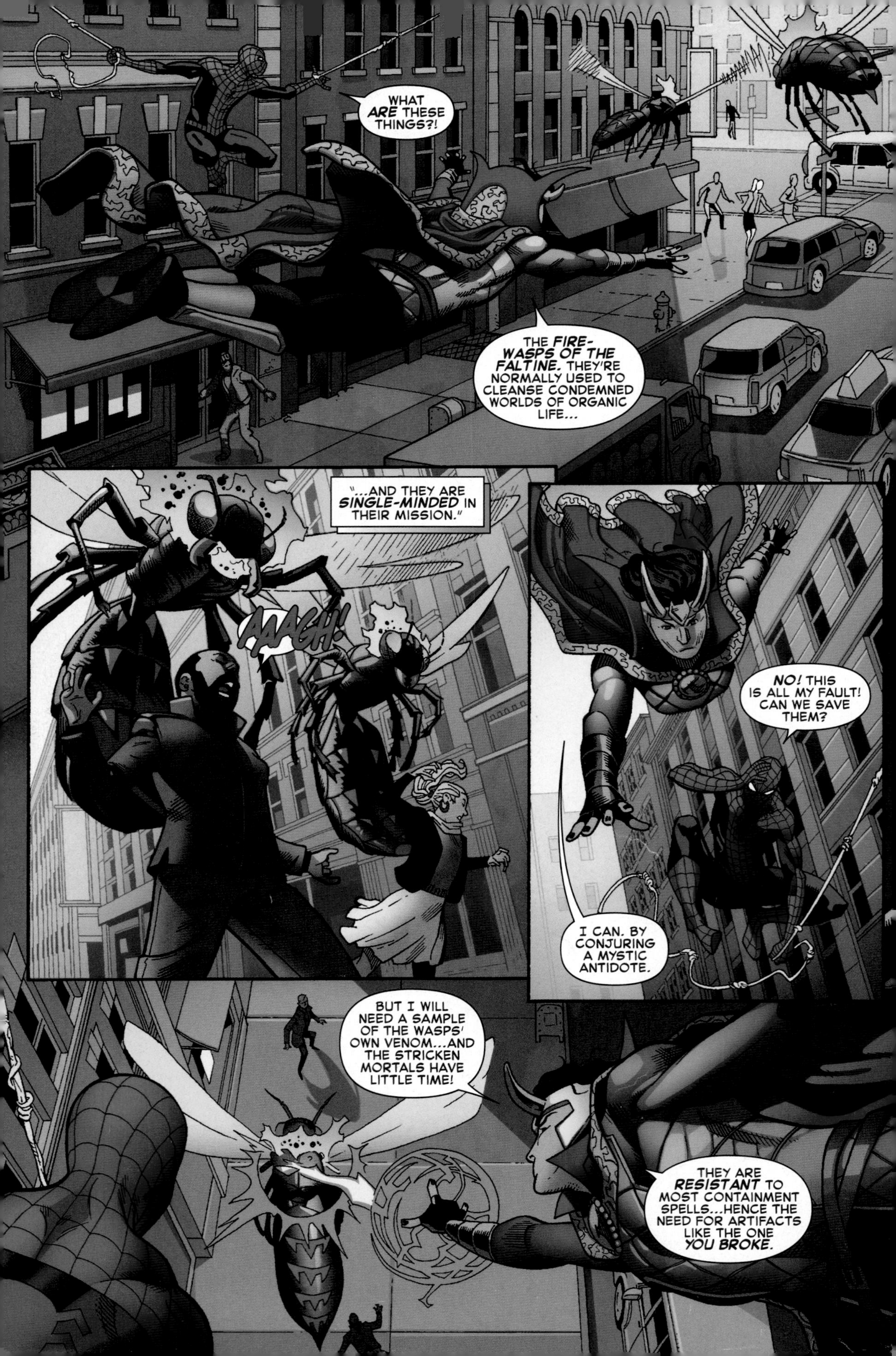
WHAT ARE THESE THINGS?!
THE FIRE-WASPS OF THE FALTINE. THEY'RE NORMALLY USED TO CLEANSE CONDEMNED WORLDS OF ORGANIC LIFE...
"...AND THEY ARE SINGLE-MINDED IN THEIR MISSION."
AAAGH!
NO! THIS IS ALL MY FAULT! CAN WE SAVE THEM?
I CAN. BY CONJURING A MYSTIC ANTIDOTE.
BUT I WILL NEED A SAMPLE OF THE WASPS' OWN VENOM...AND THE STRICKEN MORTALS HAVE LITTLE TIME!
THEY ARE RESISTANT TO MOST CONTAINMENT SPELLS...HENCE THE NEED FOR ARTIFACTS LIKE THE ONE YOU BROKE.

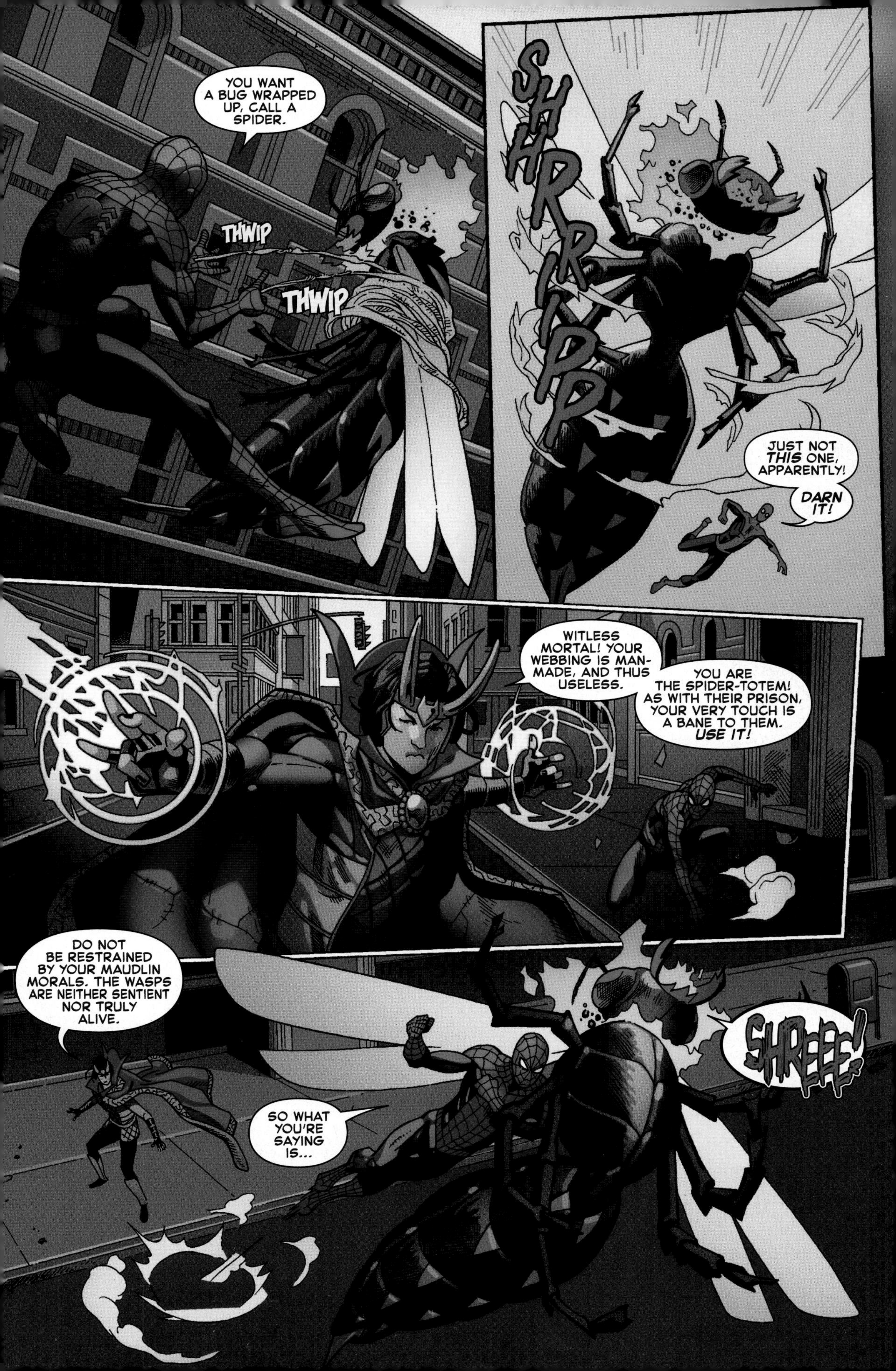
YOU WANT A BUG WRAPPED UP, CALL A SPIDER.
THWIP
THWIP
SHHRIPP
JUST NOT THIS ONE, APPARENTLY!
DARN IT!
WITLESS MORTAL! YOUR WEBBING IS MAN-MADE, AND THUS USELESS.
YOU ARE THE SPIDER-TOTEM! AS WITH THEIR PRISON, YOUR VERY TOUCH IS A BANE TO THEM. USE IT!
DO NOT BE RESTRAINED BY YOUR MAUDLIN MORALS. THE WASPS ARE NEITHER SENTIENT NOR TRULY ALIVE.
SHREEE!
SO WHAT YOU'RE SAYING IS...

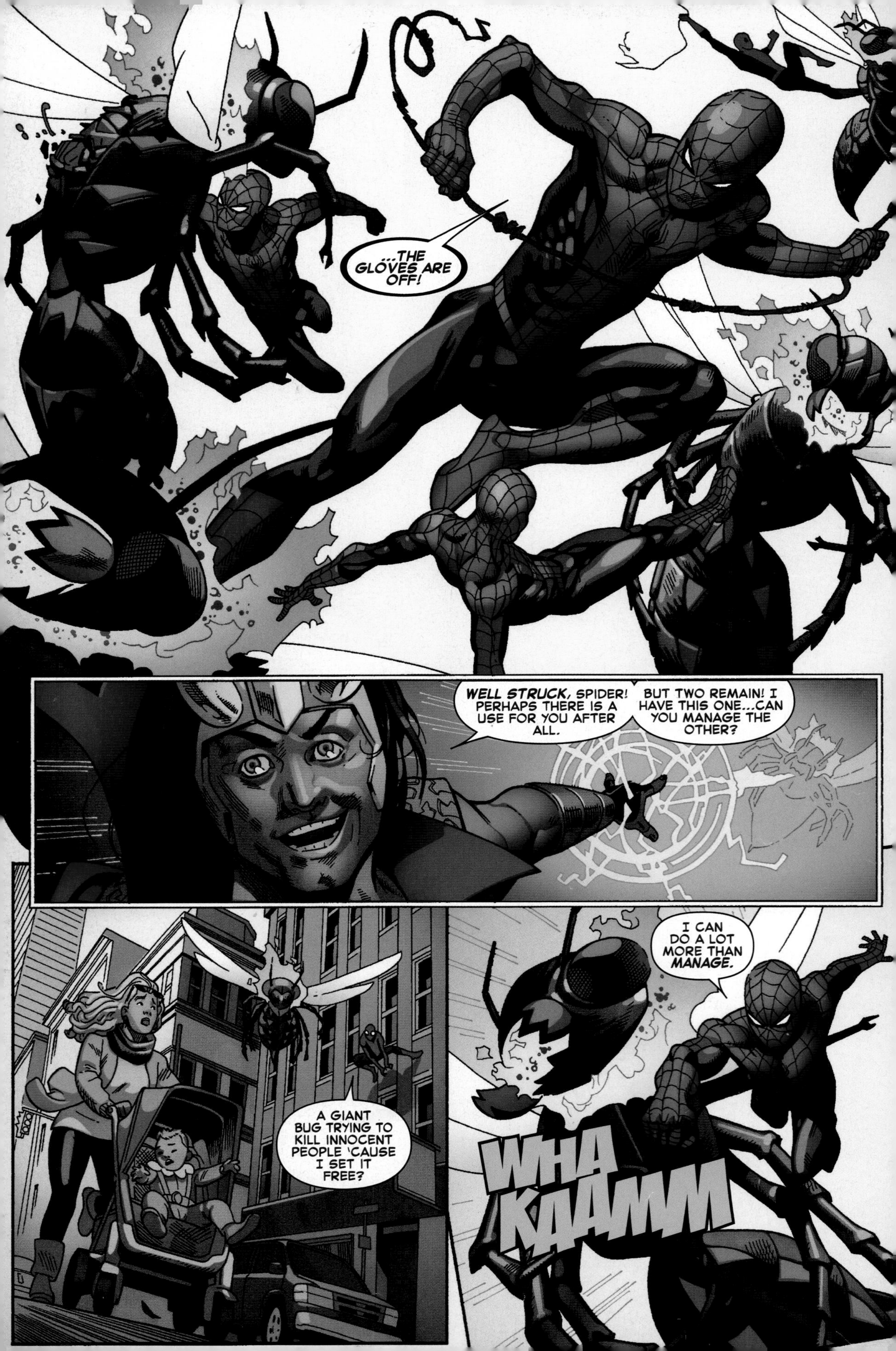
...THE GLOVES ARE OFF!
WELL STRUCK, SPIDER! PERHAPS THERE IS A USE FOR YOU AFTER ALL.
BUT TWO REMAIN! I HAVE THIS ONE...CAN YOU MANAGE THE OTHER?
A GIANT BUG TRYING TO KILL INNOCENT PEOPLE 'CAUSE I SET IT FREE?
I CAN DO A LOT MORE THAN MANAGE.
WHA KAAMMM

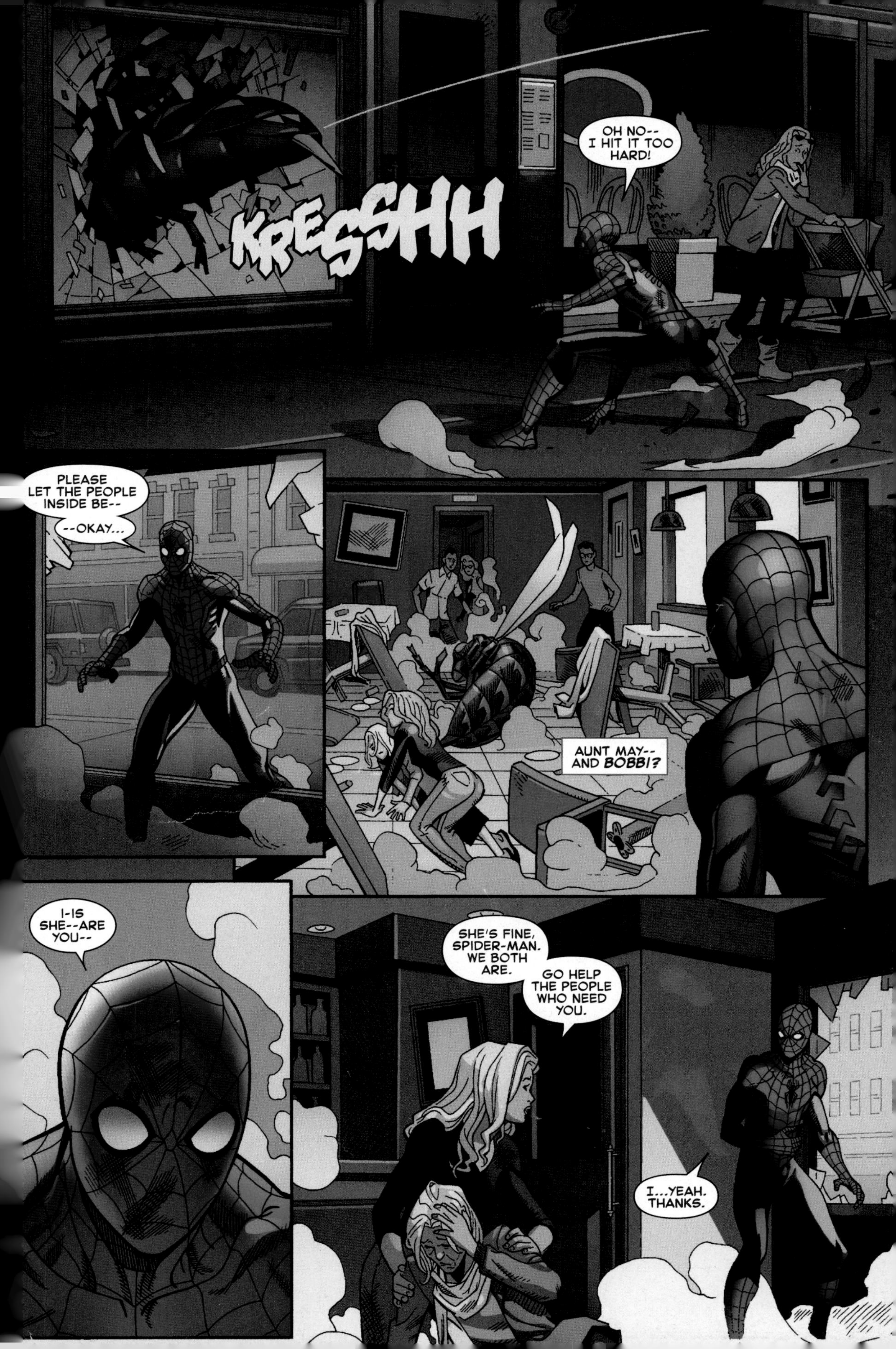
KRESSHH
OH NO-- I HIT IT TOO HARD!
PLEASE LET THE PEOPLE INSIDE BE--
--OKAY...
AUNT MAY-- AND BOBBI?
I-IS SHE--ARE YOU--
SHE'S FINE, SPIDER-MAN. WE BOTH ARE.
GO HELP THE PEOPLE WHO NEED YOU.
I...YEAH. THANKS.

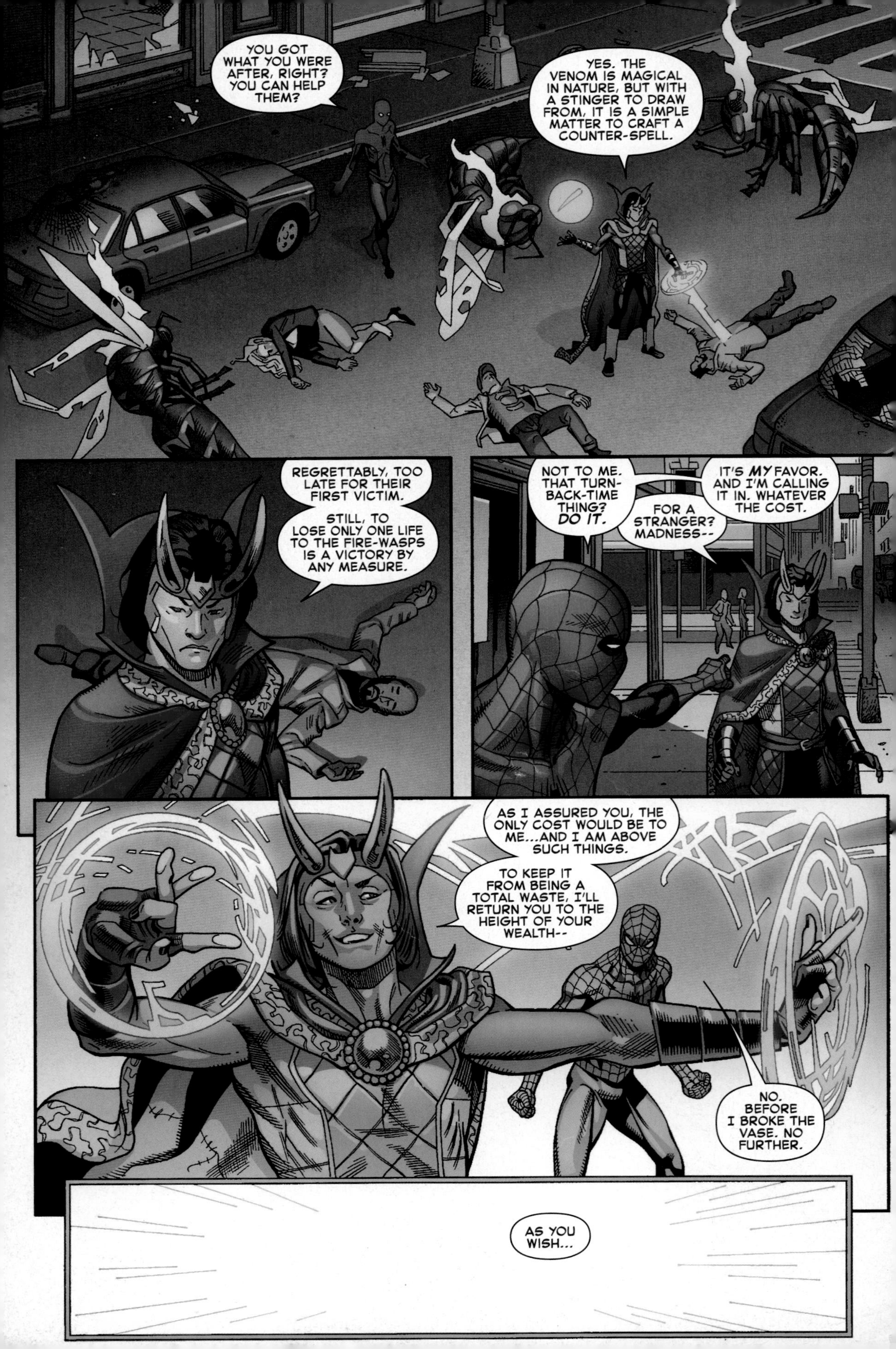
YOU GOT WHAT YOU WERE AFTER, RIGHT? YOU CAN HELP THEM?
YES. THE VENOM IS MAGICAL IN NATURE, BUT WITH A STINGER TO DRAW FROM, IT IS A SIMPLE MATTER TO CRAFT A COUNTER-SPELL.
REGRETTABLY, TOO LATE FOR THEIR FIRST VICTIM.
STILL, TO LOSE ONLY ONE LIFE TO THE FIRE-WASPS IS A VICTORY BY ANY MEASURE.
NOT TO ME. THAT TURN-BACK-TIME THING? DO IT.
FOR A STRANGER? MADNESS--
IT'S MY FAVOR. AND I'M CALLING IT IN. WHATEVER THE COST.
AS I ASSURED YOU, THE ONLY COST WOULD BE TO ME...AND I AM ABOVE SUCH THINGS.
TO KEEP IT FROM BEING A TOTAL WASTE, I'LL RETURN YOU TO THE HEIGHT OF YOUR WEALTH--
NO. BEFORE I BROKE THE VASE. NO FURTHER.
AS YOU WISH...

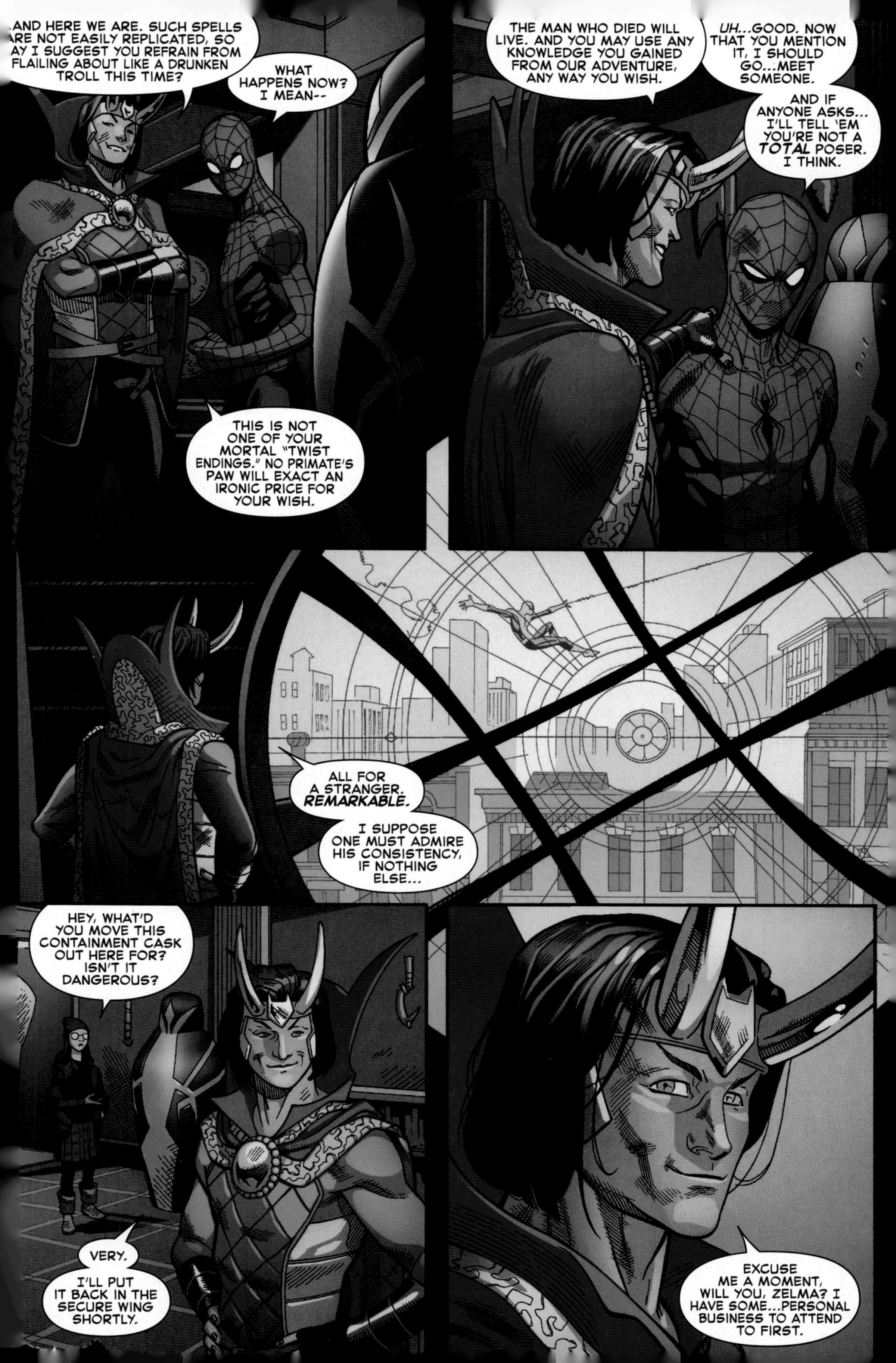
...AND HERE WE ARE. SUCH SPELLS ARE NOT EASILY REPLICATED, SO MAY I SUGGEST YOU REFRAIN FROM FLAILING ABOUT LIKE A DRUNKEN TROLL THIS TIME?
WHAT HAPPENS NOW? I MEAN--
THIS IS NOT ONE OF YOUR MORTAL "TWIST ENDINGS." NO PRIMATE'S PAW WILL EXACT AN IRONIC PRICE FOR YOUR WISH.
THE MAN WHO DIED WILL LIVE. AND YOU MAY USE ANY KNOWLEDGE YOU GAINED FROM OUR ADVENTURE, ANY WAY YOU WISH.
UH...GOOD. NOW THAT YOU MENTION IT, I SHOULD GO...MEET SOMEONE.
AND IF ANYONE ASKS... I'LL TELL 'EM YOU'RE NOT A TOTAL POSER. I THINK.
ALL FOR A STRANGER. REMARKABLE.
I SUPPOSE ONE MUST ADMIRE HIS CONSISTENCY, IF NOTHING ELSE...
HEY, WHAT'D YOU MOVE THIS CONTAINMENT CASK OUT HERE FOR? ISN'T IT DANGEROUS?
VERY.
I'LL PUT IT BACK IN THE SECURE WING SHORTLY.
EXCUSE ME A MOMENT, WILL YOU, ZELMA? I HAVE SOME...PERSONAL BUSINESS TO ATTEND TO FIRST.

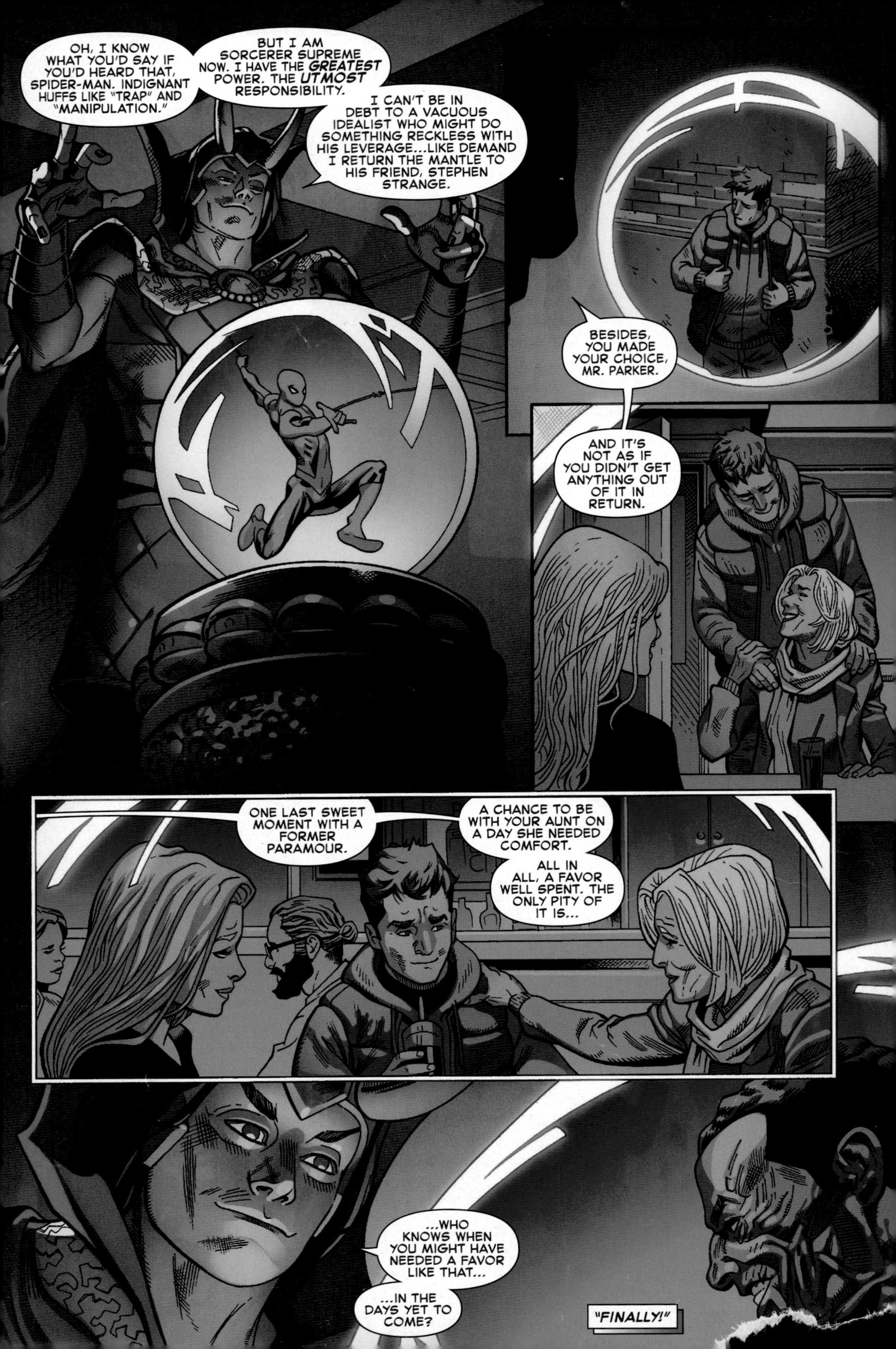
OH, I KNOW WHAT YOU'D SAY IF YOU'D HEARD THAT, SPIDER-MAN. INDIGNANT HUFFS LIKE "TRAP" AND "MANIPULATION."
BUT I AM SORCERER SUPREME NOW. I HAVE THE GREATEST POWER. THE UTMOST RESPONSIBILITY.
I CAN'T BE IN DEBT TO A VACUOUS IDEALIST WHO MIGHT DO SOMETHING RECKLESS WITH HIS LEVERAGE...LIKE DEMAND I RETURN THE MANTLE TO HIS FRIEND, STEPHEN STRANGE.
BESIDES, YOU MADE YOUR CHOICE, MR. PARKER.
AND IT'S NOT AS IF YOU DIDN'T GET ANYTHING OUT OF IT IN RETURN.
ONE LAST SWEET MOMENT WITH A FORMER PARAMOUR.
A CHANCE TO BE WITH YOUR AUNT ON A DAY SHE NEEDED COMFORT.
ALL IN ALL, A FAVOR WELL SPENT. THE ONLY PITY OF IT IS...
...WHO KNOWS WHEN YOU MIGHT HAVE NEEDED A FAVOR LIKE THAT...
...IN THE DAYS YET TO COME?
"FINALLY!"

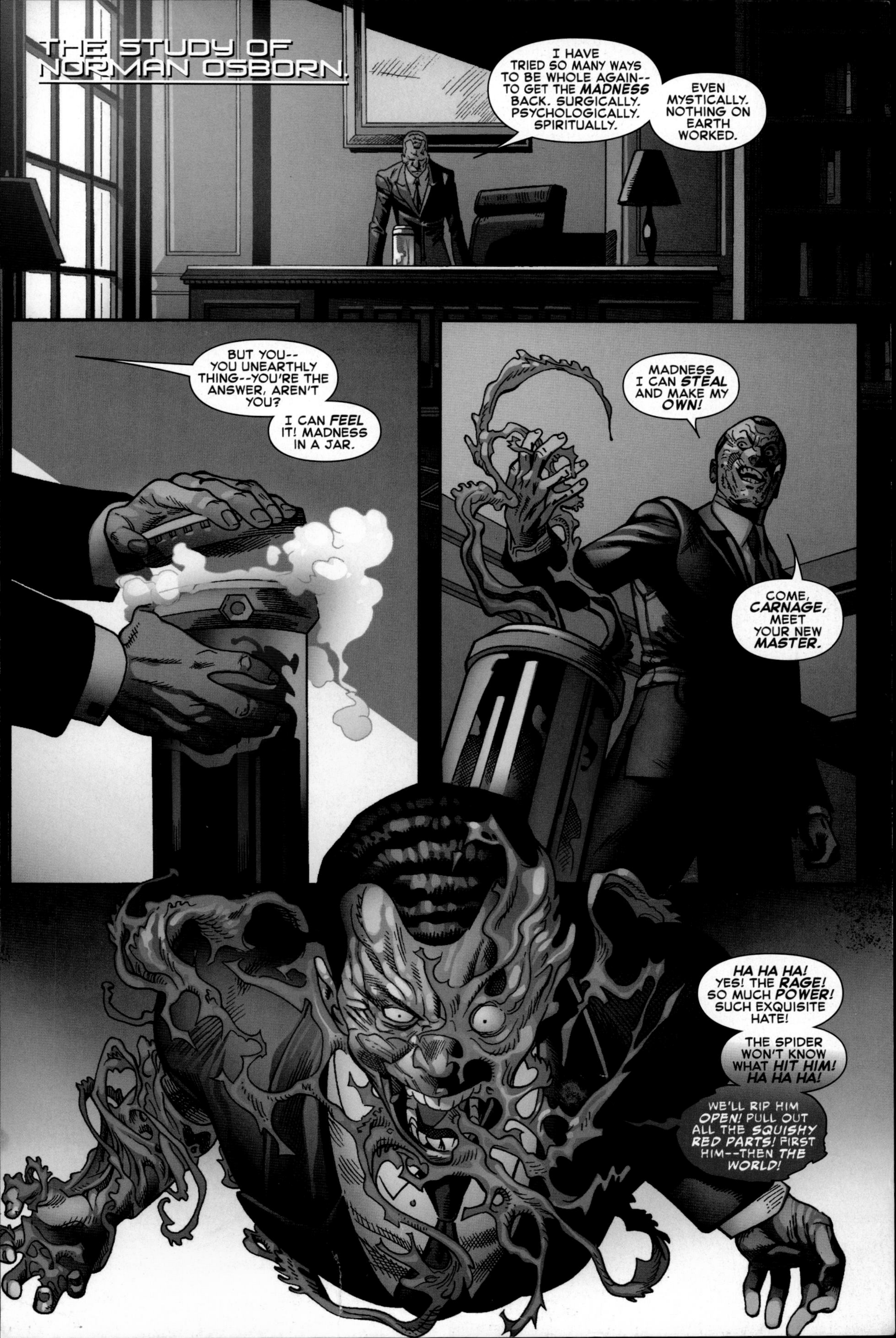

THE STUDY OF NORMAN OSBORN.
I HAVE TRIED SO MANY WAYS TO BE WHOLE AGAIN-- TO GET THE MADNESS BACK. SURGICALLY. PSYCHOLOGICALLY. SPIRITUALLY.
EVEN MYSTICALLY. NOTHING ON EARTH WORKED.
BUT YOU-- YOU UNEARTHLY THING--YOU'RE THE ANSWER, AREN'T YOU?
I CAN FEEL IT! MADNESS IN A JAR.
MADNESS I CAN STEAL AND MAKE MY OWN!
COME, CARNAGE, MEET YOUR NEW MASTER.
HA HA HA! YES! THE RAGE! SO MUCH POWER! SUCH EXQUISITE HATE!
THE SPIDER WON'T KNOW WHAT HIT HIM! HA HA HA!
WE'LL RIP HIM OPEN! PULL OUT ALL THE SQUISHY RED PARTS! FIRST HIM--THEN THE WORLD!

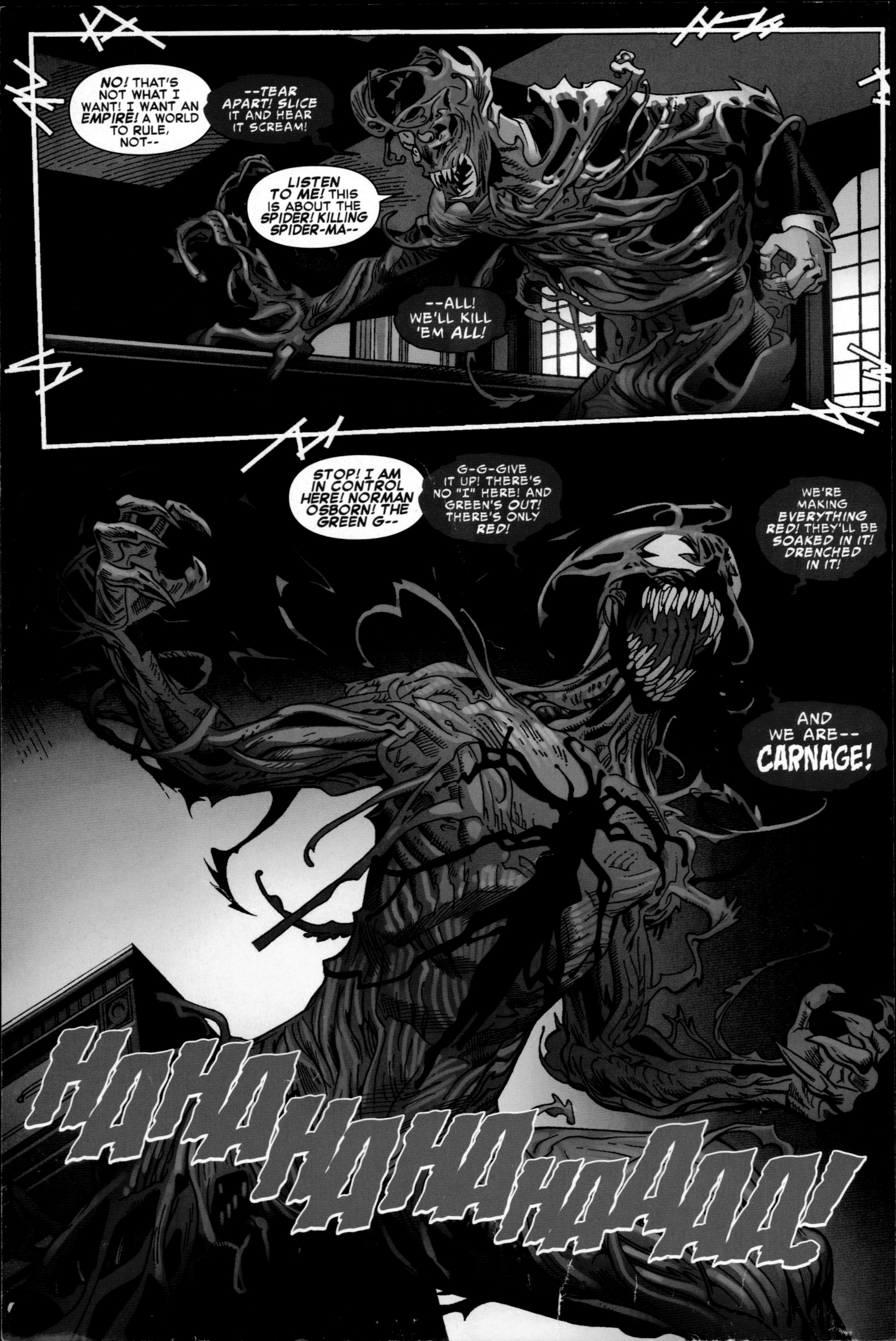
NO! THAT'S NOT WHAT I WANT! I WANT AN EMPIRE! A WORLD TO RULE, NOT--
--TEAR APART! SLICE IT AND HEAR IT SCREAM!
LISTEN TO ME! THIS IS ABOUT THE SPIDER! KILLING SPIDER-MA--
--ALL! WE'LL KILL 'EM ALL!
STOP! I AM IN CONTROL HERE! NORMAN OSBORN! THE GREEN G--
G-G-GIVE IT UP! THERE'S NO "I" HERE! AND GREEN'S OUT! THERE'S ONLY RED!
WE'RE MAKING EVERYTHING RED! THEY'LL BE SOAKED IN IT! DRENCHED IN IT!
AND WE ARE-- CARNAGE!

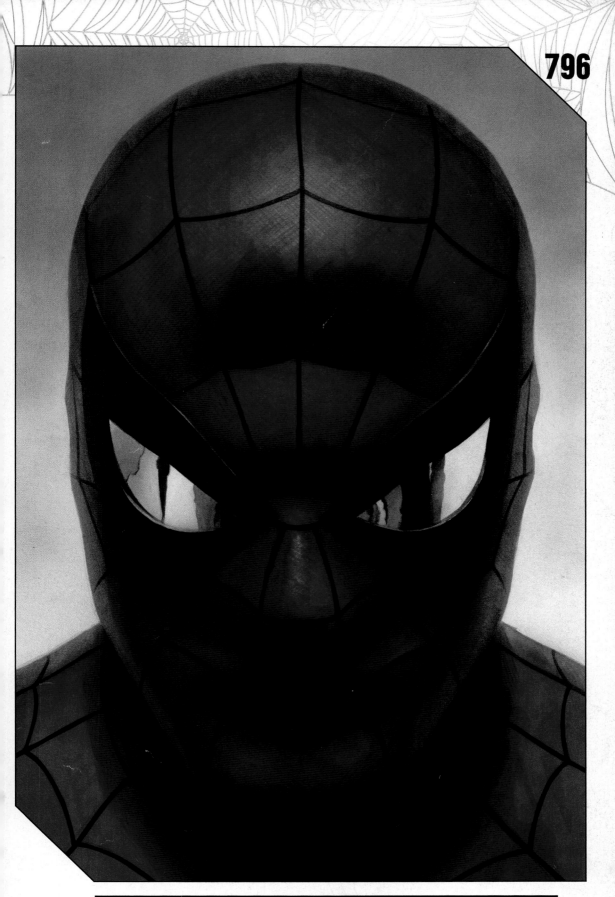

THREAT LEVEL: RED PART THREE "HIGHER PRIORITIES"

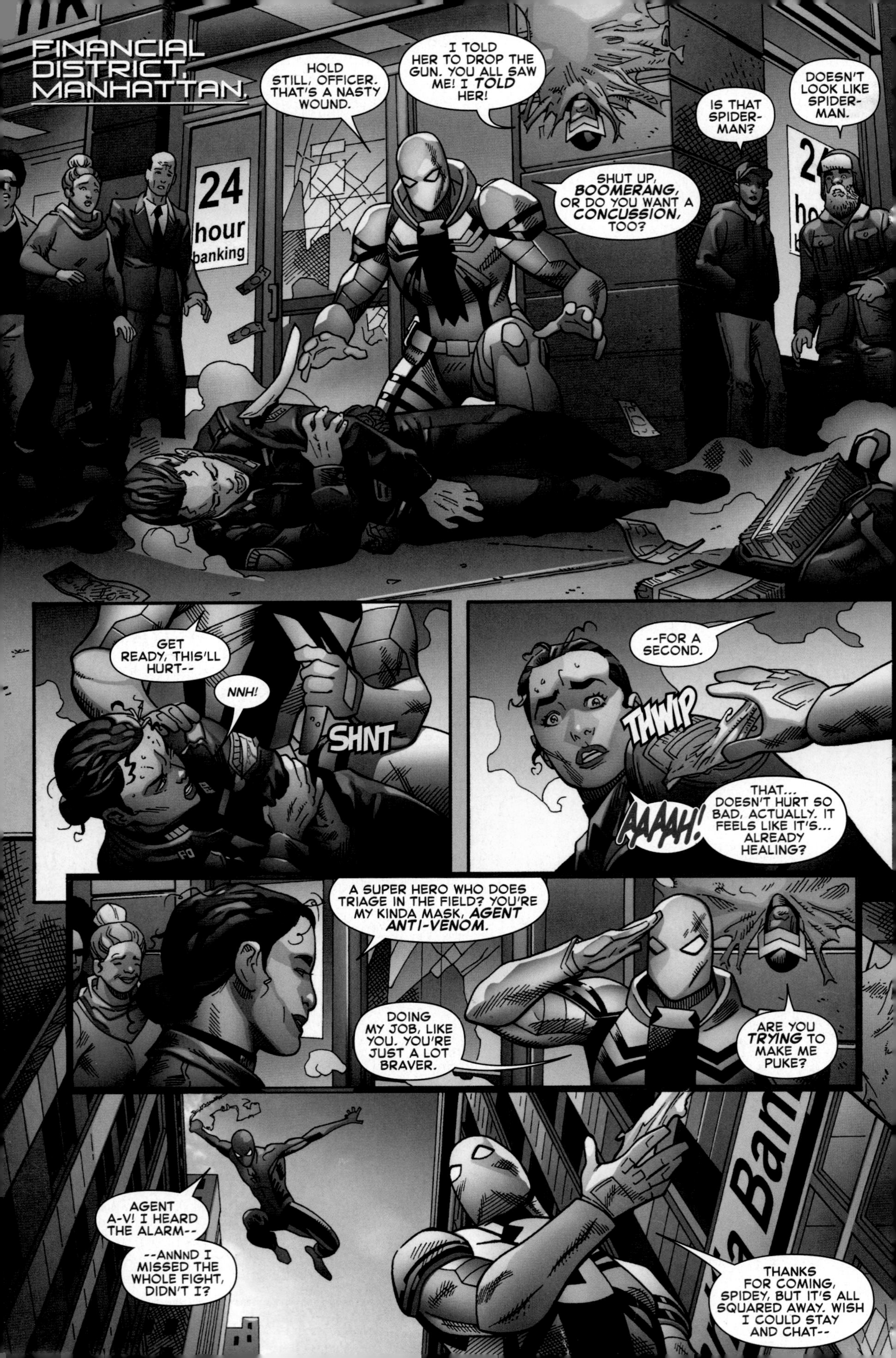
FINANCIAL DISTRICT, MANHATTAN.
HOLD STILL, OFFICER. THAT'S A NASTY WOUND.
I TOLD HER TO DROP THE GUN. YOU ALL SAW ME! I *TOLD* HER!
SHUT UP, **BOOMERANG,** OR DO YOU WANT A **CONCUSSION,** TOO?
IS THAT SPIDER-MAN?
DOESN'T LOOK LIKE SPIDER-MAN.
24 hour banking
GET READY, THIS'LL HURT--
NNH!
SHNT
--FOR A SECOND.
THWIP
AAAAH!
THAT... DOESN'T HURT SO BAD, ACTUALLY. IT FEELS LIKE IT'S... ALREADY HEALING?
A SUPER HERO WHO DOES TRIAGE IN THE FIELD? YOU'RE MY KINDA MASK, **AGENT ANTI-VENOM.**
DOING MY JOB, LIKE YOU. YOU'RE JUST A LOT BRAVER.
ARE YOU *TRYING* TO MAKE ME PUKE?
AGENT A-V! I HEARD THE ALARM--
--ANNND I MISSED THE WHOLE FIGHT, DIDN'T I?
THANKS FOR COMING, SPIDEY, BUT IT'S ALL SQUARED AWAY. WISH I COULD STAY AND CHAT--

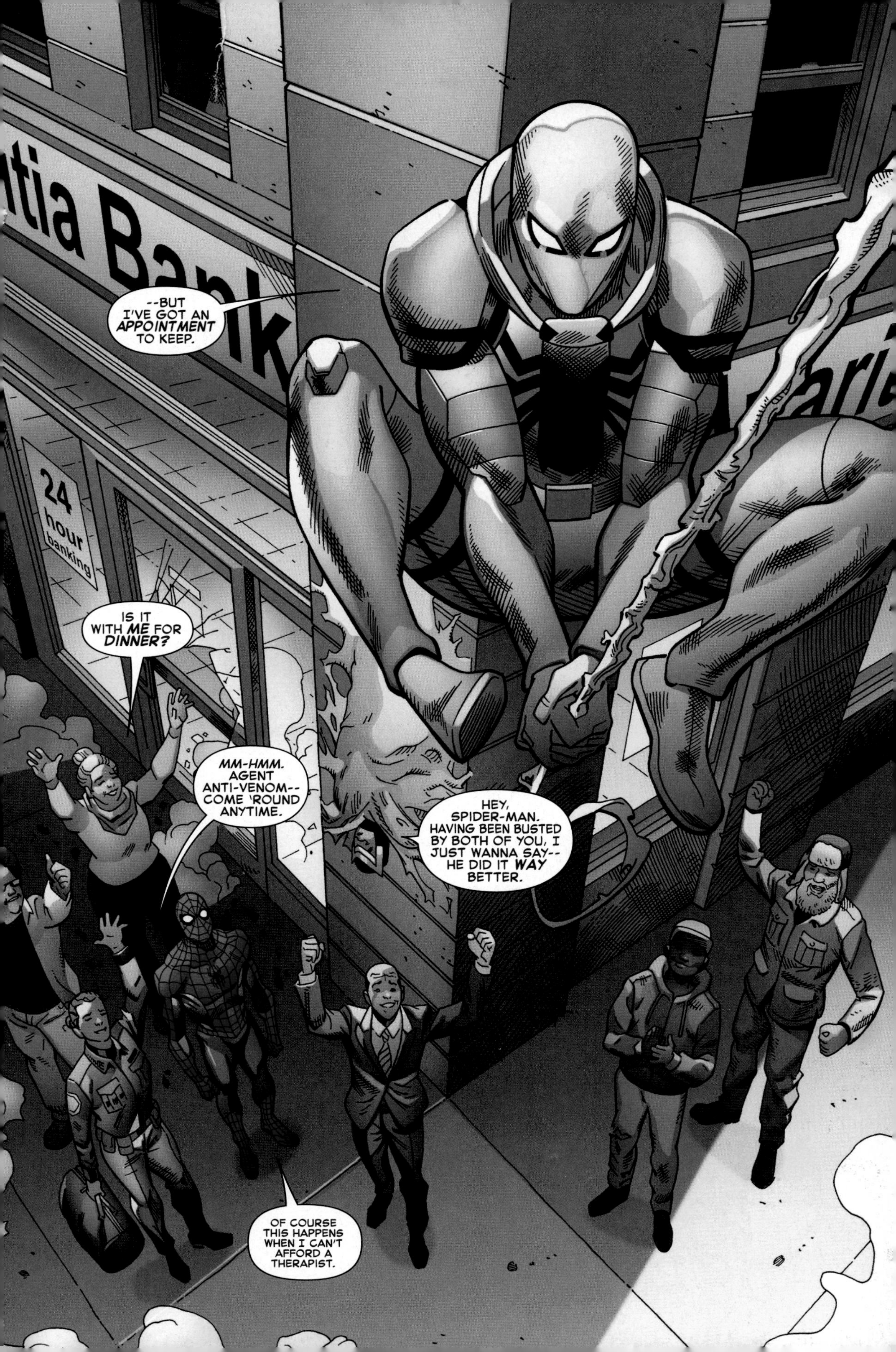

ntia Bank
--BUT I'VE GOT AN APPOINTMENT TO KEEP.
24 hour banking
IS IT WITH ME FOR DINNER?
MM-HMM. AGENT ANTI-VENOM-- COME 'ROUND ANYTIME.
HEY, SPIDER-MAN. HAVING BEEN BUSTED BY BOTH OF YOU, I JUST WANNA SAY-- HE DID IT WAY BETTER.
OF COURSE THIS HAPPENS WHEN I CAN'T AFFORD A THERAPIST.

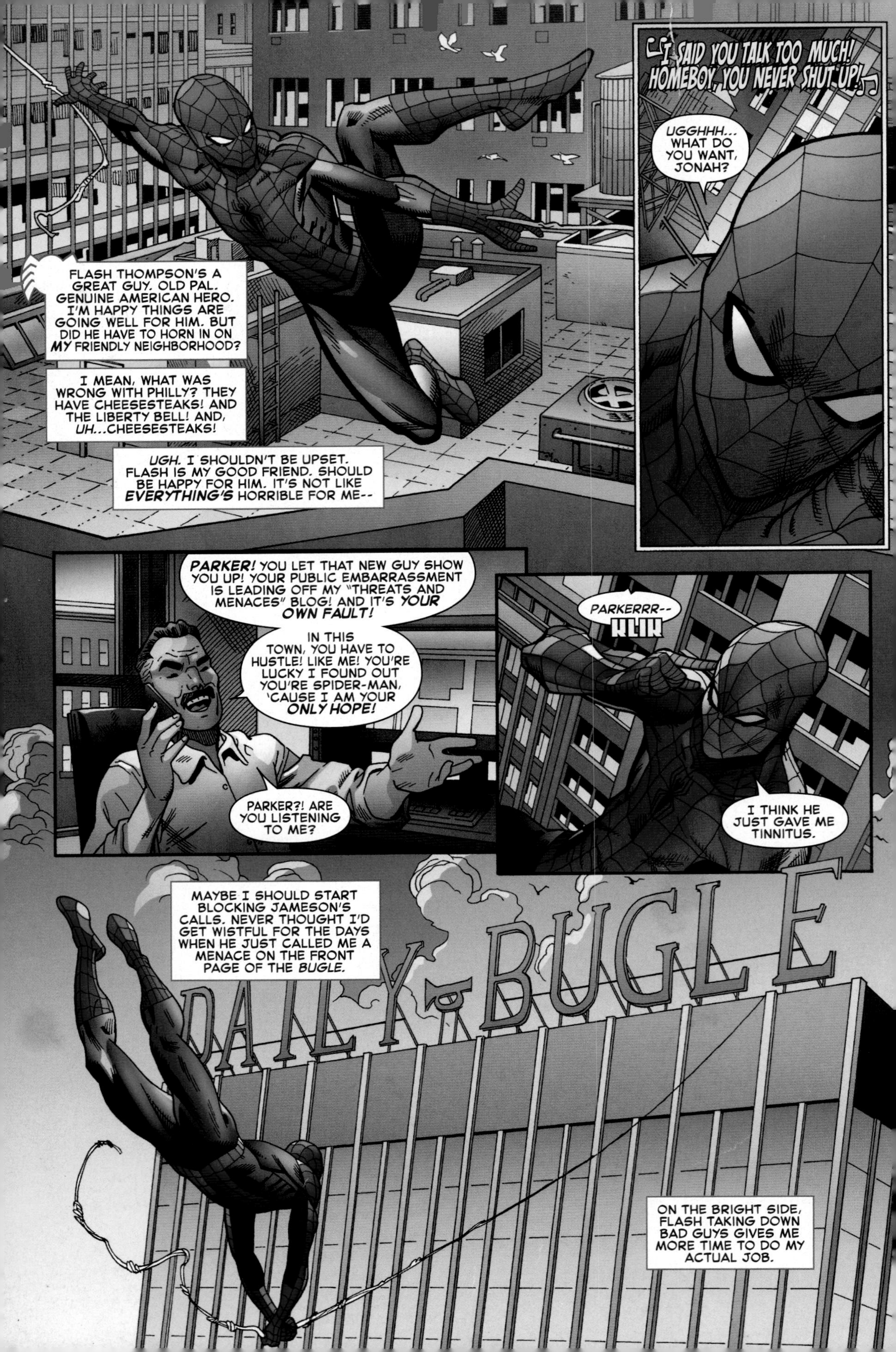
FLASH THOMPSON'S A GREAT GUY. OLD PAL. GENUINE AMERICAN HERO. I'M HAPPY THINGS ARE GOING WELL FOR HIM. BUT DID HE HAVE TO HORN IN ON MY FRIENDLY NEIGHBORHOOD?
I MEAN, WHAT WAS WRONG WITH PHILLY? THEY HAVE CHEESESTEAKS! AND THE LIBERTY BELL! AND, UH...CHEESESTEAKS!
UGH. I SHOULDN'T BE UPSET. FLASH IS MY GOOD FRIEND. SHOULD BE HAPPY FOR HIM. IT'S NOT LIKE EVERYTHING'S HORRIBLE FOR ME--
I SAID YOU TALK TOO MUCH! HOMEBOY, YOU NEVER SHUT UP!
UGGHHH... WHAT DO YOU WANT, JONAH?
PARKER! YOU LET THAT NEW GUY SHOW YOU UP! YOUR PUBLIC EMBARRASSMENT IS LEADING OFF MY "THREATS AND MENACES" BLOG! AND IT'S YOUR OWN FAULT!
IN THIS TOWN, YOU HAVE TO HUSTLE! LIKE ME! YOU'RE LUCKY I FOUND OUT YOU'RE SPIDER-MAN, 'CAUSE I AM YOUR ONLY HOPE!
PARKER?! ARE YOU LISTENING TO ME?
PARKERRR--
KLIK
I THINK HE JUST GAVE ME TINNITUS.
MAYBE I SHOULD START BLOCKING JAMESON'S CALLS. NEVER THOUGHT I'D GET WISTFUL FOR THE DAYS WHEN HE JUST CALLED ME A MENACE ON THE FRONT PAGE OF THE BUGLE.
DAILY BUGLE
ON THE BRIGHT SIDE, FLASH TAKING DOWN BAD GUYS GIVES ME MORE TIME TO DO MY ACTUAL JOB.

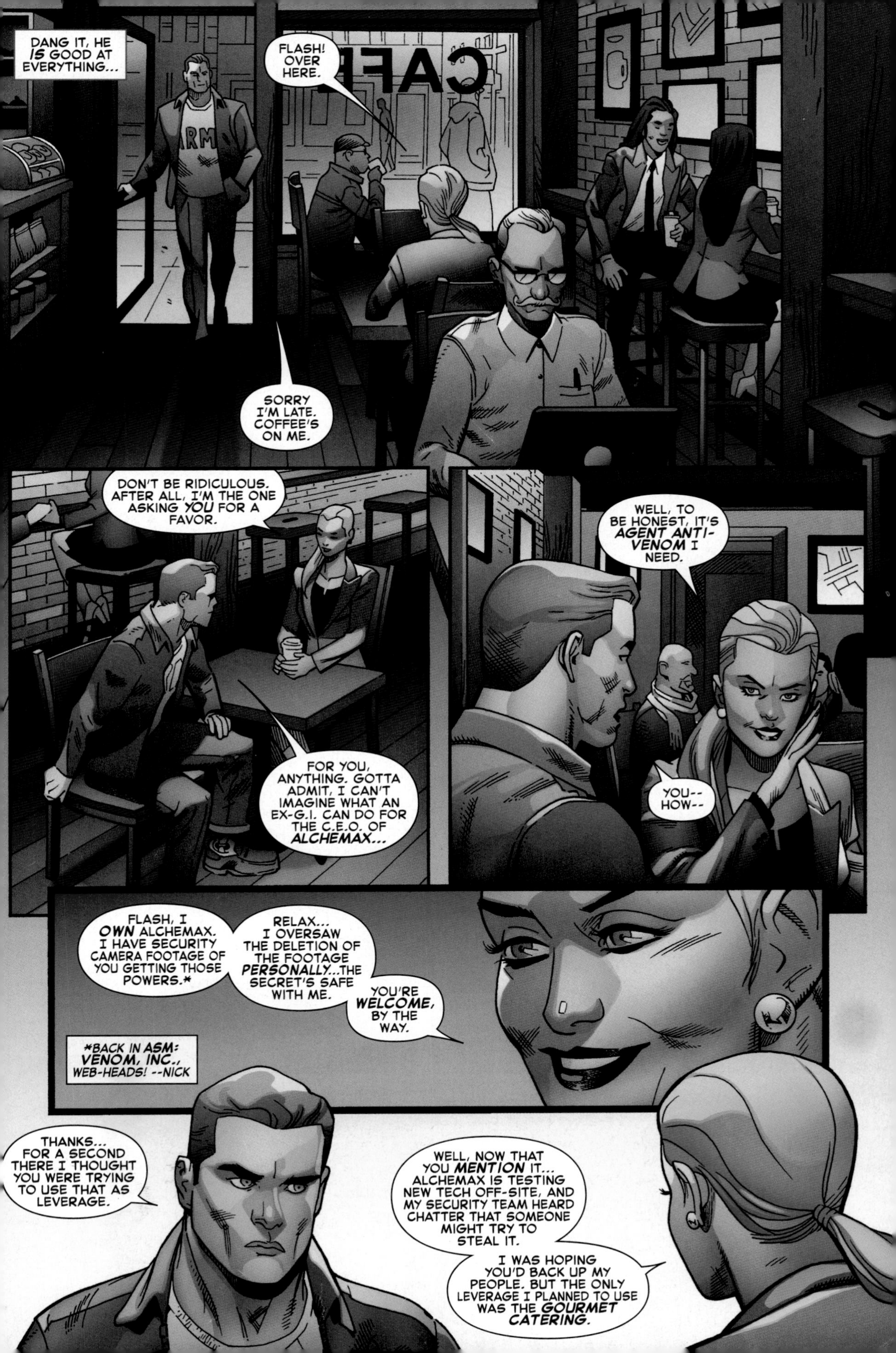
DANG IT, HE IS GOOD AT EVERYTHING...
FLASH! OVER HERE.
SORRY I'M LATE. COFFEE'S ON ME.
DON'T BE RIDICULOUS. AFTER ALL, I'M THE ONE ASKING YOU FOR A FAVOR.
FOR YOU, ANYTHING. GOTTA ADMIT, I CAN'T IMAGINE WHAT AN EX-G.I. CAN DO FOR THE C.E.O. OF ALCHEMAX...
WELL, TO BE HONEST, IT'S AGENT ANTI-VENOM I NEED.
YOU-- HOW--
FLASH, I OWN ALCHEMAX. I HAVE SECURITY CAMERA FOOTAGE OF YOU GETTING THOSE POWERS.*
RELAX... I OVERSAW THE DELETION OF THE FOOTAGE PERSONALLY...THE SECRET'S SAFE WITH ME.
YOU'RE WELCOME, BY THE WAY.
*BACK IN ASM: VENOM, INC., WEB-HEADS! --NICK
THANKS... FOR A SECOND THERE I THOUGHT YOU WERE TRYING TO USE THAT AS LEVERAGE.
WELL, NOW THAT YOU MENTION IT... ALCHEMAX IS TESTING NEW TECH OFF-SITE, AND MY SECURITY TEAM HEARD CHATTER THAT SOMEONE MIGHT TRY TO STEAL IT.
I WAS HOPING YOU'D BACK UP MY PEOPLE. BUT THE ONLY LEVERAGE I PLANNED TO USE WAS THE GOURMET CATERING.

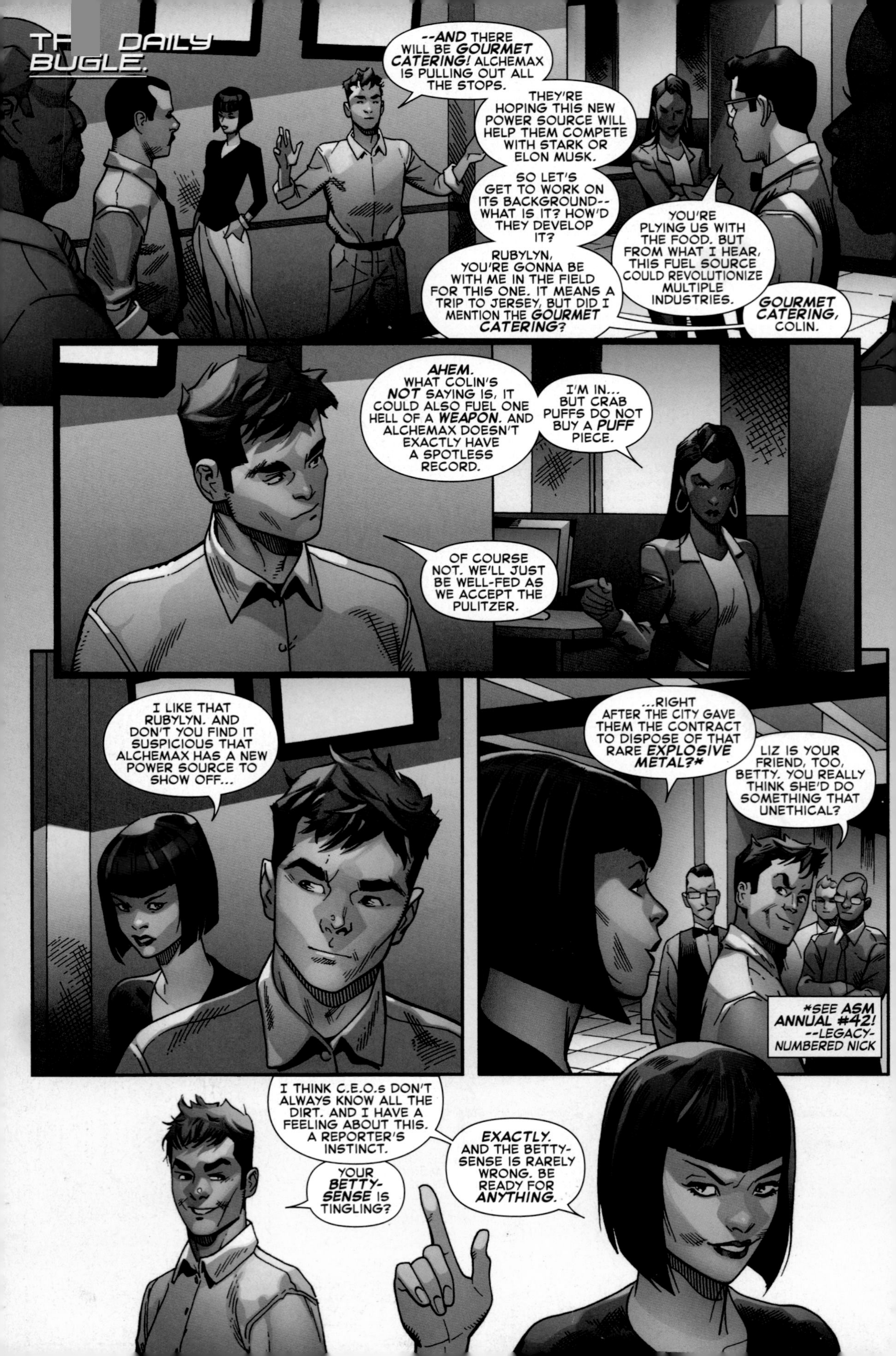

TH DAILY BUGLE.
--AND THERE WILL BE GOURMET CATERING! ALCHEMAX IS PULLING OUT ALL THE STOPS.
THEY'RE HOPING THIS NEW POWER SOURCE WILL HELP THEM COMPETE WITH STARK OR ELON MUSK.
SO LET'S GET TO WORK ON ITS BACKGROUND-- WHAT IS IT? HOW'D THEY DEVELOP IT?
RUBYLYN, YOU'RE GONNA BE WITH ME IN THE FIELD FOR THIS ONE. IT MEANS A TRIP TO JERSEY, BUT DID I MENTION THE GOURMET CATERING?
YOU'RE PLYING US WITH THE FOOD. BUT FROM WHAT I HEAR, THIS FUEL SOURCE COULD REVOLUTIONIZE MULTIPLE INDUSTRIES.
GOURMET CATERING, COLIN.
AHEM. WHAT COLIN'S NOT SAYING IS, IT COULD ALSO FUEL ONE HELL OF A WEAPON. AND ALCHEMAX DOESN'T EXACTLY HAVE A SPOTLESS RECORD.
I'M IN... BUT CRAB PUFFS DO NOT BUY A PUFF PIECE.
OF COURSE NOT. WE'LL JUST BE WELL-FED AS WE ACCEPT THE PULITZER.
I LIKE THAT RUBYLYN. AND DON'T YOU FIND IT SUSPICIOUS THAT ALCHEMAX HAS A NEW POWER SOURCE TO SHOW OFF...
...RIGHT AFTER THE CITY GAVE THEM THE CONTRACT TO DISPOSE OF THAT RARE EXPLOSIVE METAL?*
LIZ IS YOUR FRIEND, TOO, BETTY. YOU REALLY THINK SHE'D DO SOMETHING THAT UNETHICAL?
*SEE ASM ANNUAL #42! --LEGACY-NUMBERED NICK
I THINK C.E.O.s DON'T ALWAYS KNOW ALL THE DIRT. AND I HAVE A FEELING ABOUT THIS. A REPORTER'S INSTINCT.
YOUR BETTY-SENSE IS TINGLING?
EXACTLY. AND THE BETTY-SENSE IS RARELY WRONG. BE READY FOR ANYTHING.

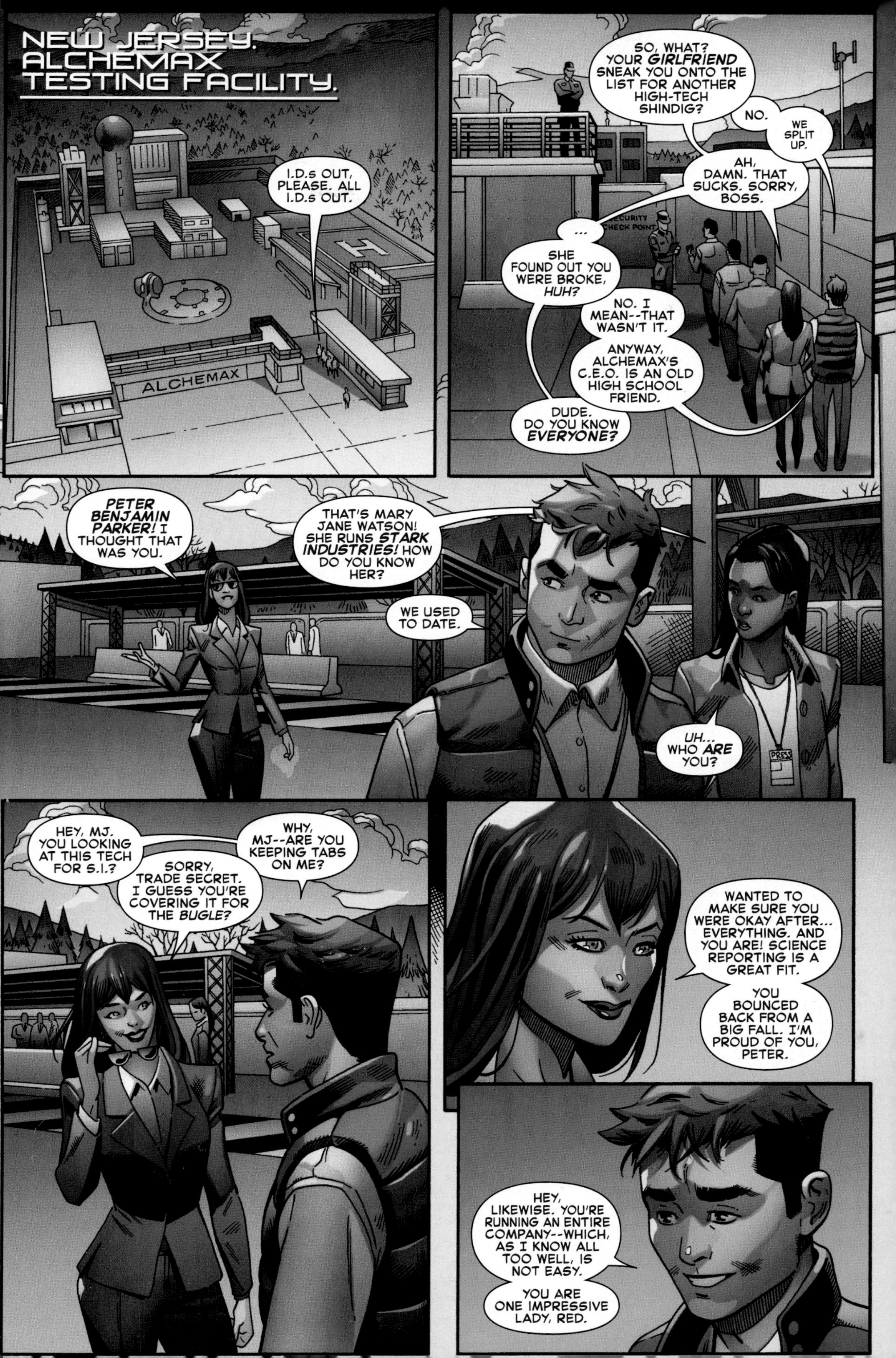
NEW JERSEY. ALCHEMAX TESTING FACILITY.
I.D.s OUT, PLEASE. ALL I.D.s OUT.
ALCHEMAX
SO, WHAT? YOUR GIRLFRIEND SNEAK YOU ONTO THE LIST FOR ANOTHER HIGH-TECH SHINDIG?
NO.
WE SPLIT UP.
AH, DAMN. THAT SUCKS. SORRY, BOSS.
...
SECURITY CHECK POINT
SHE FOUND OUT YOU WERE BROKE, HUH?
NO. I MEAN--THAT WASN'T IT.
ANYWAY, ALCHEMAX'S C.E.O. IS AN OLD HIGH SCHOOL FRIEND.
DUDE. DO YOU KNOW EVERYONE?
PETER BENJAMIN PARKER! I THOUGHT THAT WAS YOU.
THAT'S MARY JANE WATSON! SHE RUNS STARK INDUSTRIES! HOW DO YOU KNOW HER?
WE USED TO DATE.
UH... WHO ARE YOU?
PRESS
HEY, MJ. YOU LOOKING AT THIS TECH FOR S.I.?
SORRY, TRADE SECRET. I GUESS YOU'RE COVERING IT FOR THE BUGLE?
WHY, MJ--ARE YOU KEEPING TABS ON ME?
WANTED TO MAKE SURE YOU WERE OKAY AFTER... EVERYTHING. AND YOU ARE! SCIENCE REPORTING IS A GREAT FIT.
YOU BOUNCED BACK FROM A BIG FALL. I'M PROUD OF YOU, PETER.
HEY, LIKEWISE. YOU'RE RUNNING AN ENTIRE COMPANY--WHICH, AS I KNOW ALL TOO WELL, IS NOT EASY.
YOU ARE ONE IMPRESSIVE LADY, RED.

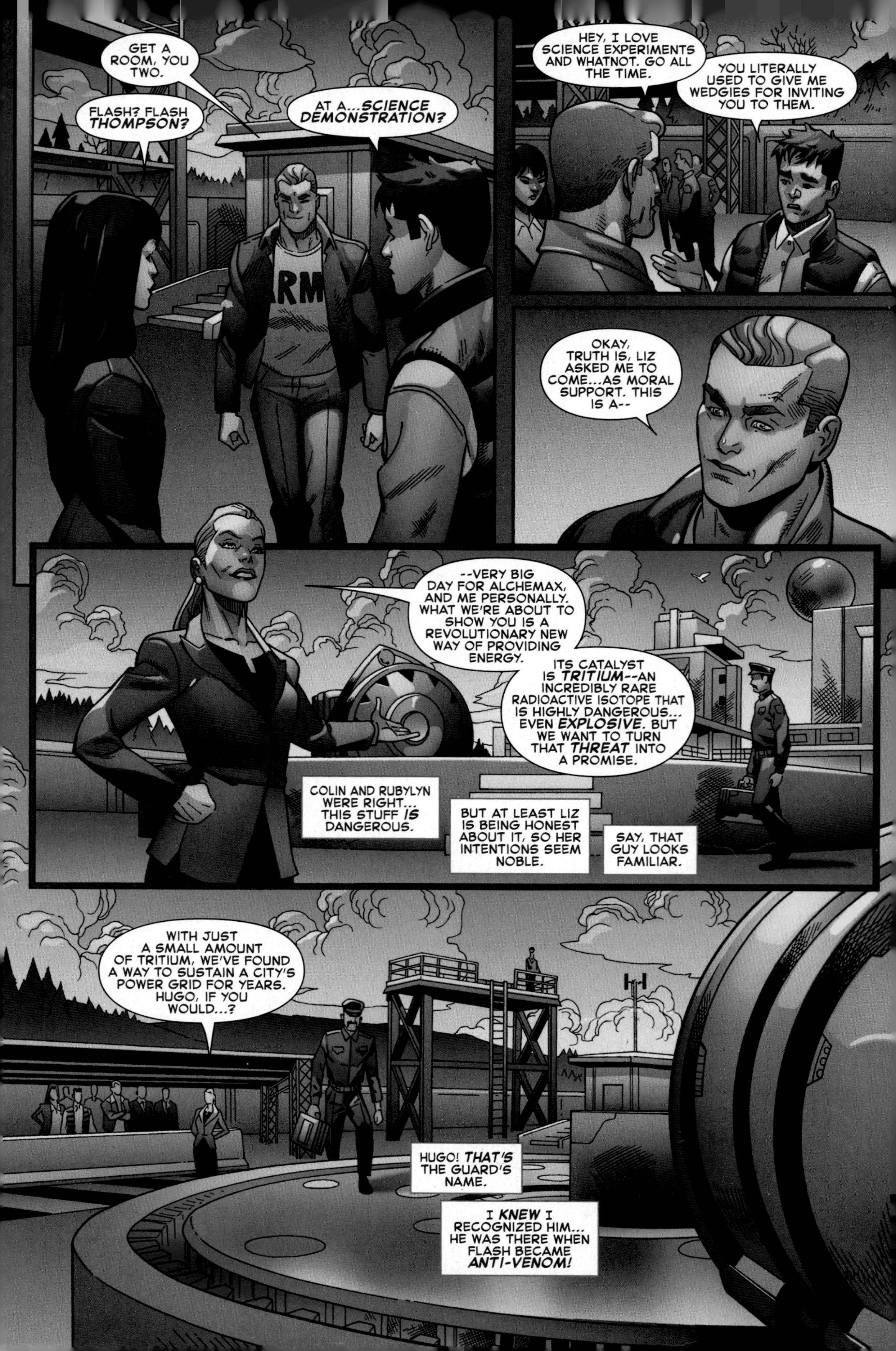
GET A ROOM, YOU TWO.
FLASH? FLASH THOMPSON?
AT A...SCIENCE DEMONSTRATION?
HEY, I LOVE SCIENCE EXPERIMENTS AND WHATNOT. GO ALL THE TIME.
YOU LITERALLY USED TO GIVE ME WEDGIES FOR INVITING YOU TO THEM.
OKAY, TRUTH IS, LIZ ASKED ME TO COME...AS MORAL SUPPORT. THIS IS A--
--VERY BIG DAY FOR ALCHEMAX, AND ME PERSONALLY. WHAT WE'RE ABOUT TO SHOW YOU IS A REVOLUTIONARY NEW WAY OF PROVIDING ENERGY.
ITS CATALYST IS TRITIUM--AN INCREDIBLY RARE RADIOACTIVE ISOTOPE THAT IS HIGHLY DANGEROUS... EVEN EXPLOSIVE. BUT WE WANT TO TURN THAT THREAT INTO A PROMISE.
COLIN AND RUBYLYN WERE RIGHT... THIS STUFF IS DANGEROUS.
BUT AT LEAST LIZ IS BEING HONEST ABOUT IT, SO HER INTENTIONS SEEM NOBLE.
SAY, THAT GUY LOOKS FAMILIAR.
WITH JUST A SMALL AMOUNT OF TRITIUM, WE'VE FOUND A WAY TO SUSTAIN A CITY'S POWER GRID FOR YEARS. HUGO, IF YOU WOULD...?
HUGO! THAT'S THE GUARD'S NAME.
I KNEW I RECOGNIZED HIM... HE WAS THERE WHEN FLASH BECAME ANTI-VENOM!

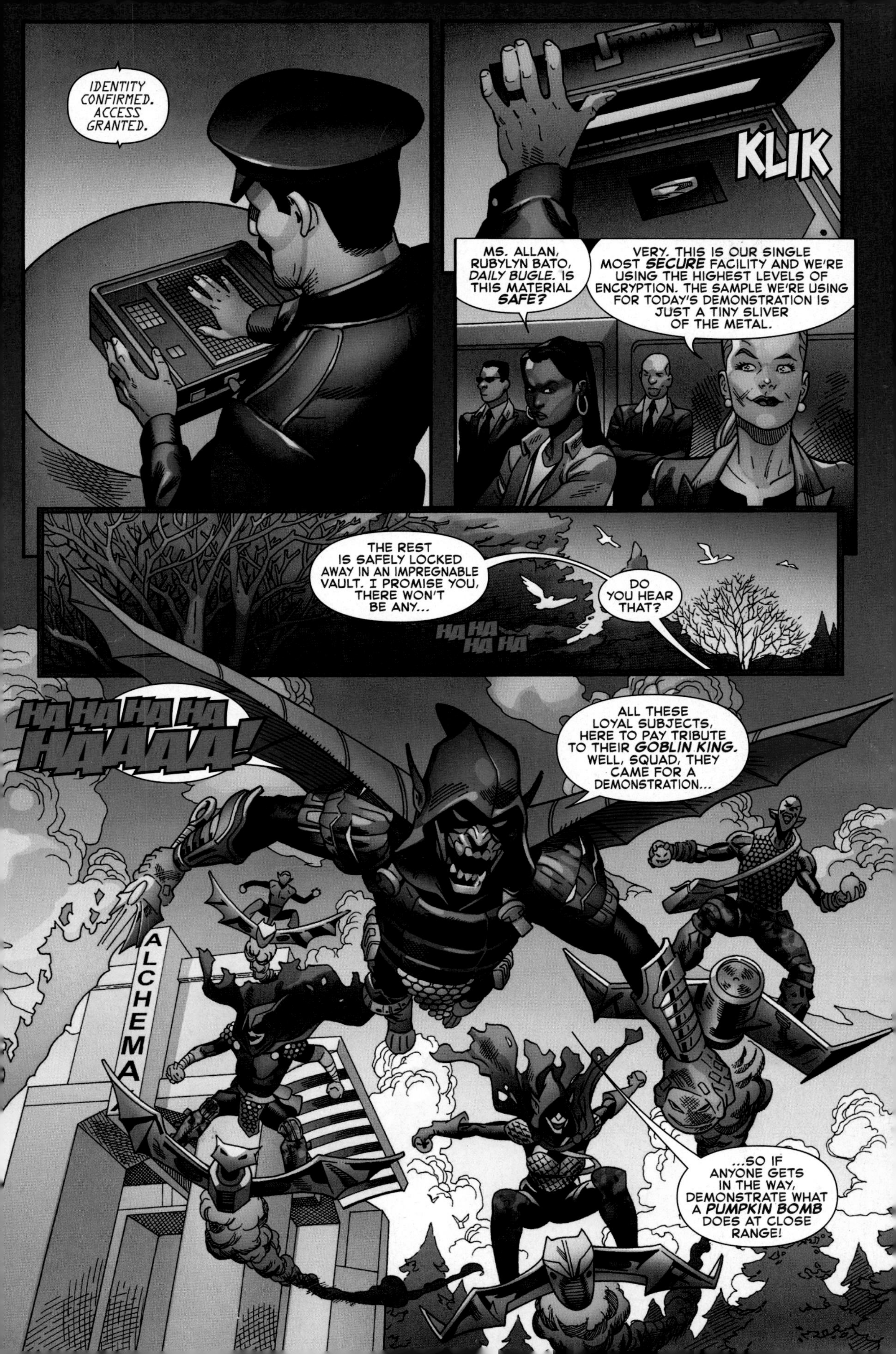
IDENTITY CONFIRMED. ACCESS GRANTED.
KLIK
MS. ALLAN, RUBYLYN BATO, DAILY BUGLE. IS THIS MATERIAL SAFE?
VERY. THIS IS OUR SINGLE MOST SECURE FACILITY AND WE'RE USING THE HIGHEST LEVELS OF ENCRYPTION. THE SAMPLE WE'RE USING FOR TODAY'S DEMONSTRATION IS JUST A TINY SLIVER OF THE METAL.
THE REST IS SAFELY LOCKED AWAY IN AN IMPREGNABLE VAULT. I PROMISE YOU, THERE WON'T BE ANY...
DO YOU HEAR THAT?
HA HA HA HA
HA HA HA HA HAAAAA!
ALL THESE LOYAL SUBJECTS, HERE TO PAY TRIBUTE TO THEIR GOBLIN KING. WELL, SQUAD, THEY CAME FOR A DEMONSTRATION...
ALCHEMA
...SO IF ANYONE GETS IN THE WAY, DEMONSTRATE WHAT A PUMPKIN BOMB DOES AT CLOSE RANGE!

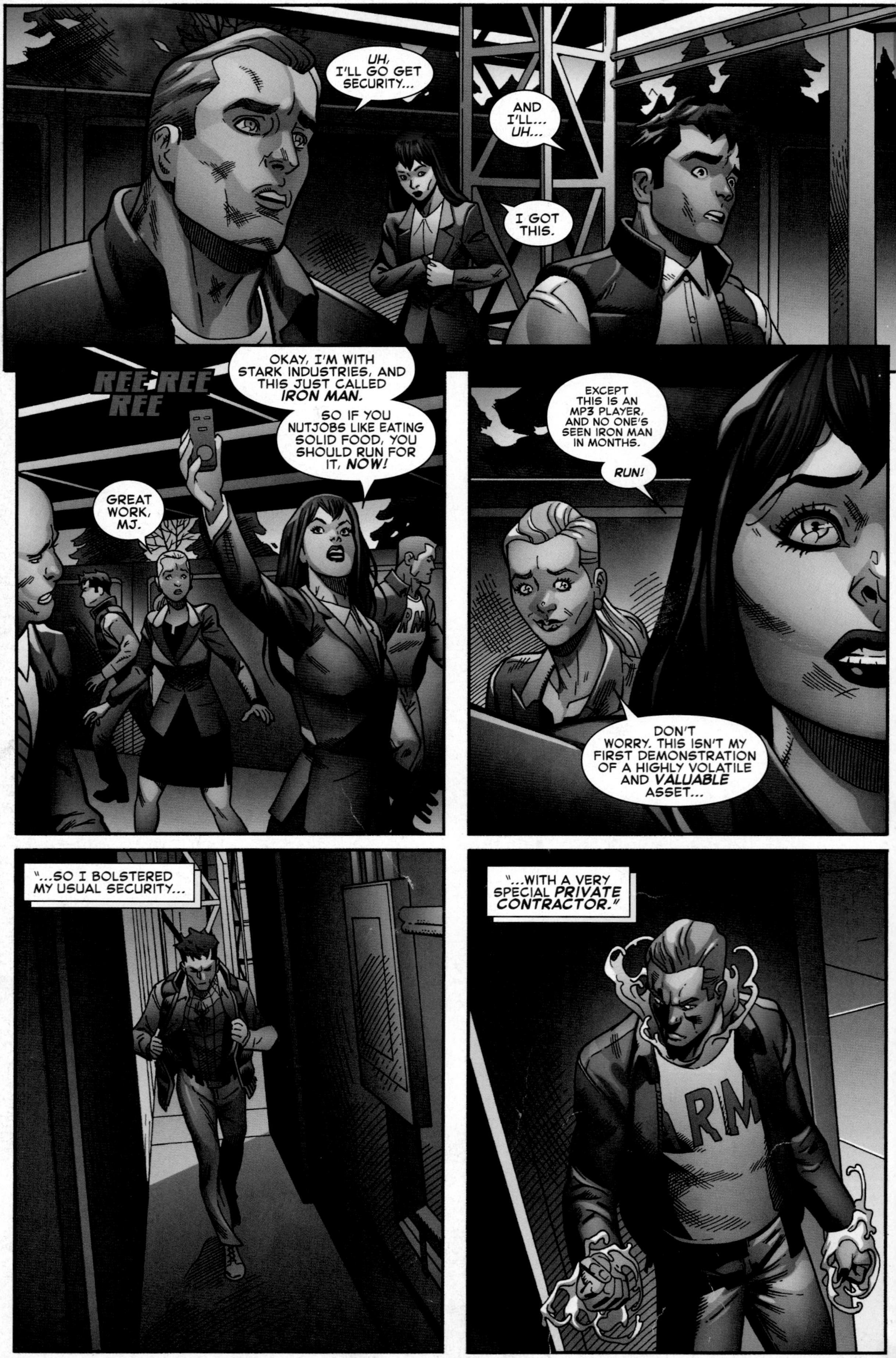
UH, I'LL GO GET SECURITY...
AND I'LL... UH...
I GOT THIS.
REE REE REE
OKAY, I'M WITH STARK INDUSTRIES, AND THIS JUST CALLED IRON MAN.
SO IF YOU NUTJOBS LIKE EATING SOLID FOOD, YOU SHOULD RUN FOR IT, NOW!
GREAT WORK, MJ.
EXCEPT THIS IS AN MP3 PLAYER, AND NO ONE'S SEEN IRON MAN IN MONTHS.
RUN!
DON'T WORRY. THIS ISN'T MY FIRST DEMONSTRATION OF A HIGHLY VOLATILE AND VALUABLE ASSET...
"...SO I BOLSTERED MY USUAL SECURITY...
"...WITH A VERY SPECIAL PRIVATE CONTRACTOR."

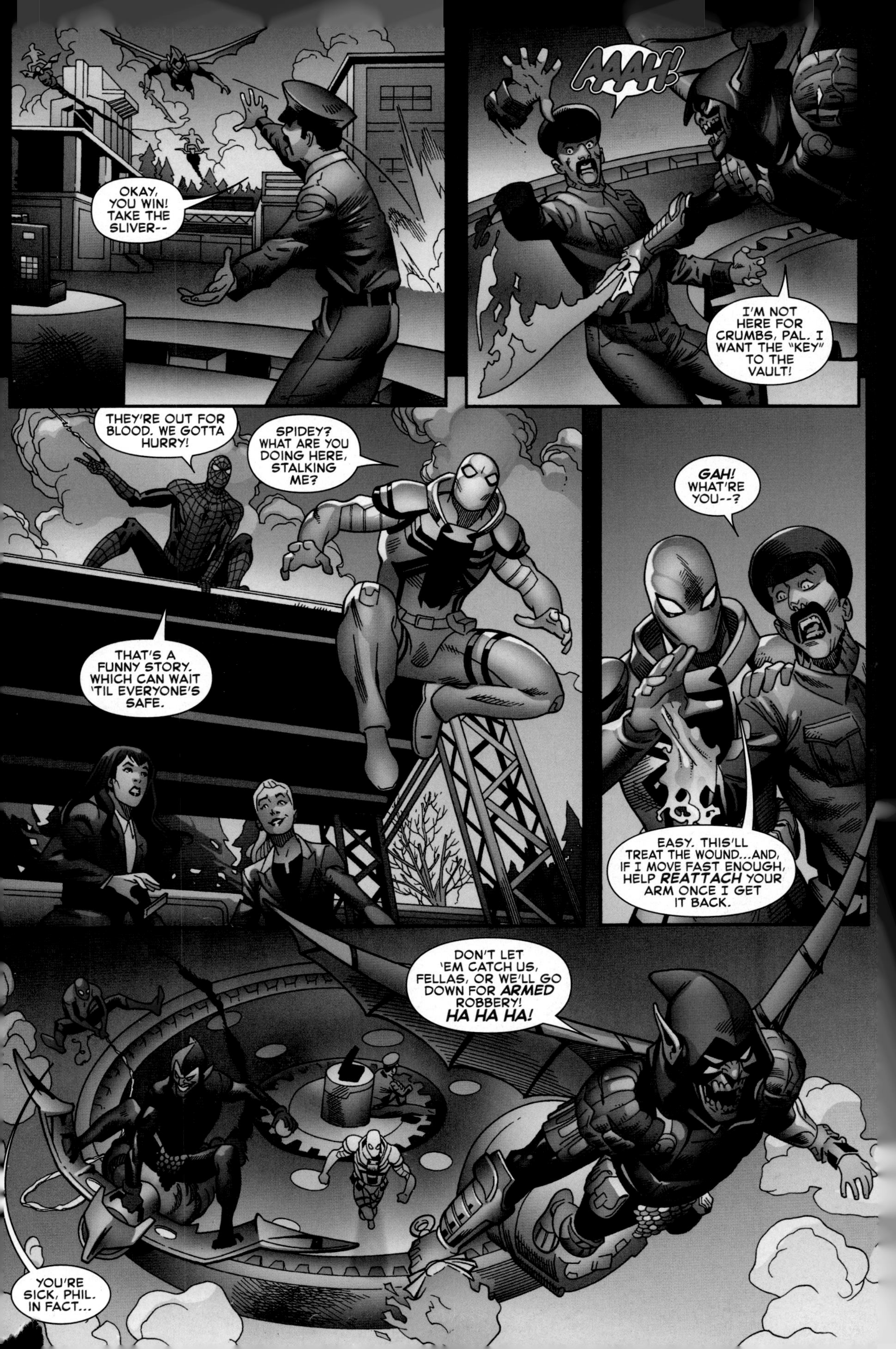
OKAY, YOU WIN! TAKE THE SLIVER--
AAAH!
I'M NOT HERE FOR CRUMBS, PAL. I WANT THE "KEY" TO THE VAULT!
THEY'RE OUT FOR BLOOD. WE GOTTA HURRY!
SPIDEY? WHAT ARE YOU DOING HERE, STALKING ME?
THAT'S A FUNNY STORY. WHICH CAN WAIT 'TIL EVERYONE'S SAFE.
GAH! WHAT'RE YOU--?
EASY. THIS'LL TREAT THE WOUND...AND, IF I MOVE FAST ENOUGH, HELP REATTACH YOUR ARM ONCE I GET IT BACK.
DON'T LET 'EM CATCH US, FELLAS, OR WE'LL GO DOWN FOR ARMED ROBBERY! HA HA HA!
YOU'RE SICK, PHIL. IN FACT...

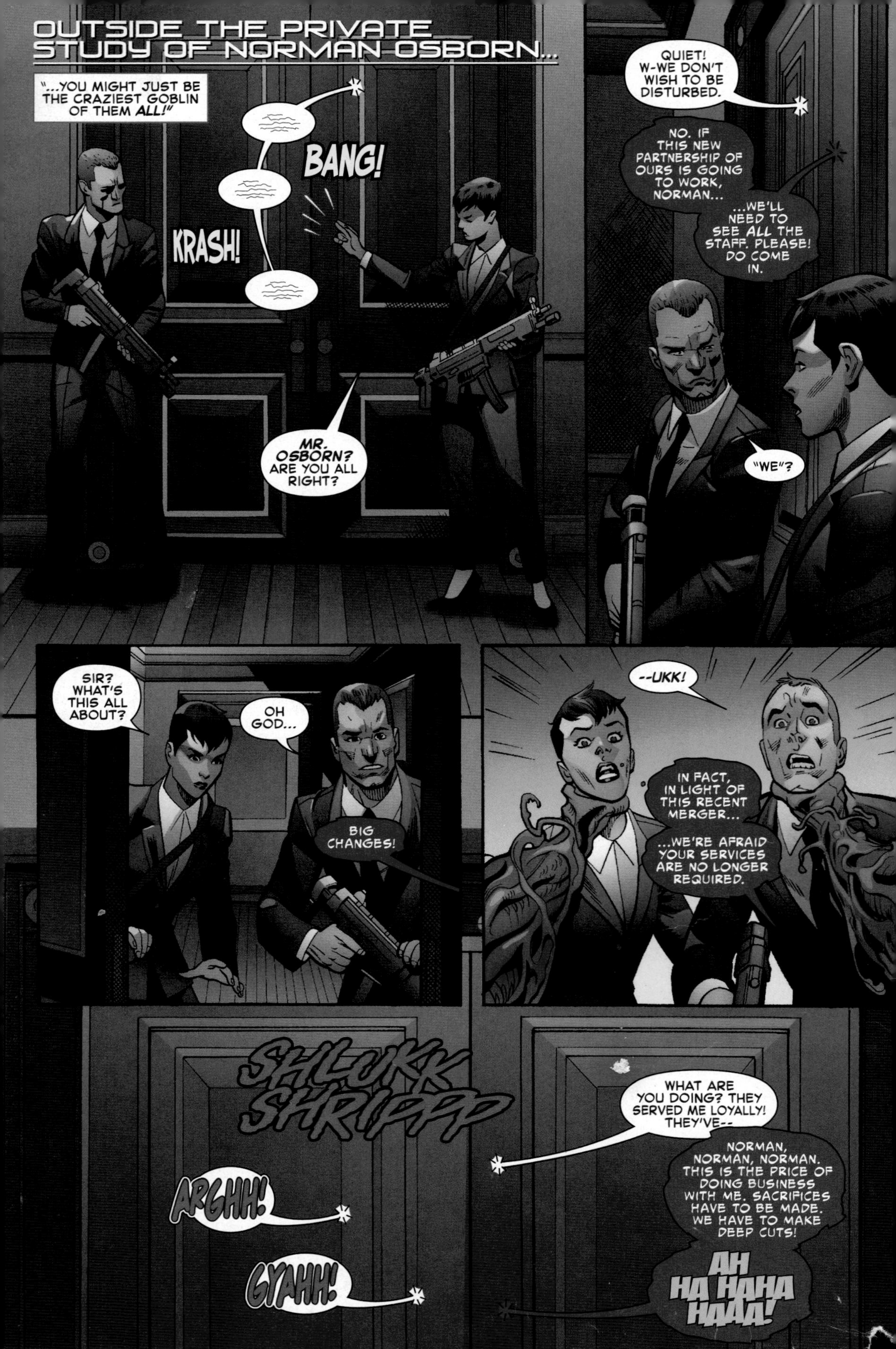

OUTSIDE THE PRIVATE STUDY OF NORMAN OSBORN...
"...YOU MIGHT JUST BE THE CRAZIEST GOBLIN OF THEM ALL!"
BANG!
KRASH!
MR. OSBORN? ARE YOU ALL RIGHT?
QUIET! W-WE DON'T WISH TO BE DISTURBED.
NO. IF THIS NEW PARTNERSHIP OF OURS IS GOING TO WORK, NORMAN...
...WE'LL NEED TO SEE ALL THE STAFF. PLEASE! DO COME IN.
"WE"?
SIR? WHAT'S THIS ALL ABOUT?
OH GOD...
BIG CHANGES!
--UKK!
IN FACT, IN LIGHT OF THIS RECENT MERGER...
...WE'RE AFRAID YOUR SERVICES ARE NO LONGER REQUIRED.
SHLUKK SHRIPPP
ARGHH!
GYAHH!
WHAT ARE YOU DOING? THEY SERVED ME LOYALLY! THEY'VE--
NORMAN, NORMAN, NORMAN. THIS IS THE PRICE OF DOING BUSINESS WITH ME. SACRIFICES HAVE TO BE MADE. WE HAVE TO MAKE DEEP CUTS!
AH HA HAHAHA HAAA!

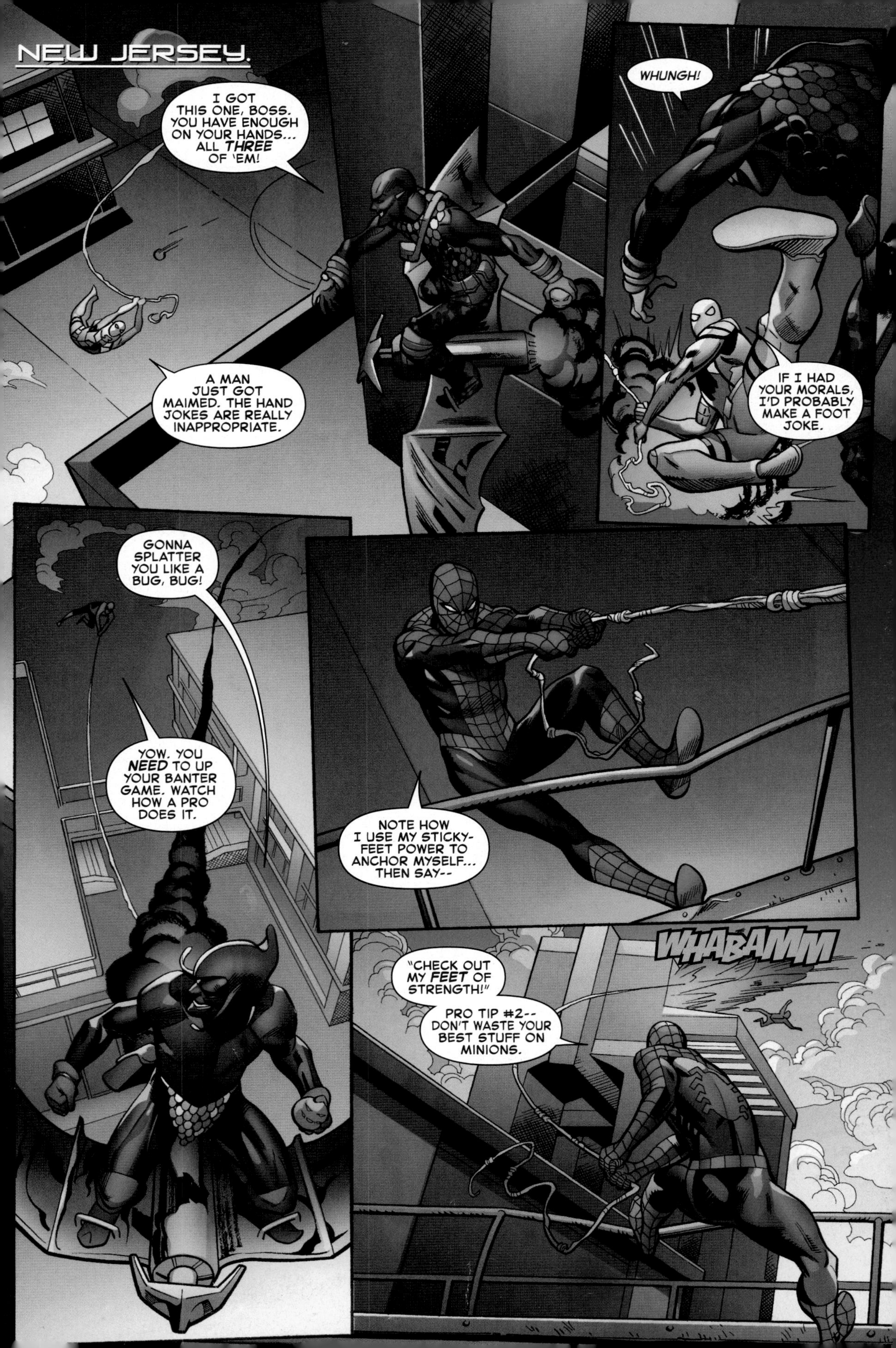
NEW JERSEY.
I GOT THIS ONE, BOSS. YOU HAVE ENOUGH ON YOUR HANDS... ALL THREE OF 'EM!
A MAN JUST GOT MAIMED. THE HAND JOKES ARE REALLY INAPPROPRIATE.
WHUNGH!
IF I HAD YOUR MORALS, I'D PROBABLY MAKE A FOOT JOKE.
GONNA SPLATTER YOU LIKE A BUG, BUG!
YOW. YOU NEED TO UP YOUR BANTER GAME. WATCH HOW A PRO DOES IT.
NOTE HOW I USE MY STICKY-FEET POWER TO ANCHOR MYSELF... THEN SAY--
WHABAMM
"CHECK OUT MY FEET OF STRENGTH!"
PRO TIP #2-- DON'T WASTE YOUR BEST STUFF ON MINIONS.

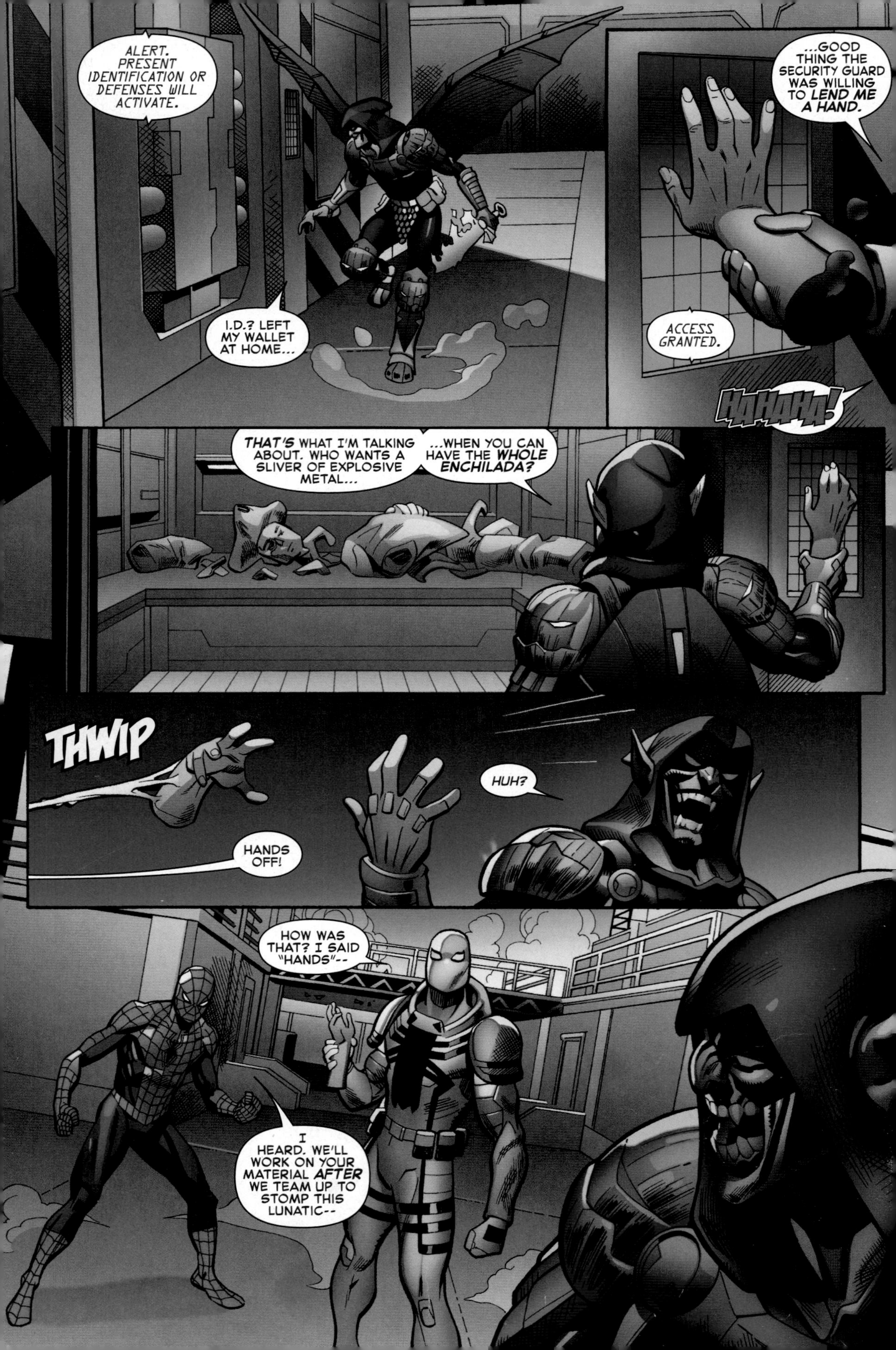
ALERT. PRESENT IDENTIFICATION OR DEFENSES WILL ACTIVATE.
I.D.? LEFT MY WALLET AT HOME...
...GOOD THING THE SECURITY GUARD WAS WILLING TO LEND ME A HAND.
ACCESS GRANTED.
HAHAHA!
THAT'S WHAT I'M TALKING ABOUT. WHO WANTS A SLIVER OF EXPLOSIVE METAL...
...WHEN YOU CAN HAVE THE WHOLE ENCHILADA?
THWIP
HUH?
HANDS OFF!
HOW WAS THAT? I SAID "HANDS"--
I HEARD. WE'LL WORK ON YOUR MATERIAL AFTER WE TEAM UP TO STOMP THIS LUNATIC--

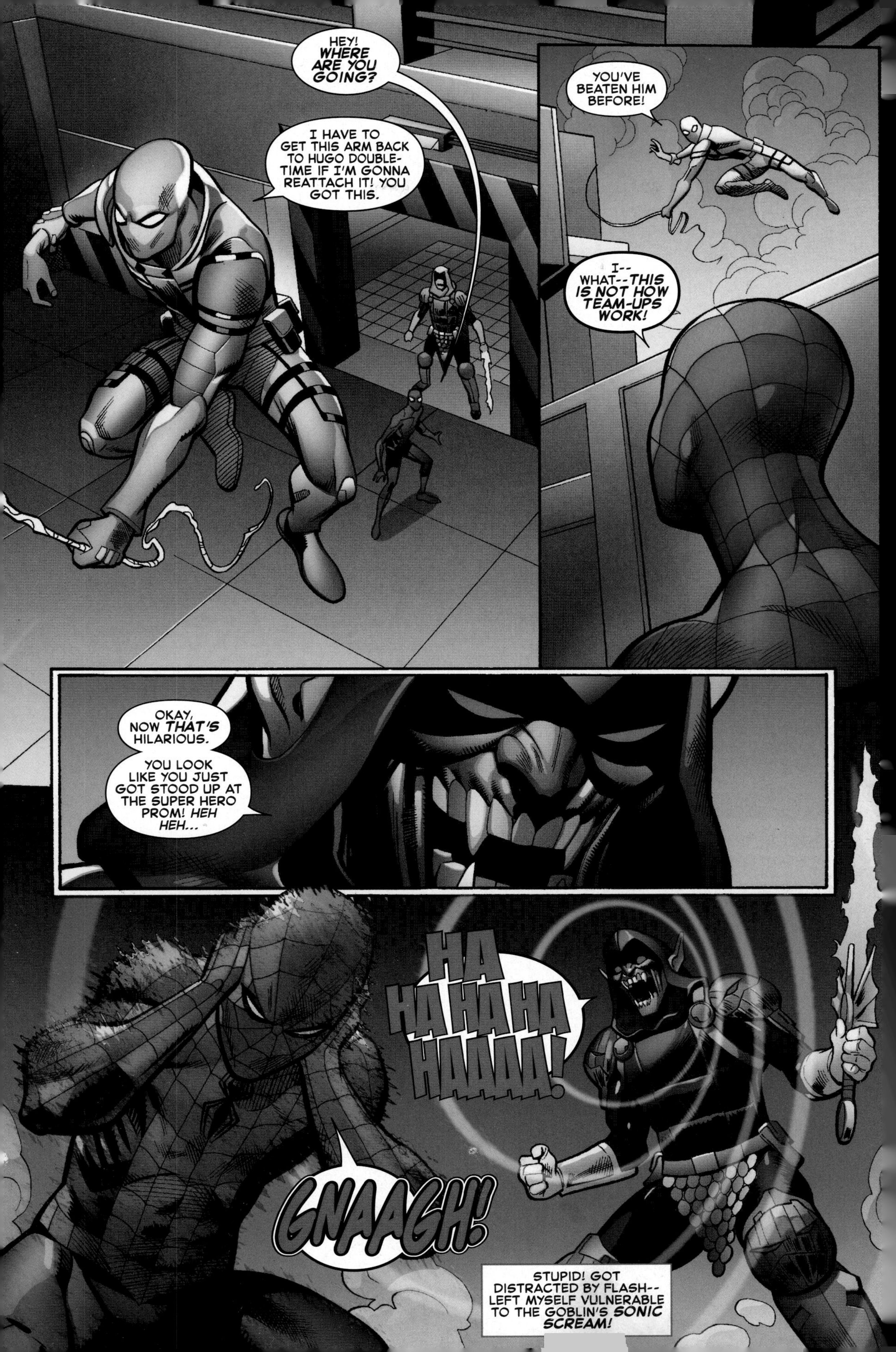
HEY! WHERE ARE YOU GOING?
I HAVE TO GET THIS ARM BACK TO HUGO DOUBLE-TIME IF I'M GONNA REATTACH IT! YOU GOT THIS.
YOU'VE BEATEN HIM BEFORE!
I-- WHAT--THIS IS NOT HOW TEAM-UPS WORK!
OKAY, NOW THAT'S HILARIOUS.
YOU LOOK LIKE YOU JUST GOT STOOD UP AT THE SUPER HERO PROM! HEH HEH...
HA HA HA HA HAAAA!
GNAAGH!
STUPID! GOT DISTRACTED BY FLASH-- LEFT MYSELF VULNERABLE TO THE GOBLIN'S SONIC SCREAM!

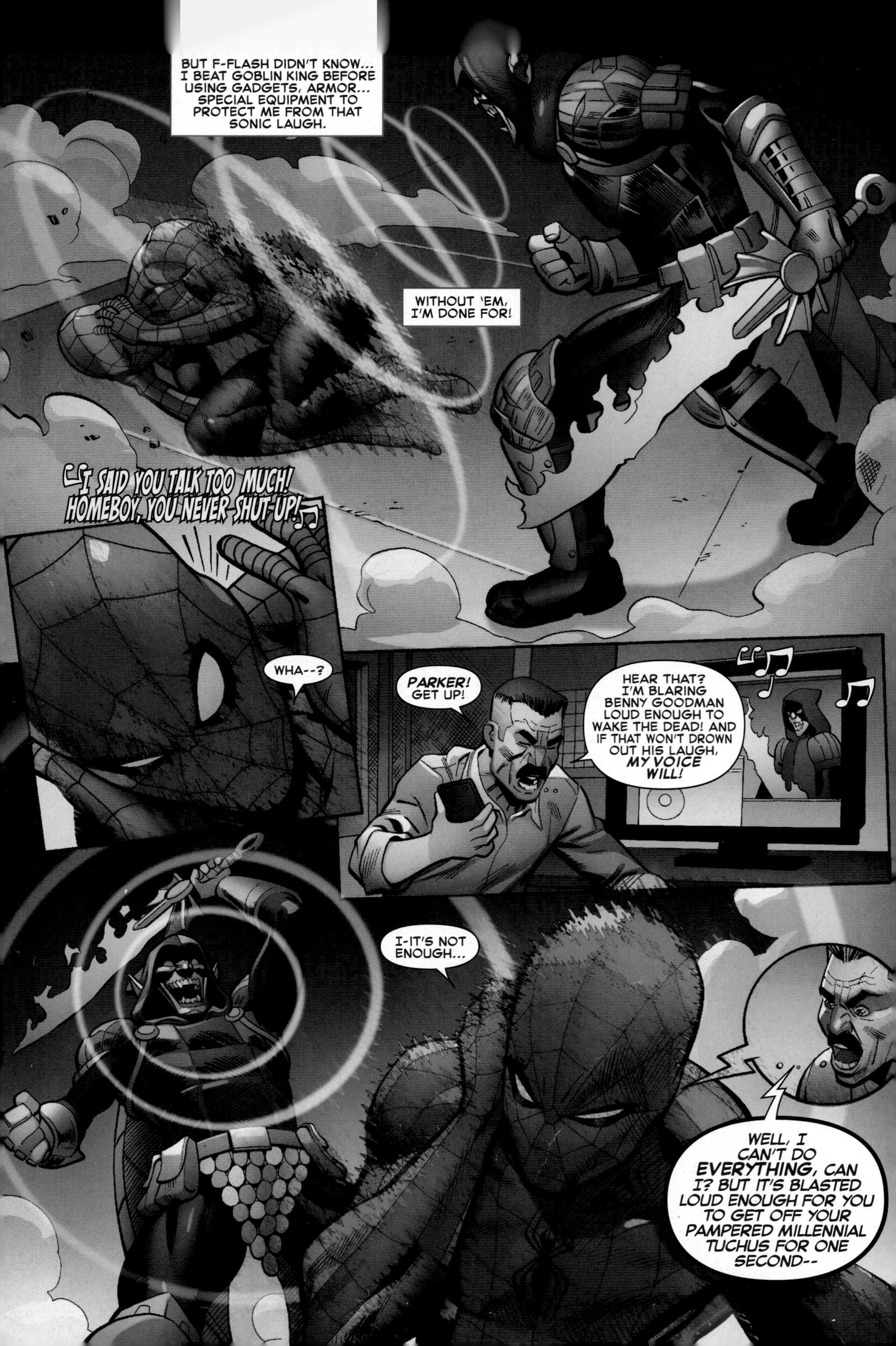
BUT F-FLASH DIDN'T KNOW... I BEAT GOBLIN KING BEFORE USING GADGETS, ARMOR... SPECIAL EQUIPMENT TO PROTECT ME FROM THAT SONIC LAUGH.
WITHOUT 'EM, I'M DONE FOR!
I SAID YOU TALK TOO MUCH! HOMEBOY, YOU NEVER SHUT UP!
WHA--?
PARKER! GET UP!
HEAR THAT? I'M BLARING BENNY GOODMAN LOUD ENOUGH TO WAKE THE DEAD! AND IF THAT WON'T DROWN OUT HIS LAUGH, MY VOICE WILL!
I-IT'S NOT ENOUGH...
WELL, I CAN'T DO EVERYTHING, CAN I? BUT IT'S BLASTED LOUD ENOUGH FOR YOU TO GET OFF YOUR PAMPERED MILLENNIAL TUCHUS FOR ONE SECOND--

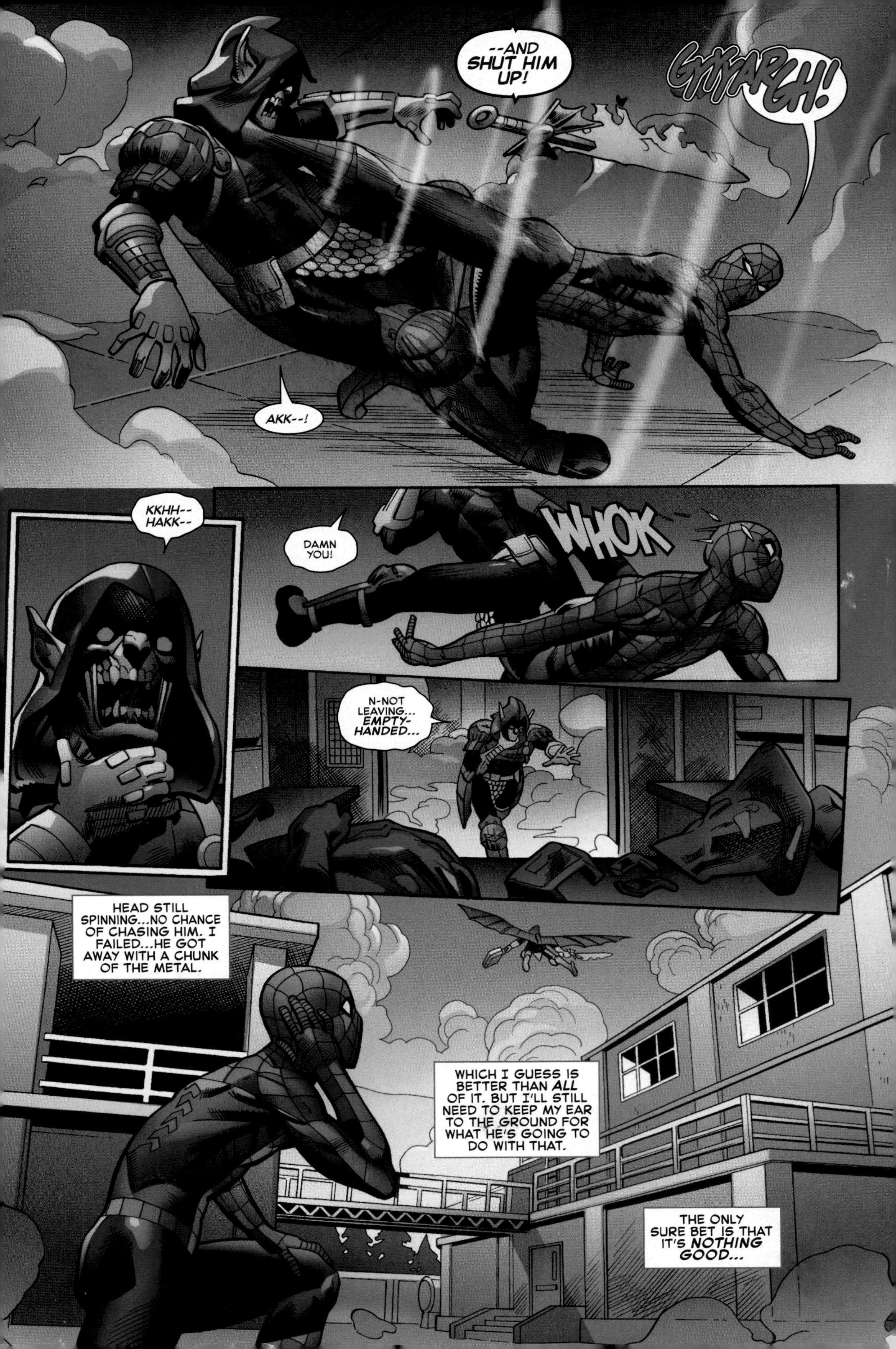
--AND SHUT HIM UP!
GYYAARGH!
AKK--!
KKHH-- HAKK--
DAMN YOU!
WHOK
N-NOT LEAVING... EMPTY-HANDED...
HEAD STILL SPINNING...NO CHANCE OF CHASING HIM. I FAILED...HE GOT AWAY WITH A CHUNK OF THE METAL.
WHICH I GUESS IS BETTER THAN ALL OF IT. BUT I'LL STILL NEED TO KEEP MY EAR TO THE GROUND FOR WHAT HE'S GOING TO DO WITH THAT.
THE ONLY SURE BET IS THAT IT'S NOTHING GOOD...

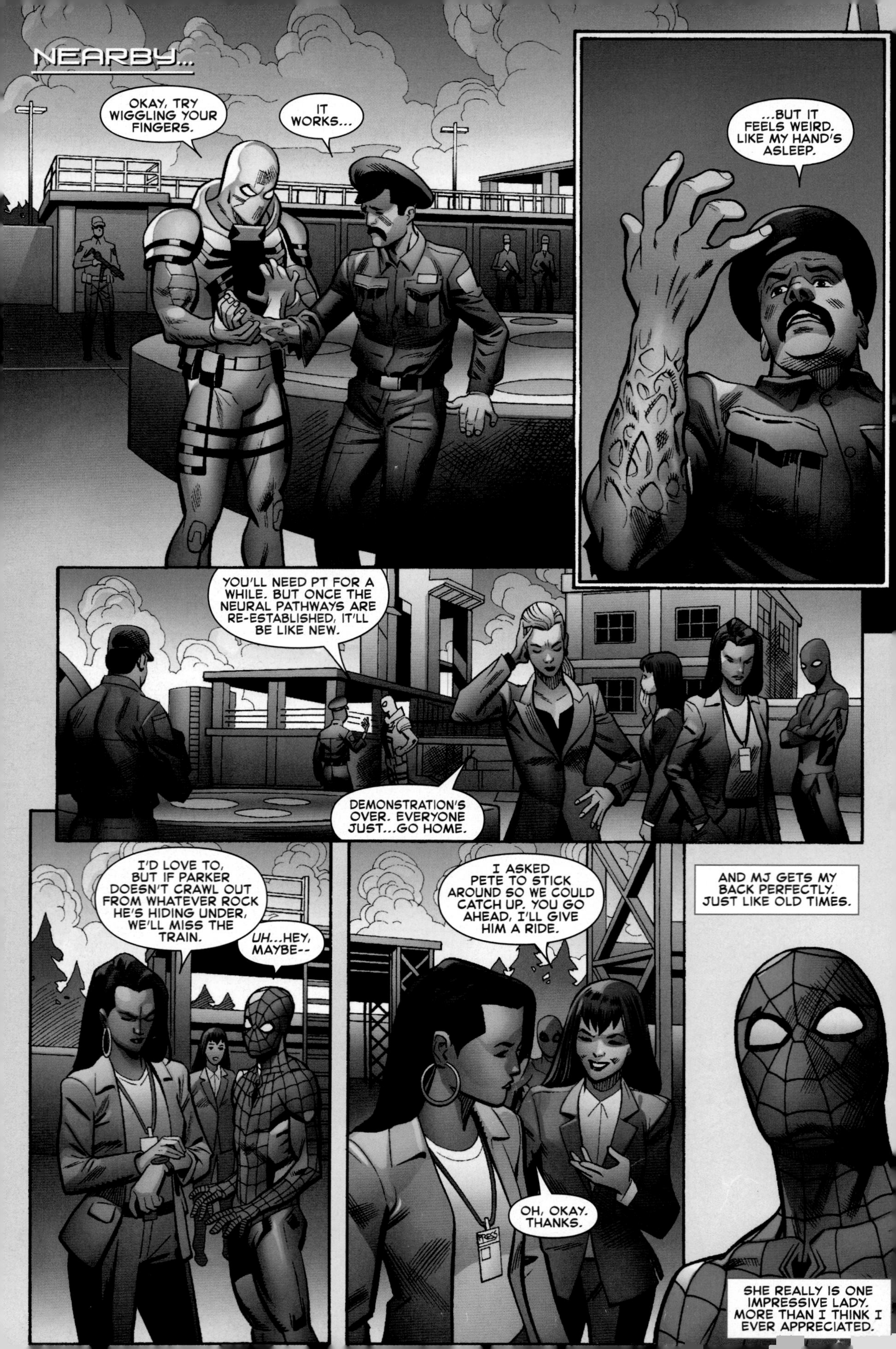
NEARBY...
OKAY, TRY WIGGLING YOUR FINGERS.
IT WORKS...
...BUT IT FEELS WEIRD. LIKE MY HAND'S ASLEEP.
YOU'LL NEED PT FOR A WHILE. BUT ONCE THE NEURAL PATHWAYS ARE RE-ESTABLISHED, IT'LL BE LIKE NEW.
DEMONSTRATION'S OVER. EVERYONE JUST...GO HOME.
I'D LOVE TO, BUT IF PARKER DOESN'T CRAWL OUT FROM WHATEVER ROCK HE'S HIDING UNDER, WE'LL MISS THE TRAIN.
UH...HEY, MAYBE--
I ASKED PETE TO STICK AROUND SO WE COULD CATCH UP. YOU GO AHEAD, I'LL GIVE HIM A RIDE.
OH, OKAY. THANKS.
AND MJ GETS MY BACK PERFECTLY. JUST LIKE OLD TIMES.
SHE REALLY IS ONE IMPRESSIVE LADY. MORE THAN I THINK I EVER APPRECIATED.

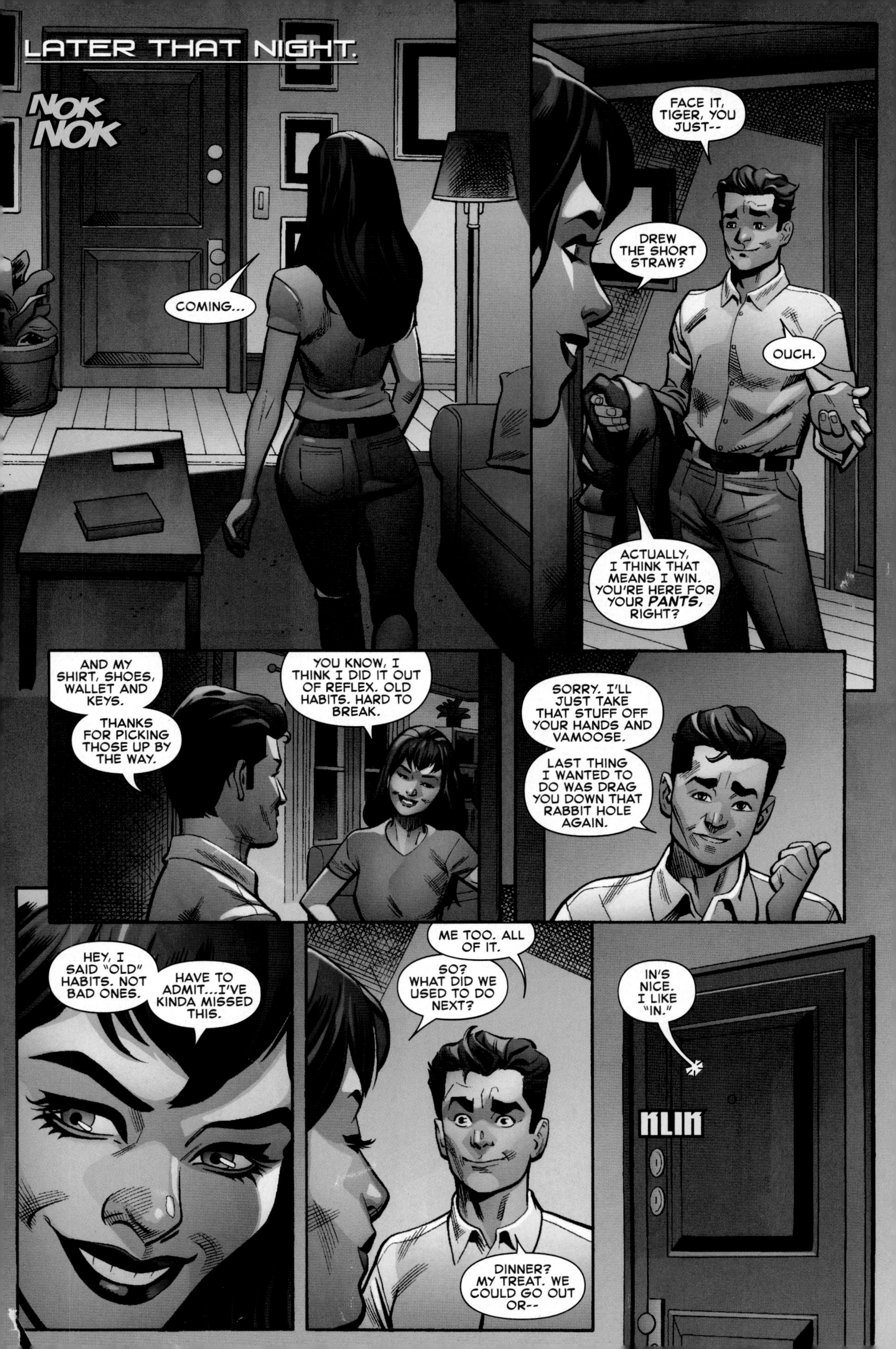
LATER THAT NIGHT.
NOK NOK
COMING...
FACE IT, TIGER, YOU JUST--
DREW THE SHORT STRAW?
OUCH.
ACTUALLY, I THINK THAT MEANS I WIN. YOU'RE HERE FOR YOUR *PANTS*, RIGHT?
AND MY SHIRT, SHOES, WALLET AND KEYS.
THANKS FOR PICKING THOSE UP BY THE WAY.
YOU KNOW, I THINK I DID IT OUT OF REFLEX. OLD HABITS. HARD TO BREAK.
SORRY. I'LL JUST TAKE THAT STUFF OFF YOUR HANDS AND VAMOOSE.
LAST THING I WANTED TO DO WAS DRAG YOU DOWN THAT RABBIT HOLE AGAIN.
HEY, I SAID "OLD" HABITS. NOT BAD ONES.
HAVE TO ADMIT...I'VE KINDA MISSED THIS.
ME TOO. ALL OF IT.
SO? WHAT DID WE USED TO DO NEXT?
DINNER? MY TREAT. WE COULD GO OUT OR--
IN'S NICE. I LIKE "IN."
KLIK

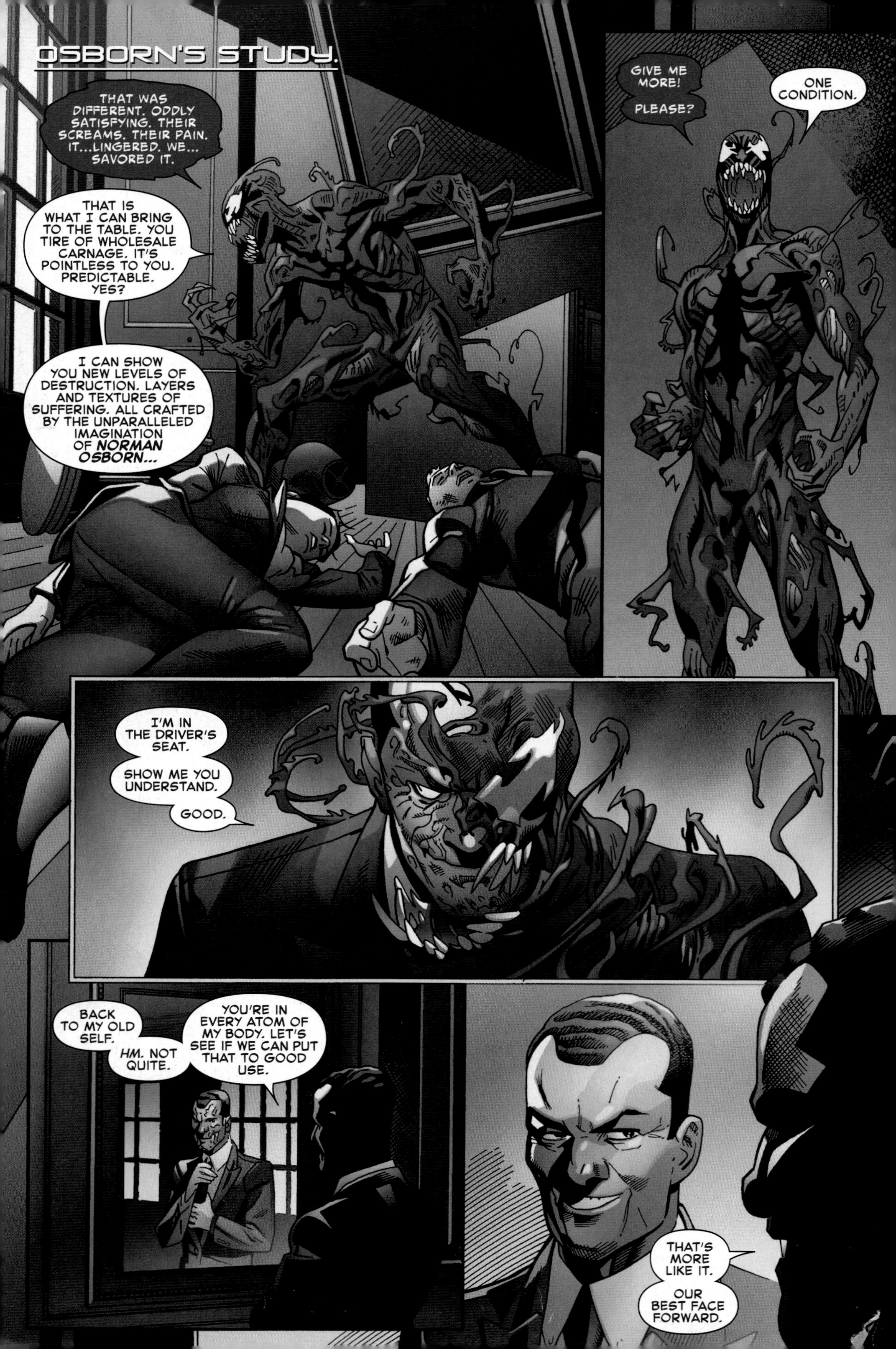
OSBORN'S STUDY.
THAT WAS DIFFERENT. ODDLY SATISFYING. THEIR SCREAMS. THEIR PAIN. IT...LINGERED. WE... SAVORED IT.
THAT IS WHAT I CAN BRING TO THE TABLE. YOU TIRE OF WHOLESALE CARNAGE. IT'S POINTLESS TO YOU. PREDICTABLE. YES?
I CAN SHOW YOU NEW LEVELS OF DESTRUCTION. LAYERS AND TEXTURES OF SUFFERING. ALL CRAFTED BY THE UNPARALLELED IMAGINATION OF ***NORMAN OSBORN...***
GIVE ME MORE!
PLEASE?
ONE CONDITION.
I'M IN THE DRIVER'S SEAT.
SHOW ME YOU UNDERSTAND.
GOOD.
BACK TO MY OLD SELF.
HM. NOT QUITE.
YOU'RE IN EVERY ATOM OF MY BODY. LET'S SEE IF WE CAN PUT THAT TO GOOD USE.
THAT'S MORE LIKE IT.
OUR BEST FACE FORWARD.

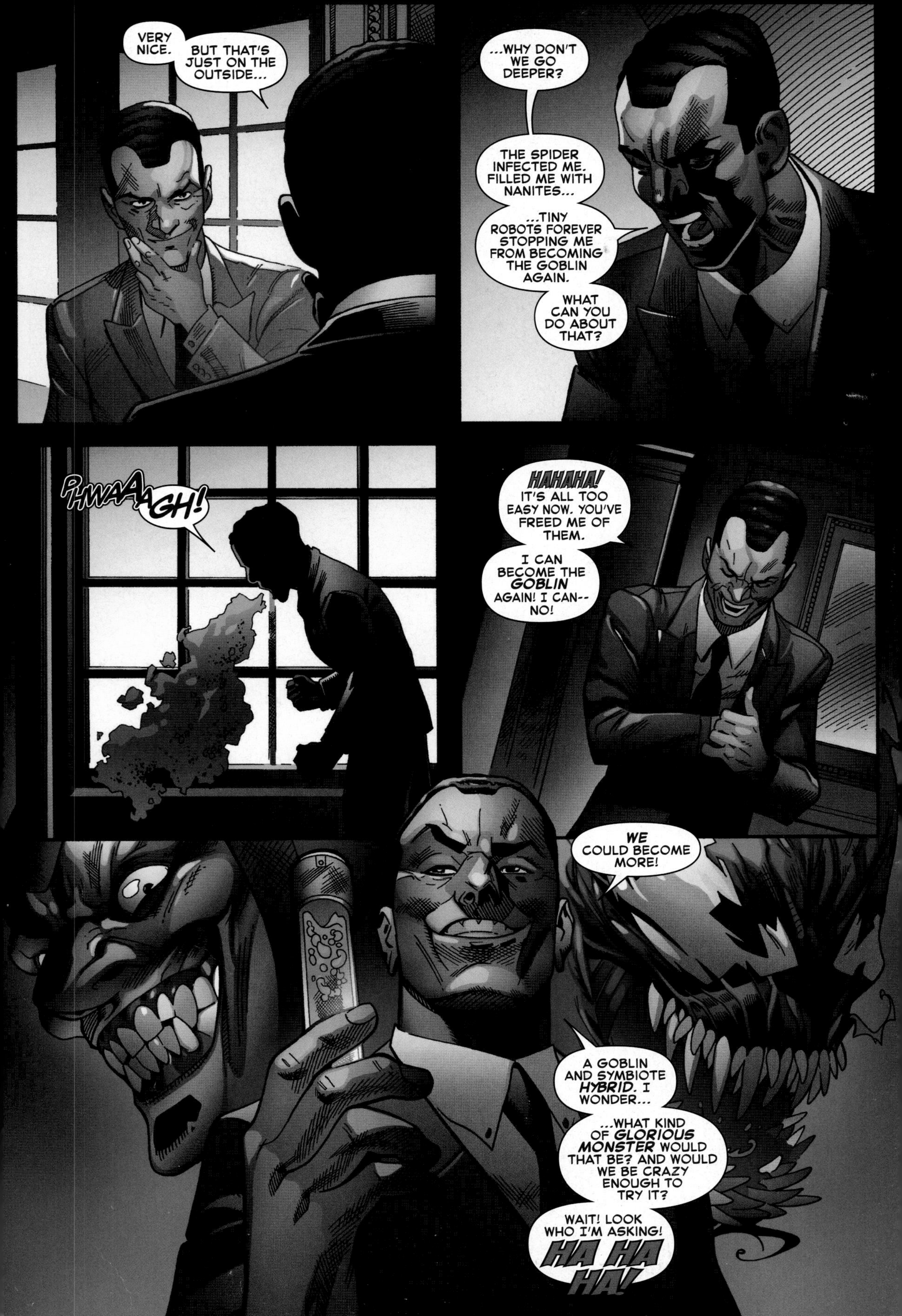
VERY NICE.
BUT THAT'S JUST ON THE OUTSIDE...
...WHY DON'T WE GO DEEPER?
THE SPIDER INFECTED ME. FILLED ME WITH NANITES...
...TINY ROBOTS FOREVER STOPPING ME FROM BECOMING THE GOBLIN AGAIN.
WHAT CAN YOU DO ABOUT THAT?
PHWAAAAGH!
HAHAHA! IT'S ALL TOO EASY NOW. YOU'VE FREED ME OF THEM.
I CAN BECOME THE GOBLIN AGAIN! I CAN-- NO!
WE COULD BECOME MORE!
A GOBLIN AND SYMBIOTE HYBRID. I WONDER...
...WHAT KIND OF GLORIOUS MONSTER WOULD THAT BE? AND WOULD WE BE CRAZY ENOUGH TO TRY IT?
WAIT! LOOK WHO I'M ASKING! HA HA HA!

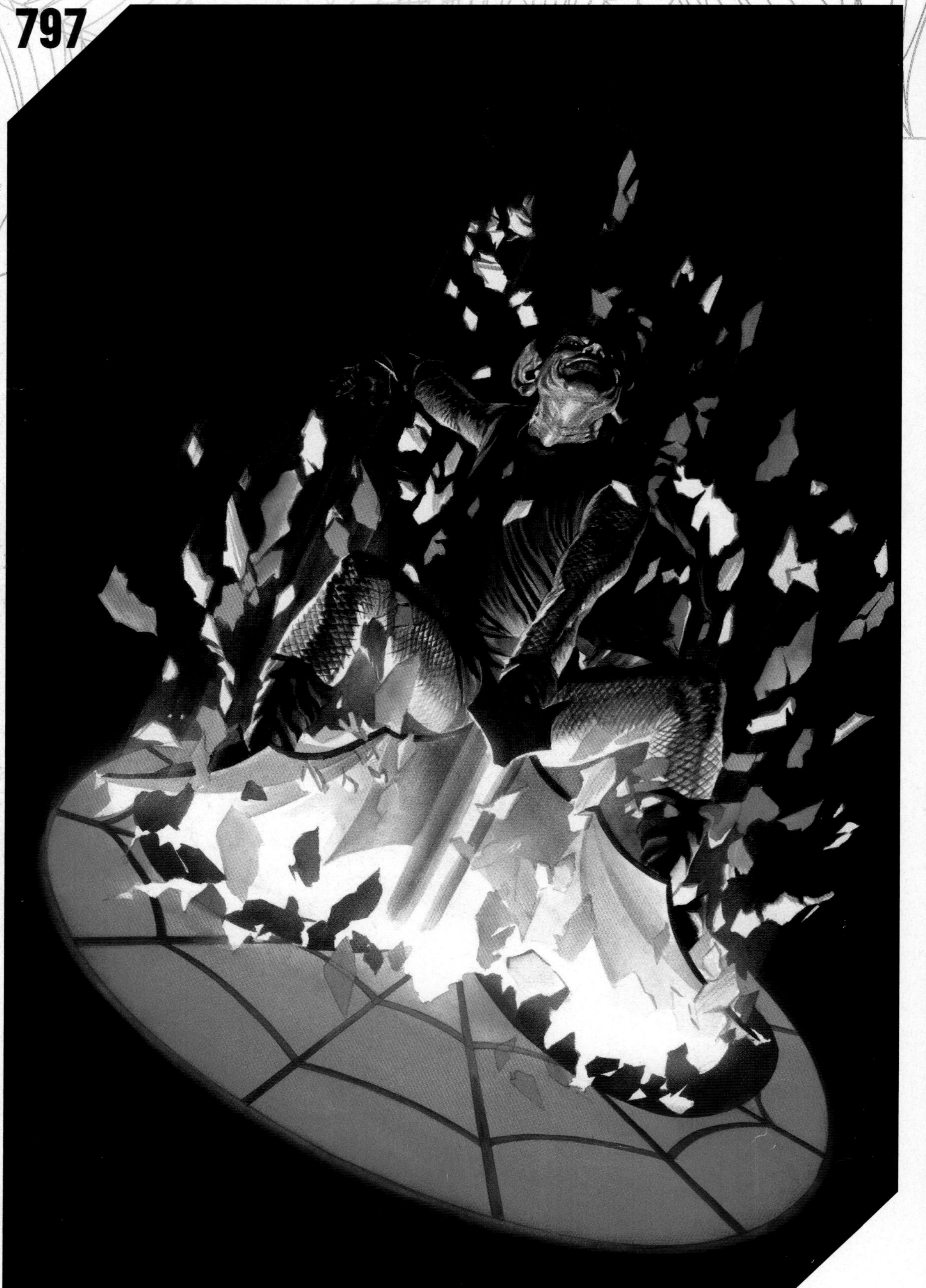

GO DOWN SWINGING PART ONE "THE LOOSE THREAD"

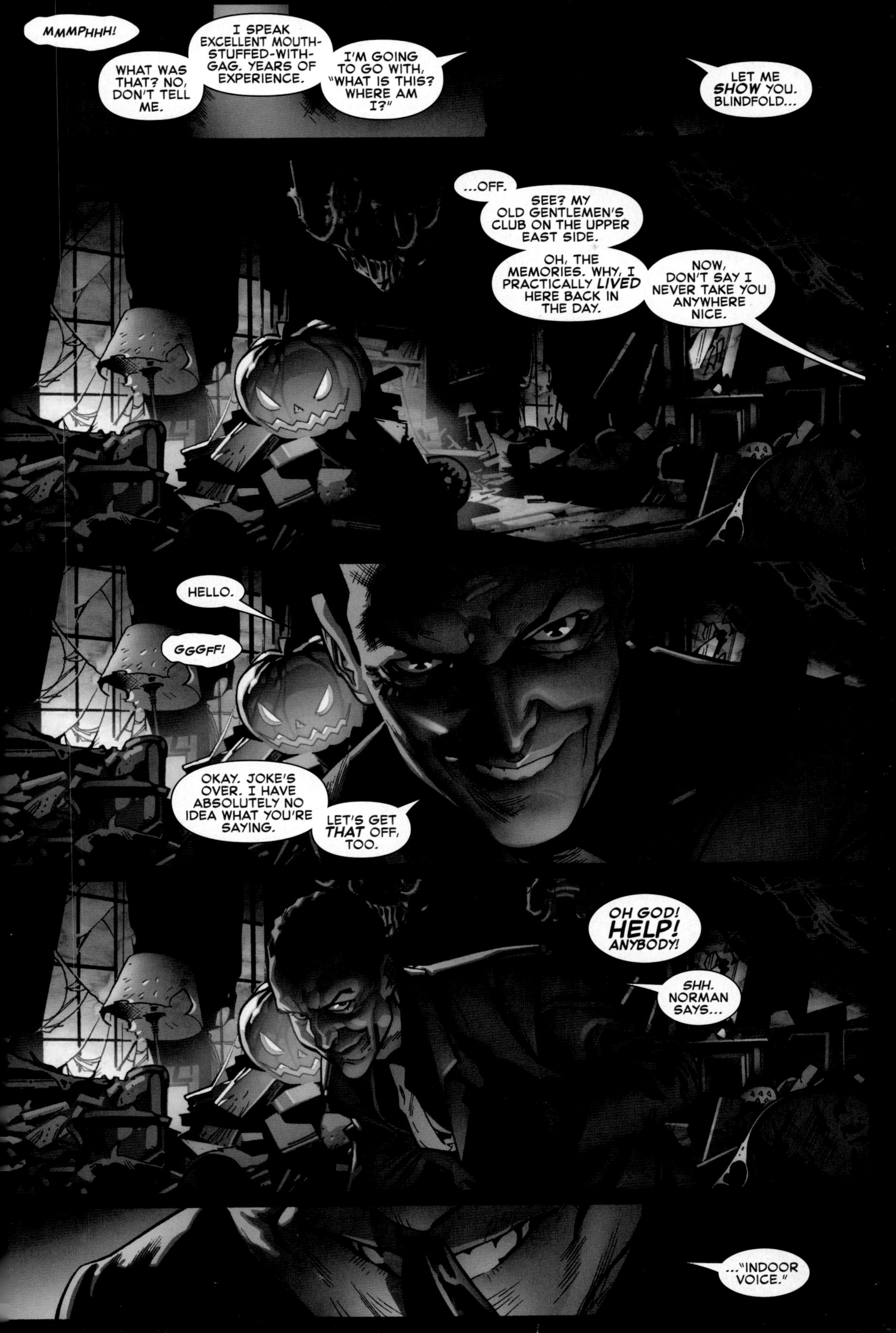
MMMPHHH!
WHAT WAS THAT? NO, DON'T TELL ME.
I SPEAK EXCELLENT MOUTH-STUFFED-WITH-GAG. YEARS OF EXPERIENCE.
I'M GOING TO GO WITH, "WHAT IS THIS? WHERE AM I?"
LET ME SHOW YOU. BLINDFOLD...
...OFF.
SEE? MY OLD GENTLEMEN'S CLUB ON THE UPPER EAST SIDE.
OH, THE MEMORIES. WHY, I PRACTICALLY LIVED HERE BACK IN THE DAY.
NOW, DON'T SAY I NEVER TAKE YOU ANYWHERE NICE.
HELLO.
GGGFF!
OKAY. JOKE'S OVER. I HAVE ABSOLUTELY NO IDEA WHAT YOU'RE SAYING.
LET'S GET THAT OFF, TOO.
OH GOD! HELP! ANYBODY!
SHH. NORMAN SAYS...
..."INDOOR VOICE."

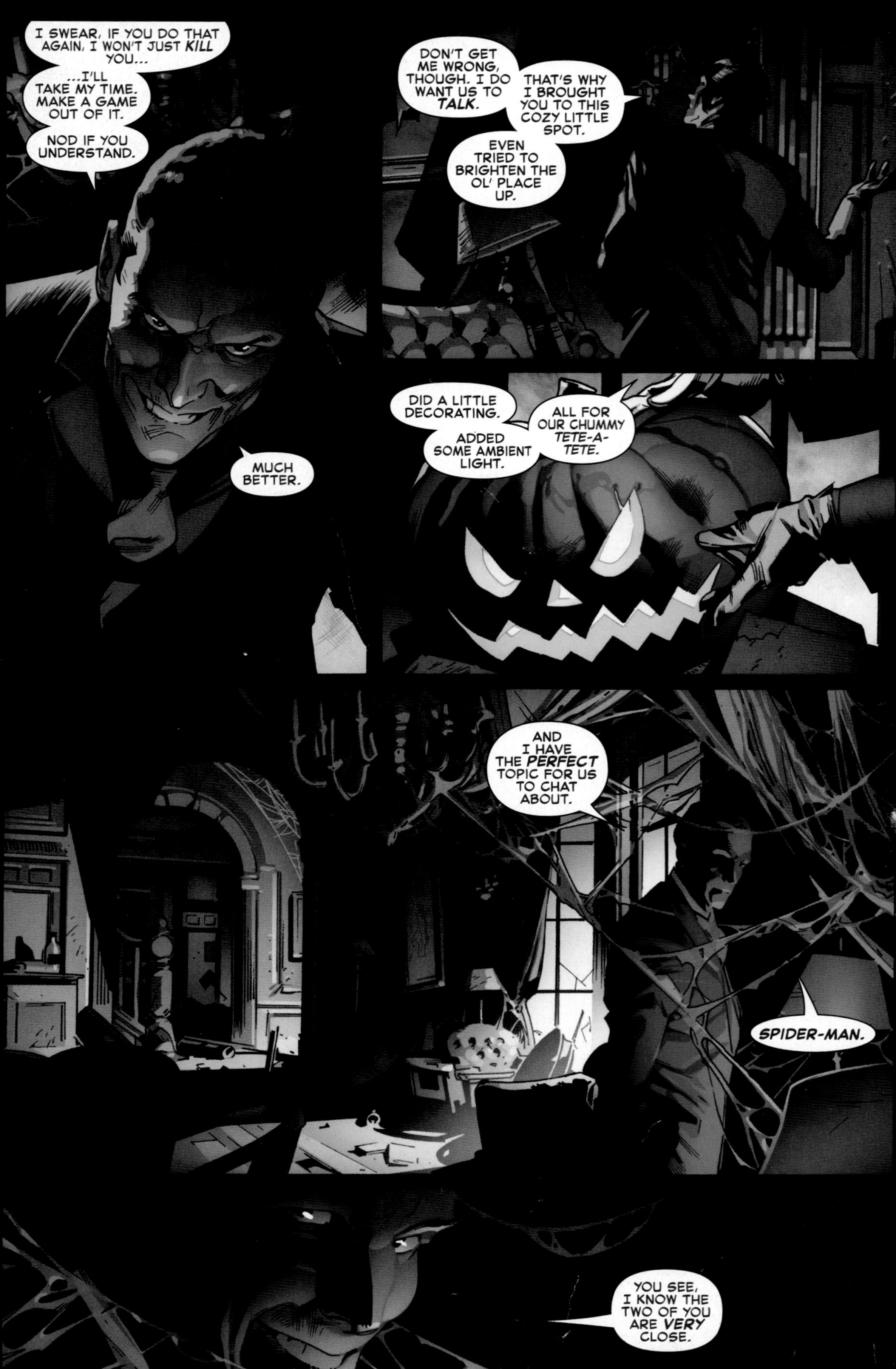
I SWEAR, IF YOU DO THAT AGAIN, I WON'T JUST KILL YOU...
...I'LL TAKE MY TIME. MAKE A GAME OUT OF IT.
NOD IF YOU UNDERSTAND.
MUCH BETTER.
DON'T GET ME WRONG, THOUGH. I DO WANT US TO TALK.
THAT'S WHY I BROUGHT YOU TO THIS COZY LITTLE SPOT.
EVEN TRIED TO BRIGHTEN THE OL' PLACE UP.
DID A LITTLE DECORATING.
ADDED SOME AMBIENT LIGHT.
ALL FOR OUR CHUMMY TETE-A-TETE.
AND I HAVE THE PERFECT TOPIC FOR US TO CHAT ABOUT.
SPIDER-MAN.
YOU SEE, I KNOW THE TWO OF YOU ARE VERY CLOSE.

FOUR HOURS AGO. THE APARTMENT OF MARY JANE WATSON.
YOU'RE ONE HELL OF A SCIENTIST, PARKER.
HOW'S THAT?
YOU JUST PROVED TIME TRAVEL'S POSSIBLE.
ONE KISS, AND WE'RE BACK TO HOW EVERYTHING'S SUPPOSED TO--
I--I'M SORRY. WE CAN'T DO THIS. NOT AGAIN.
WHAT? DON'T SAY IT'S BECAUSE OF--
SPIDER-MAN.
BUT YOU KNOW THAT. MORE THAN ANYONE ON EARTH. YOU KNOW.

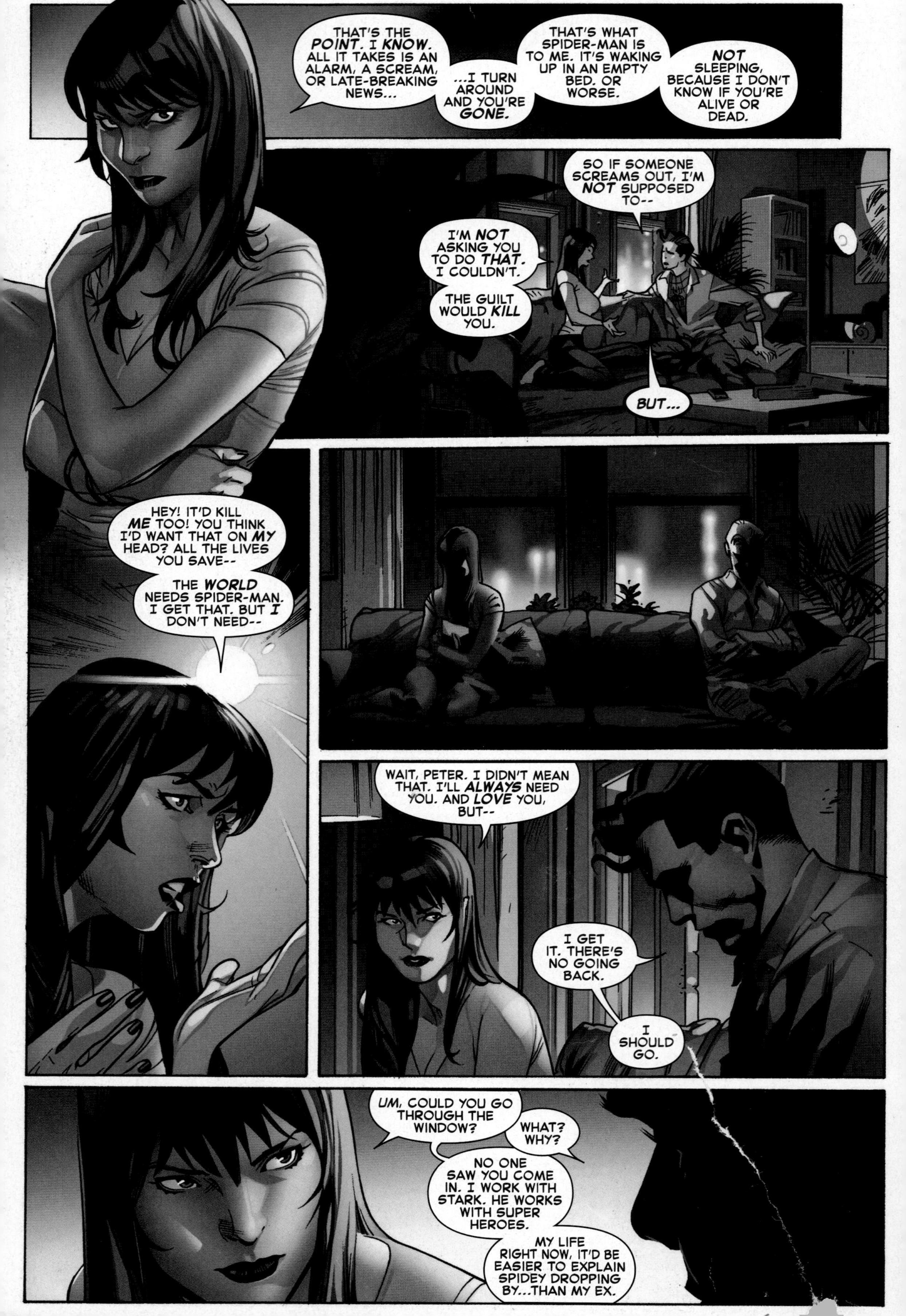
THAT'S THE POINT. I KNOW. ALL IT TAKES IS AN ALARM, A SCREAM, OR LATE-BREAKING NEWS...
...I TURN AROUND AND YOU'RE GONE.
THAT'S WHAT SPIDER-MAN IS TO ME. IT'S WAKING UP IN AN EMPTY BED. OR WORSE.
NOT SLEEPING, BECAUSE I DON'T KNOW IF YOU'RE ALIVE OR DEAD.
SO IF SOMEONE SCREAMS OUT, I'M NOT SUPPOSED TO--
I'M NOT ASKING YOU TO DO THAT. I COULDN'T.
THE GUILT WOULD KILL YOU.
BUT...
HEY! IT'D KILL ME TOO! YOU THINK I'D WANT THAT ON MY HEAD? ALL THE LIVES YOU SAVE--
THE WORLD NEEDS SPIDER-MAN. I GET THAT. BUT I DON'T NEED--
WAIT, PETER. I DIDN'T MEAN THAT. I'LL ALWAYS NEED YOU. AND LOVE YOU, BUT--
I GET IT. THERE'S NO GOING BACK.
I SHOULD GO.
UM, COULD YOU GO THROUGH THE WINDOW?
WHAT? WHY?
NO ONE SAW YOU COME IN. I WORK WITH STARK. HE WORKS WITH SUPER HEROES.
MY LIFE RIGHT NOW, IT'D BE EASIER TO EXPLAIN SPIDEY DROPPING BY...THAN MY EX.

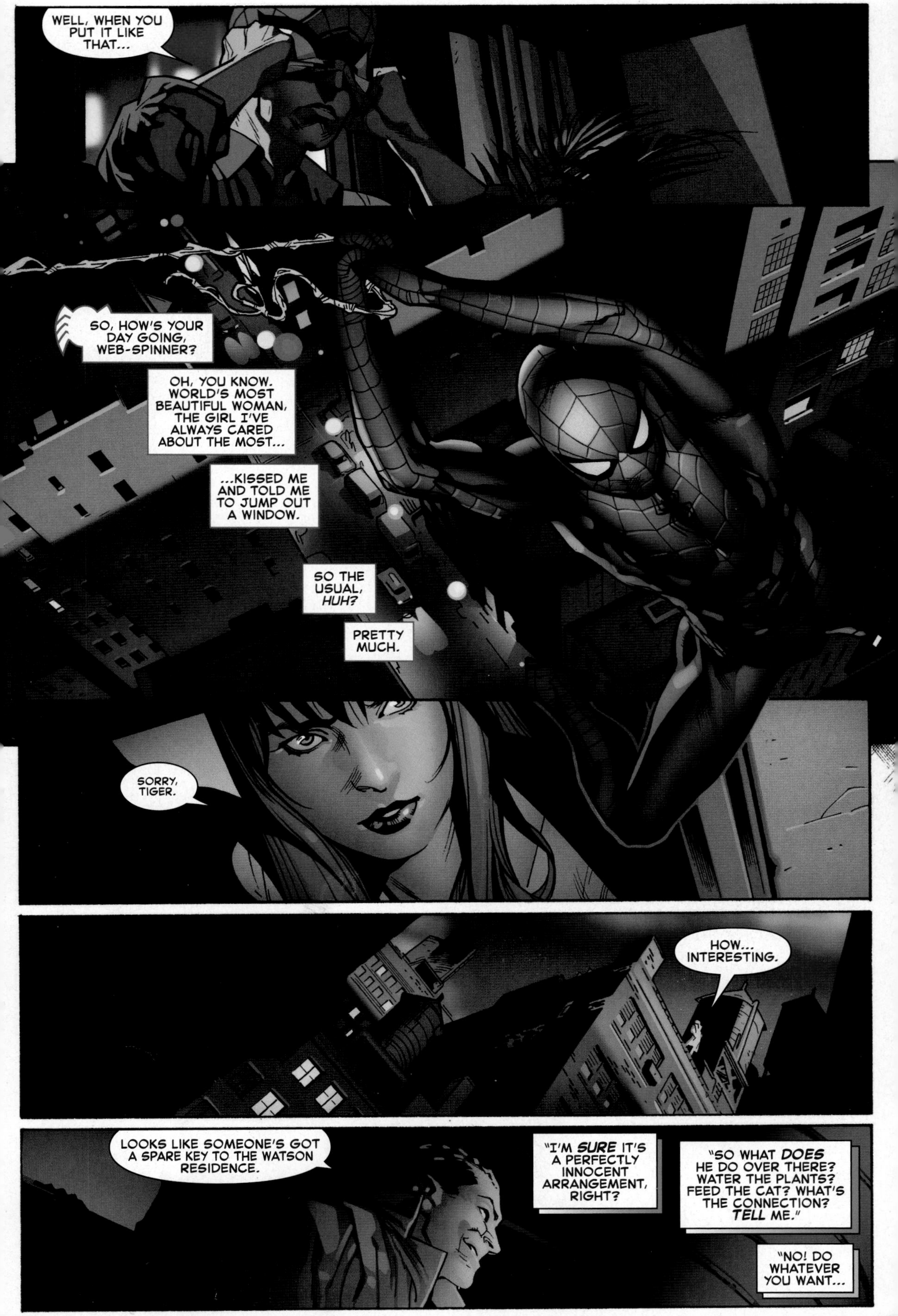

WELL, WHEN YOU PUT IT LIKE THAT...
SO, HOW'S YOUR DAY GOING, WEB-SPINNER?
OH, YOU KNOW. WORLD'S MOST BEAUTIFUL WOMAN, THE GIRL I'VE ALWAYS CARED ABOUT THE MOST...
...KISSED ME AND TOLD ME TO JUMP OUT A WINDOW.
SO THE USUAL, *HUH?*
PRETTY MUCH.
SORRY, TIGER.
HOW... INTERESTING.
LOOKS LIKE SOMEONE'S GOT A SPARE KEY TO THE WATSON RESIDENCE.
"I'M *SURE* IT'S A PERFECTLY INNOCENT ARRANGEMENT, RIGHT?
"SO WHAT *DOES* HE DO OVER THERE? WATER THE PLANTS? FEED THE CAT? WHAT'S THE CONNECTION? *TELL* ME."
"NO! DO WHATEVER YOU WANT...

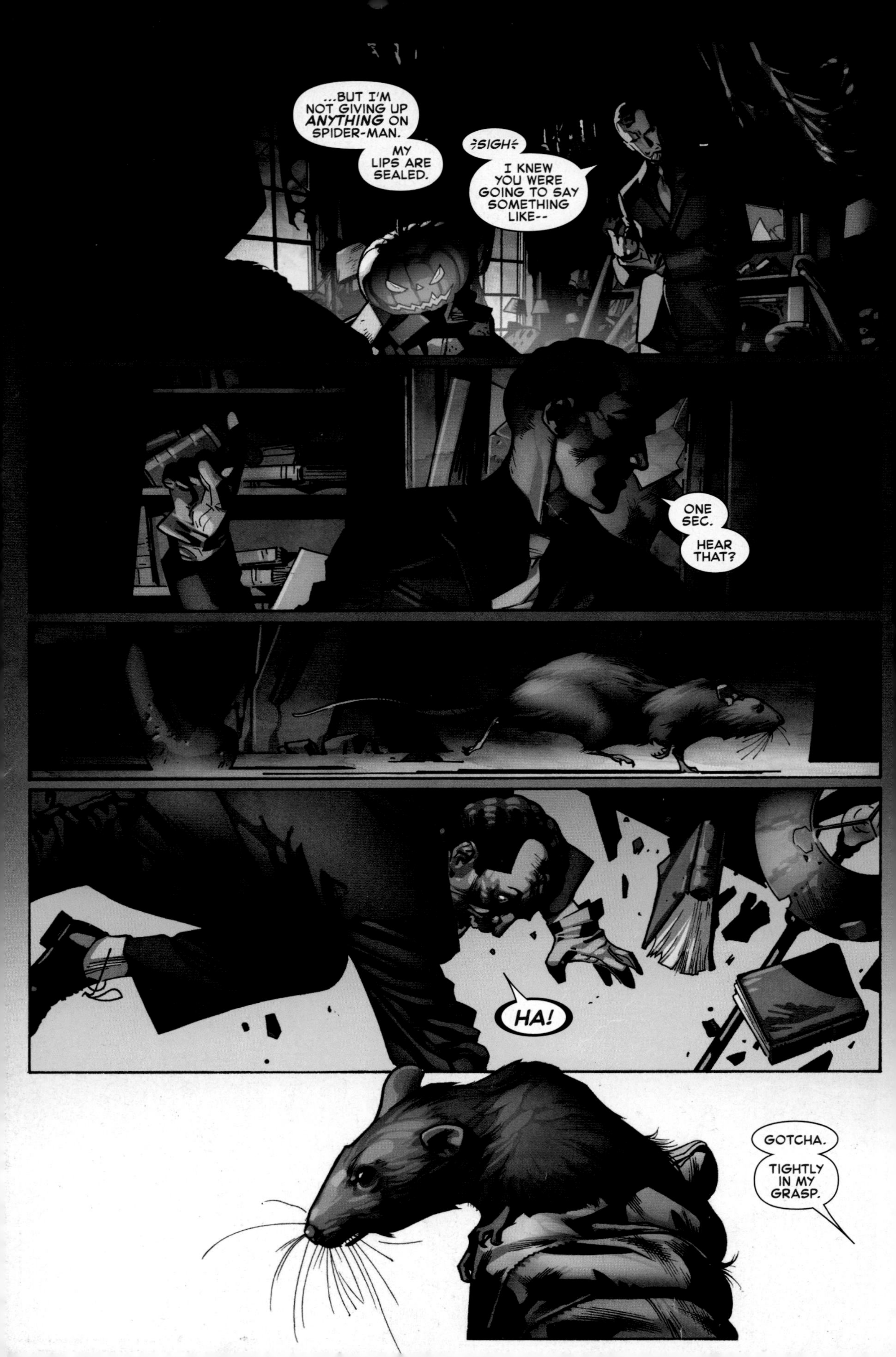
...BUT I'M NOT GIVING UP *ANYTHING* ON SPIDER-MAN.
MY LIPS ARE SEALED.
SIGH
I KNEW YOU WERE GOING TO SAY SOMETHING LIKE--
ONE SEC.
HEAR THAT?
HA!
GOTCHA.
TIGHTLY IN MY GRASP.

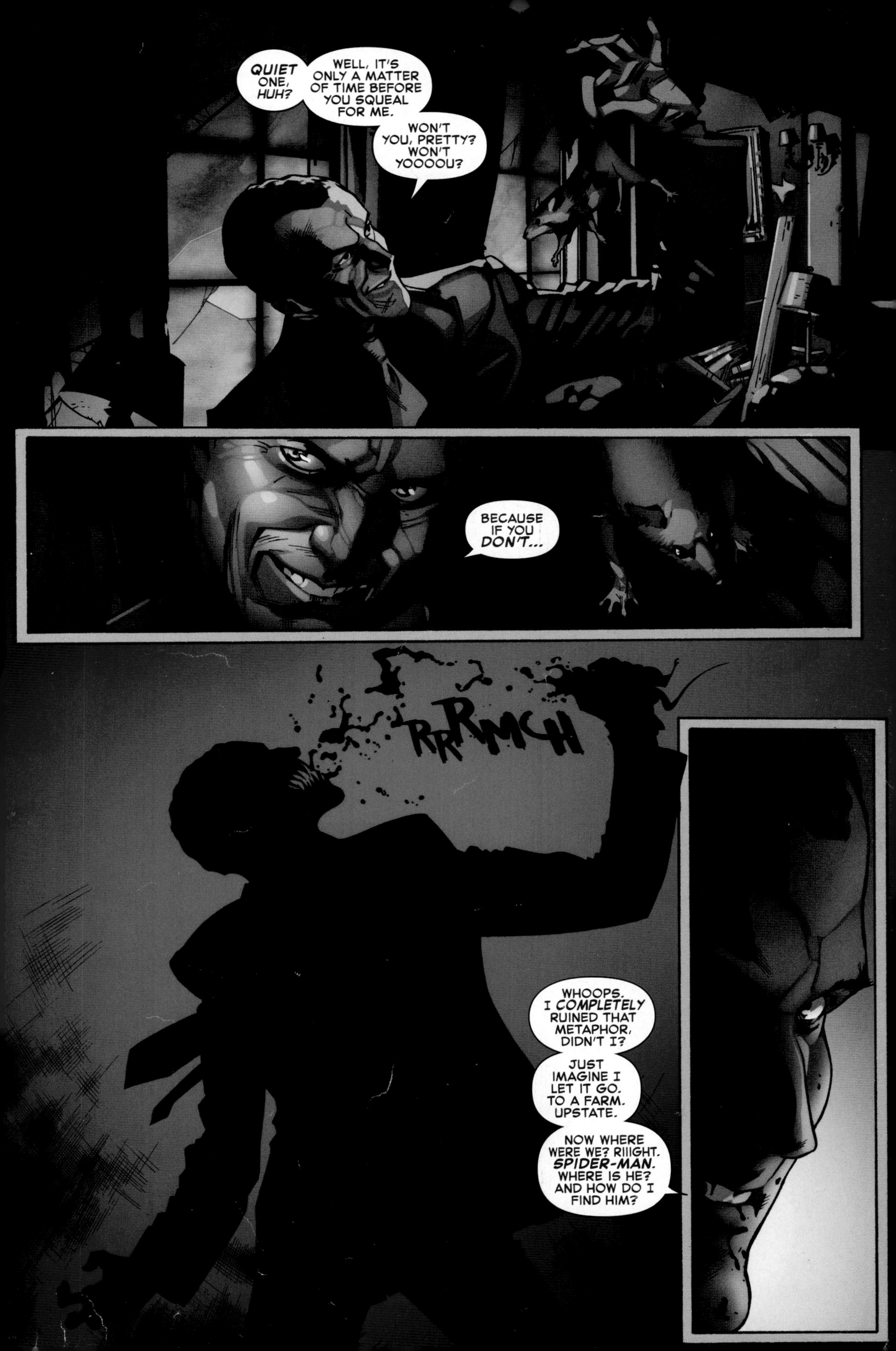
QUIET ONE, HUH?
WELL, IT'S ONLY A MATTER OF TIME BEFORE YOU SQUEAL FOR ME.
WON'T YOU, PRETTY? WON'T YOOOOU?
BECAUSE IF YOU DON'T...
RRRRMCH
WHOOPS. I COMPLETELY RUINED THAT METAPHOR, DIDN'T I?
JUST IMAGINE I LET IT GO. TO A FARM. UPSTATE.
NOW WHERE WERE WE? RIIIGHT. SPIDER-MAN. WHERE IS HE? AND HOW DO I FIND HIM?

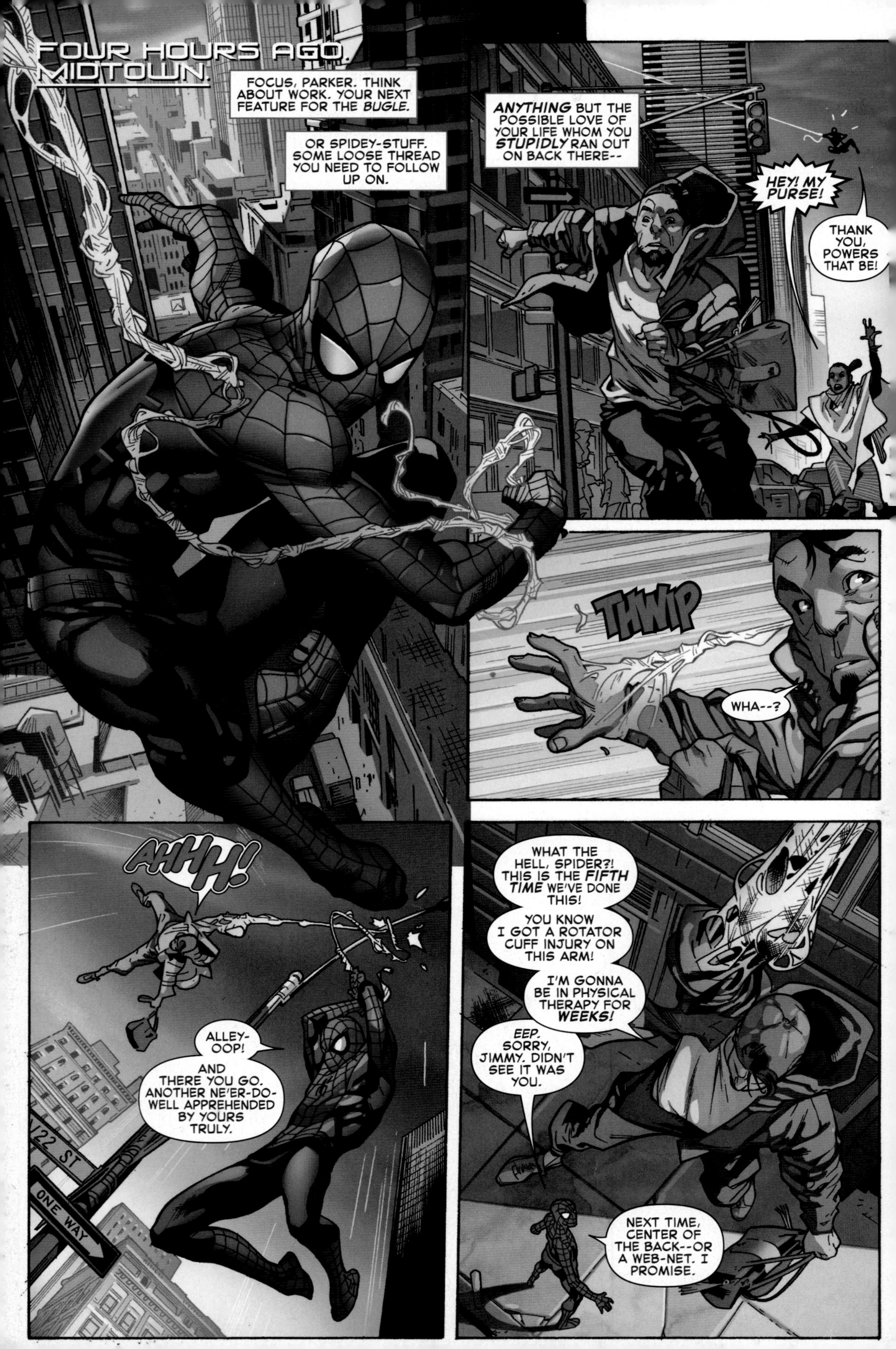
FOUR HOURS AGO. MIDTOWN.
FOCUS, PARKER. THINK ABOUT WORK. YOUR NEXT FEATURE FOR THE *BUGLE.*
OR SPIDEY-STUFF. SOME LOOSE THREAD YOU NEED TO FOLLOW UP ON.
ANYTHING BUT THE POSSIBLE LOVE OF YOUR LIFE WHOM YOU *STUPIDLY* RAN OUT ON BACK THERE--
HEY! MY PURSE!
THANK YOU, POWERS THAT BE!
THWIP
WHA--?
AHHH!
ALLEY-OOP!
AND THERE YOU GO. ANOTHER NE'ER-DO-WELL APPREHENDED BY YOURS TRULY.
122 ST
ONE WAY
WHAT THE HELL, SPIDER?! THIS IS THE *FIFTH TIME* WE'VE DONE THIS!
YOU KNOW I GOT A ROTATOR CUFF INJURY ON THIS ARM!
I'M GONNA BE IN PHYSICAL THERAPY FOR *WEEKS!*
EEP. SORRY, JIMMY. DIDN'T SEE IT WAS YOU.
NEXT TIME, CENTER OF THE BACK--OR A WEB-NET. I PROMISE.

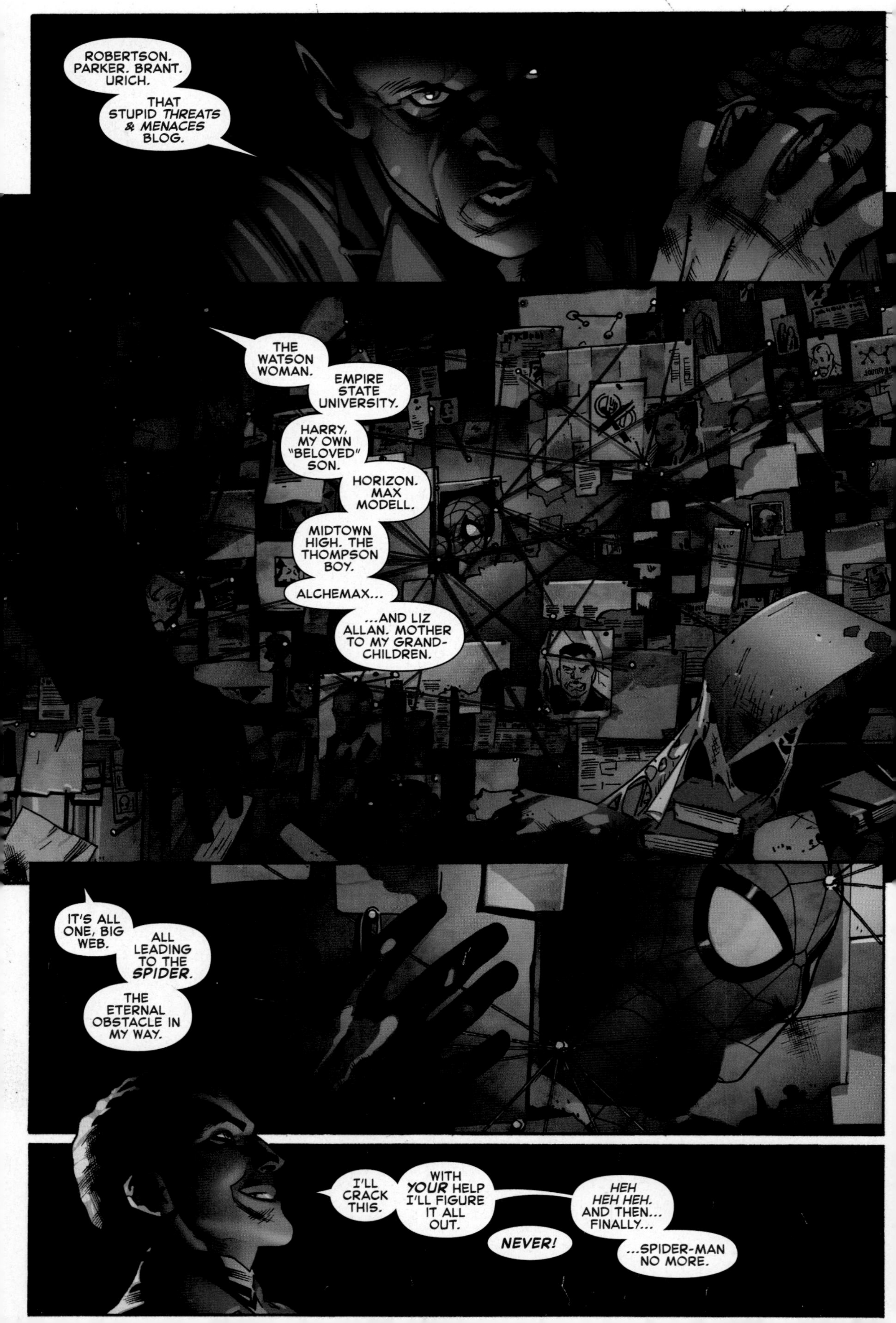
ROBERTSON. PARKER. BRANT. URICH.
THAT STUPID *THREATS & MENACES* BLOG.
THE WATSON WOMAN.
EMPIRE STATE UNIVERSITY.
HARRY, MY OWN "BELOVED" SON.
HORIZON. MAX MODELL.
MIDTOWN HIGH. THE THOMPSON BOY.
ALCHEMAX...
...AND LIZ ALLAN. MOTHER TO MY GRAND-CHILDREN.
IT'S ALL ONE, BIG WEB.
ALL LEADING TO THE *SPIDER*.
THE ETERNAL OBSTACLE IN MY WAY.
I'LL CRACK THIS.
WITH ***YOUR*** HELP I'LL FIGURE IT ALL OUT.
NEVER!
HEH HEH HEH. AND THEN... FINALLY...
...SPIDER-MAN NO MORE.

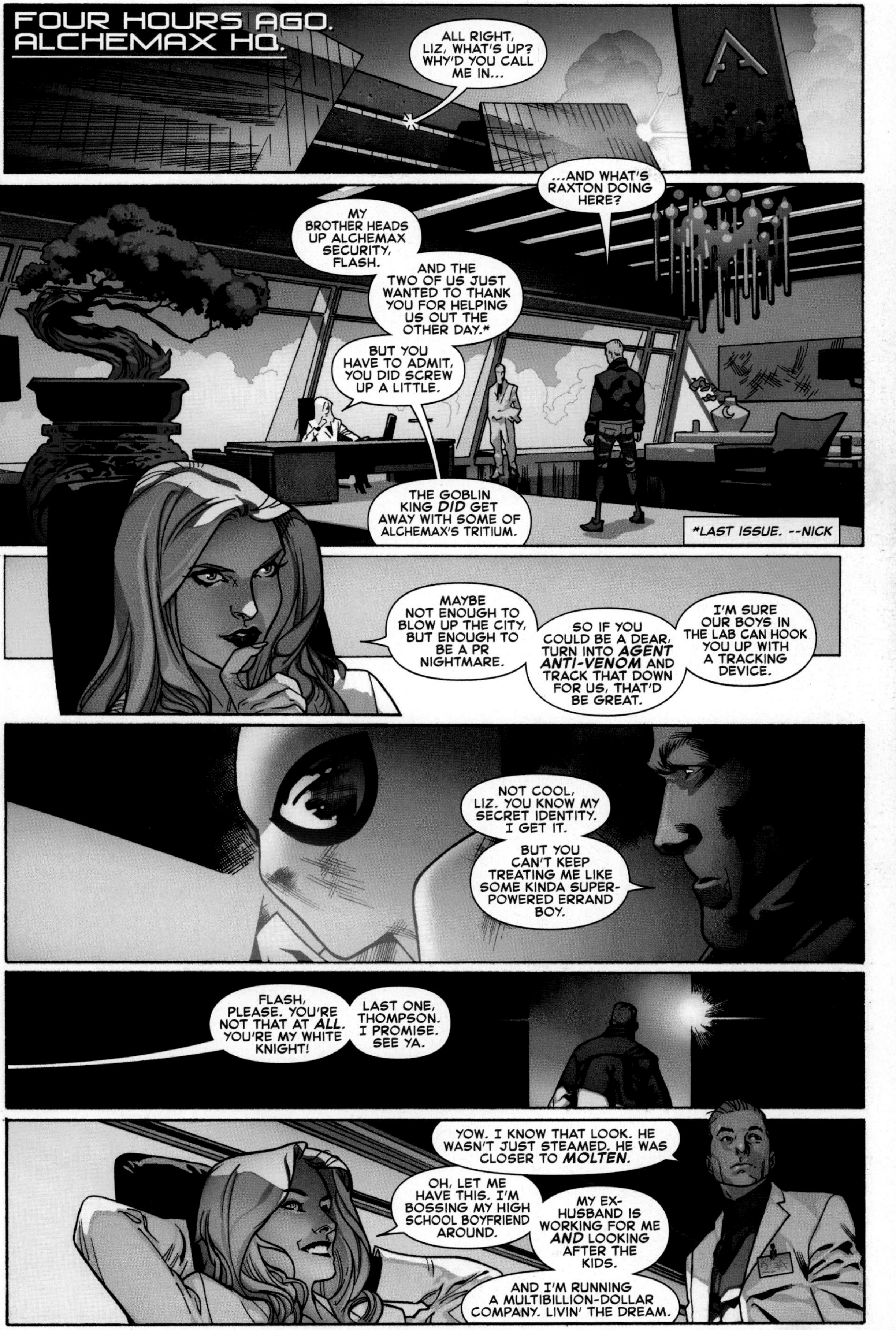
FOUR HOURS AGO. ALCHEMAX HQ.
ALL RIGHT, LIZ, WHAT'S UP? WHY'D YOU CALL ME IN...
...AND WHAT'S RAXTON DOING HERE?
MY BROTHER HEADS UP ALCHEMAX SECURITY, FLASH.
AND THE TWO OF US JUST WANTED TO THANK YOU FOR HELPING US OUT THE OTHER DAY.*
BUT YOU HAVE TO ADMIT, YOU DID SCREW UP A LITTLE.
THE GOBLIN KING DID GET AWAY WITH SOME OF ALCHEMAX'S TRITIUM.
*LAST ISSUE. --NICK
MAYBE NOT ENOUGH TO BLOW UP THE CITY, BUT ENOUGH TO BE A PR NIGHTMARE.
SO IF YOU COULD BE A DEAR, TURN INTO AGENT ANTI-VENOM AND TRACK THAT DOWN FOR US, THAT'D BE GREAT.
I'M SURE OUR BOYS IN THE LAB CAN HOOK YOU UP WITH A TRACKING DEVICE.
NOT COOL, LIZ. YOU KNOW MY SECRET IDENTITY. I GET IT.
BUT YOU CAN'T KEEP TREATING ME LIKE SOME KINDA SUPER-POWERED ERRAND BOY.
FLASH, PLEASE. YOU'RE NOT THAT AT ALL. YOU'RE MY WHITE KNIGHT!
LAST ONE, THOMPSON. I PROMISE. SEE YA.
YOW. I KNOW THAT LOOK. HE WASN'T JUST STEAMED. HE WAS CLOSER TO MOLTEN.
OH, LET ME HAVE THIS. I'M BOSSING MY HIGH SCHOOL BOYFRIEND AROUND.
MY EX-HUSBAND IS WORKING FOR ME AND LOOKING AFTER THE KIDS.
AND I'M RUNNING A MULTIBILLION-DOLLAR COMPANY. LIVIN' THE DREAM.

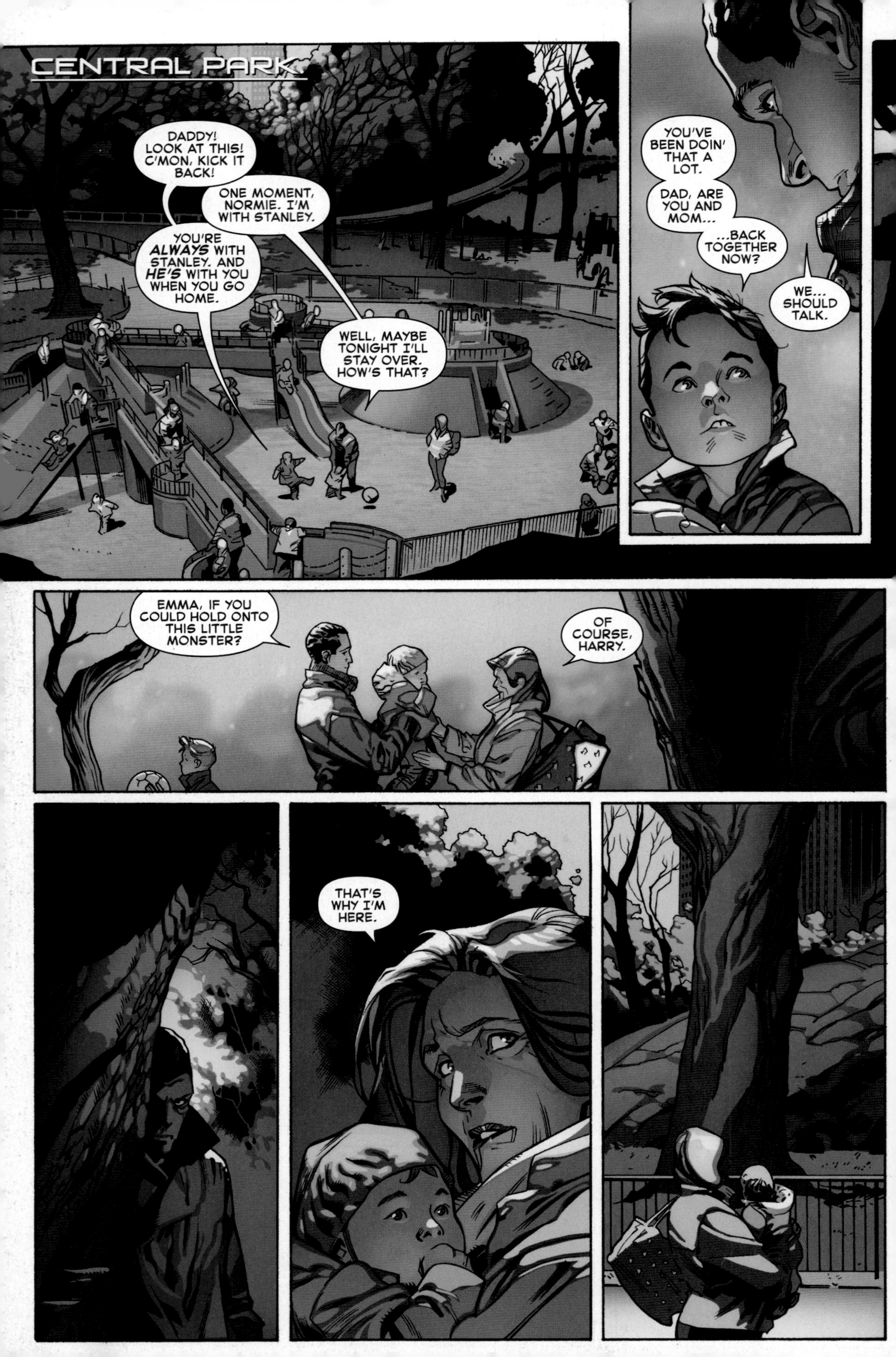
CENTRAL PARK
DADDY! LOOK AT THIS! C'MON, KICK IT BACK!
ONE MOMENT, NORMIE. I'M WITH STANLEY.
YOU'RE ALWAYS WITH STANLEY. AND HE'S WITH YOU WHEN YOU GO HOME.
WELL, MAYBE TONIGHT I'LL STAY OVER. HOW'S THAT?
YOU'VE BEEN DOIN' THAT A LOT.
DAD, ARE YOU AND MOM...
...BACK TOGETHER NOW?
WE... SHOULD TALK.
EMMA, IF YOU COULD HOLD ONTO THIS LITTLE MONSTER?
OF COURSE, HARRY.
THAT'S WHY I'M HERE.

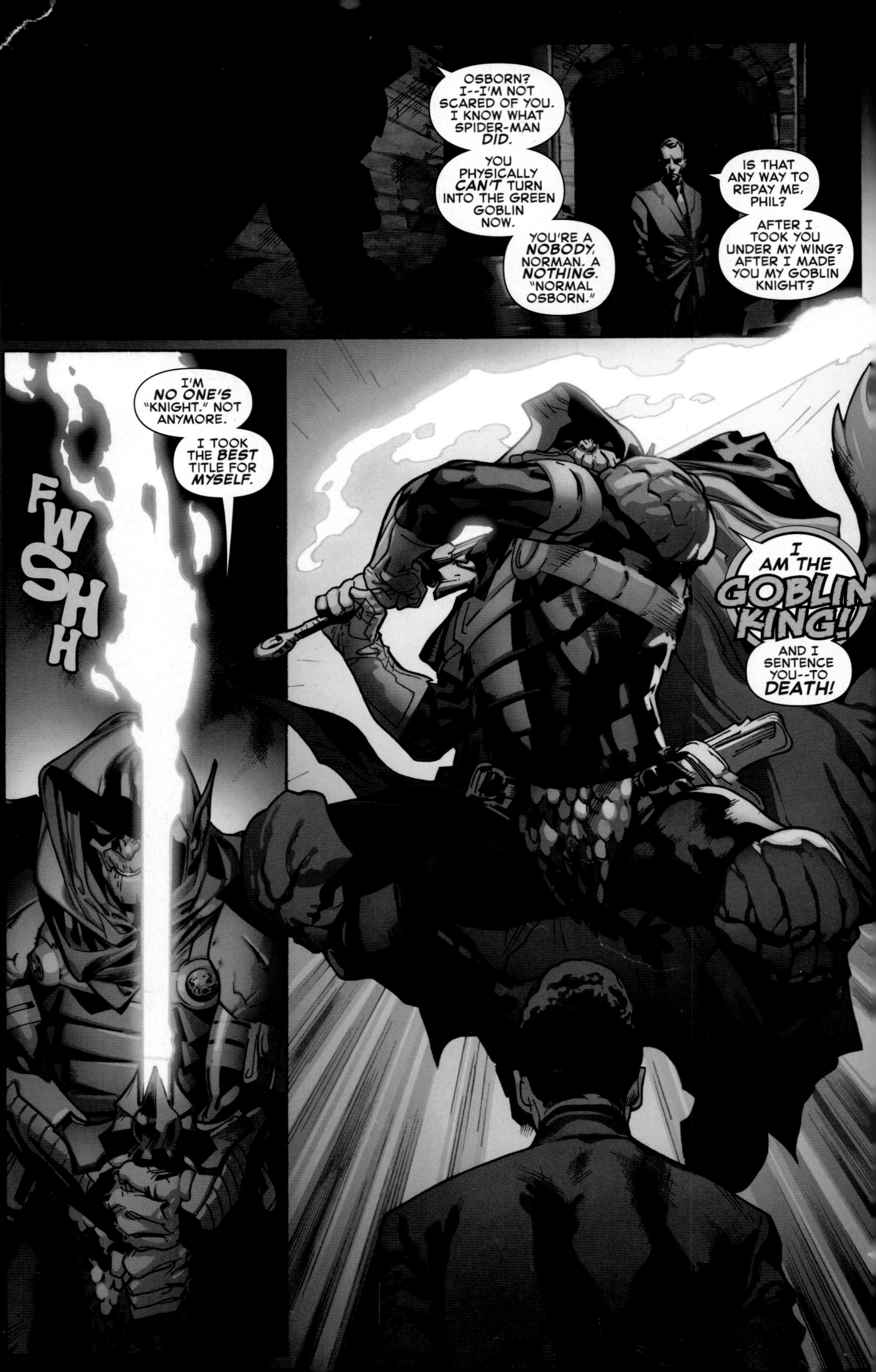

OSBORN? I--I'M NOT SCARED OF YOU. I KNOW WHAT SPIDER-MAN DID.
YOU PHYSICALLY CAN'T TURN INTO THE GREEN GOBLIN NOW.
YOU'RE A NOBODY, NORMAN. A NOTHING. "NORMAL OSBORN."
IS THAT ANY WAY TO REPAY ME, PHIL?
AFTER I TOOK YOU UNDER MY WING? AFTER I MADE YOU MY GOBLIN KNIGHT?
I'M NO ONE'S "KNIGHT." NOT ANYMORE.
I TOOK THE BEST TITLE FOR MYSELF.
FWSHH
I AM THE GOBLIN KING!
AND I SENTENCE YOU--TO DEATH!

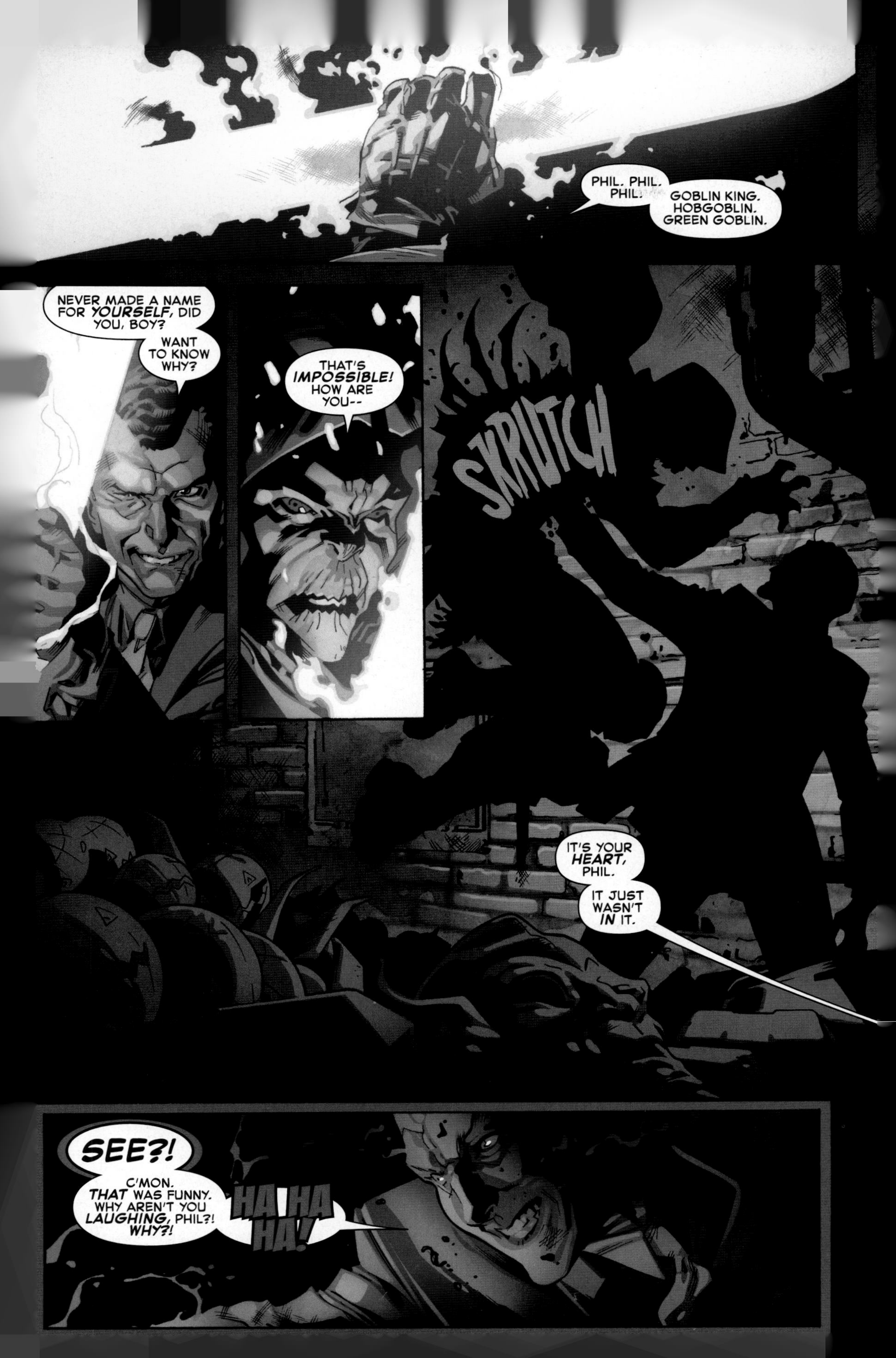
PHIL. PHIL. PHIL.
GOBLIN KING. HOBGOBLIN. GREEN GOBLIN.
NEVER MADE A NAME FOR YOURSELF, DID YOU, BOY?
WANT TO KNOW WHY?
THAT'S IMPOSSIBLE! HOW ARE YOU--
SKRUTCH
IT'S YOUR HEART, PHIL.
IT JUST WASN'T IN IT.
SEE?!
C'MON. THAT WAS FUNNY. WHY AREN'T YOU LAUGHING, PHIL?! WHY?!
HA HA HA!

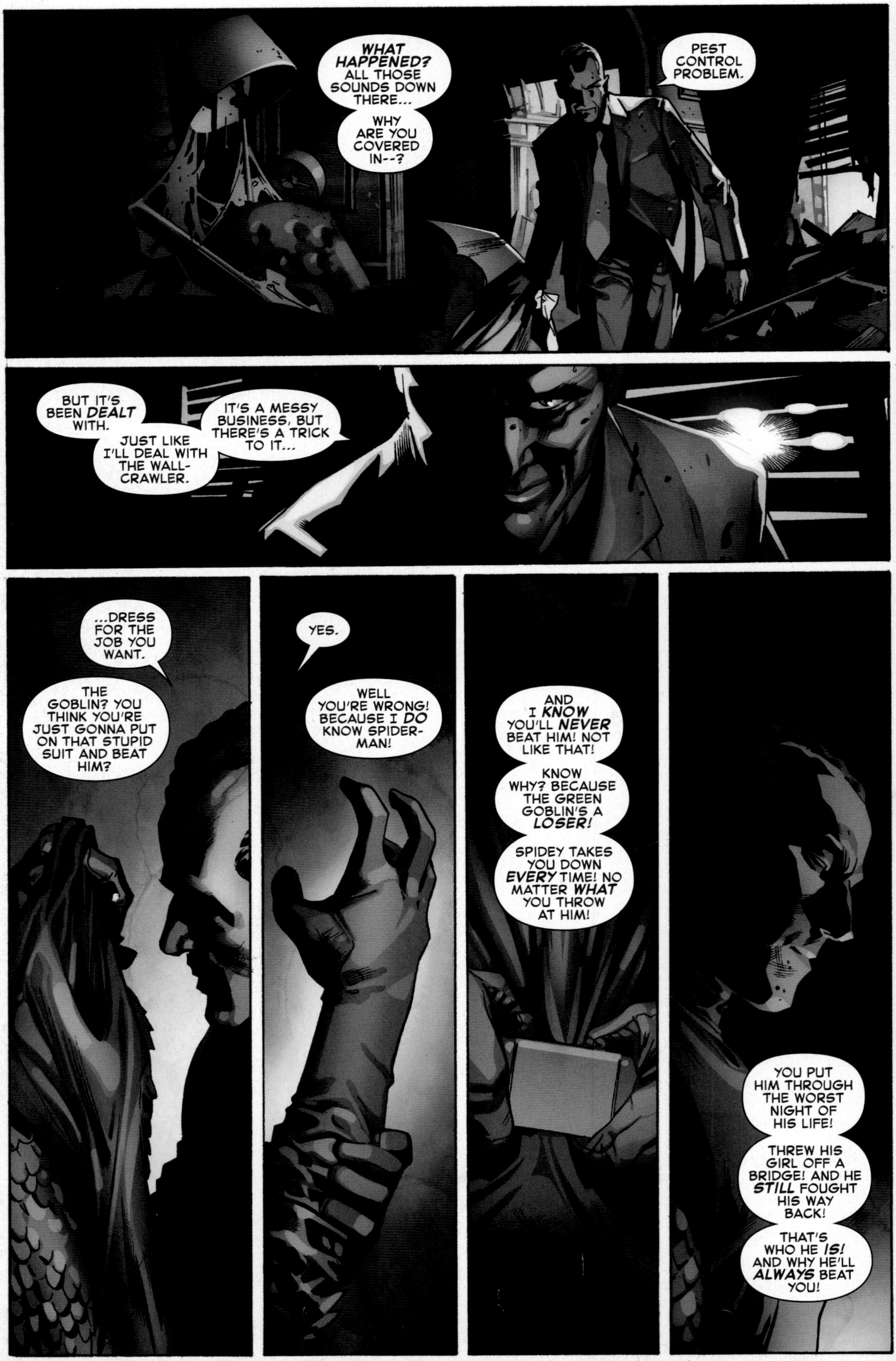
WHAT HAPPENED? ALL THOSE SOUNDS DOWN THERE...
WHY ARE YOU COVERED IN--?
PEST CONTROL PROBLEM.
BUT IT'S BEEN DEALT WITH.
JUST LIKE I'LL DEAL WITH THE WALL-CRAWLER.
IT'S A MESSY BUSINESS, BUT THERE'S A TRICK TO IT...
...DRESS FOR THE JOB YOU WANT.
THE GOBLIN? YOU THINK YOU'RE JUST GONNA PUT ON THAT STUPID SUIT AND BEAT HIM?
YES.
WELL YOU'RE WRONG! BECAUSE I DO KNOW SPIDER-MAN!
AND I KNOW YOU'LL NEVER BEAT HIM! NOT LIKE THAT!
KNOW WHY? BECAUSE THE GREEN GOBLIN'S A LOSER!
SPIDEY TAKES YOU DOWN EVERY TIME! NO MATTER WHAT YOU THROW AT HIM!
YOU PUT HIM THROUGH THE WORST NIGHT OF HIS LIFE!
THREW HIS GIRL OFF A BRIDGE! AND HE STILL FOUGHT HIS WAY BACK!
THAT'S WHO HE IS! AND WHY HE'LL ALWAYS BEAT YOU!

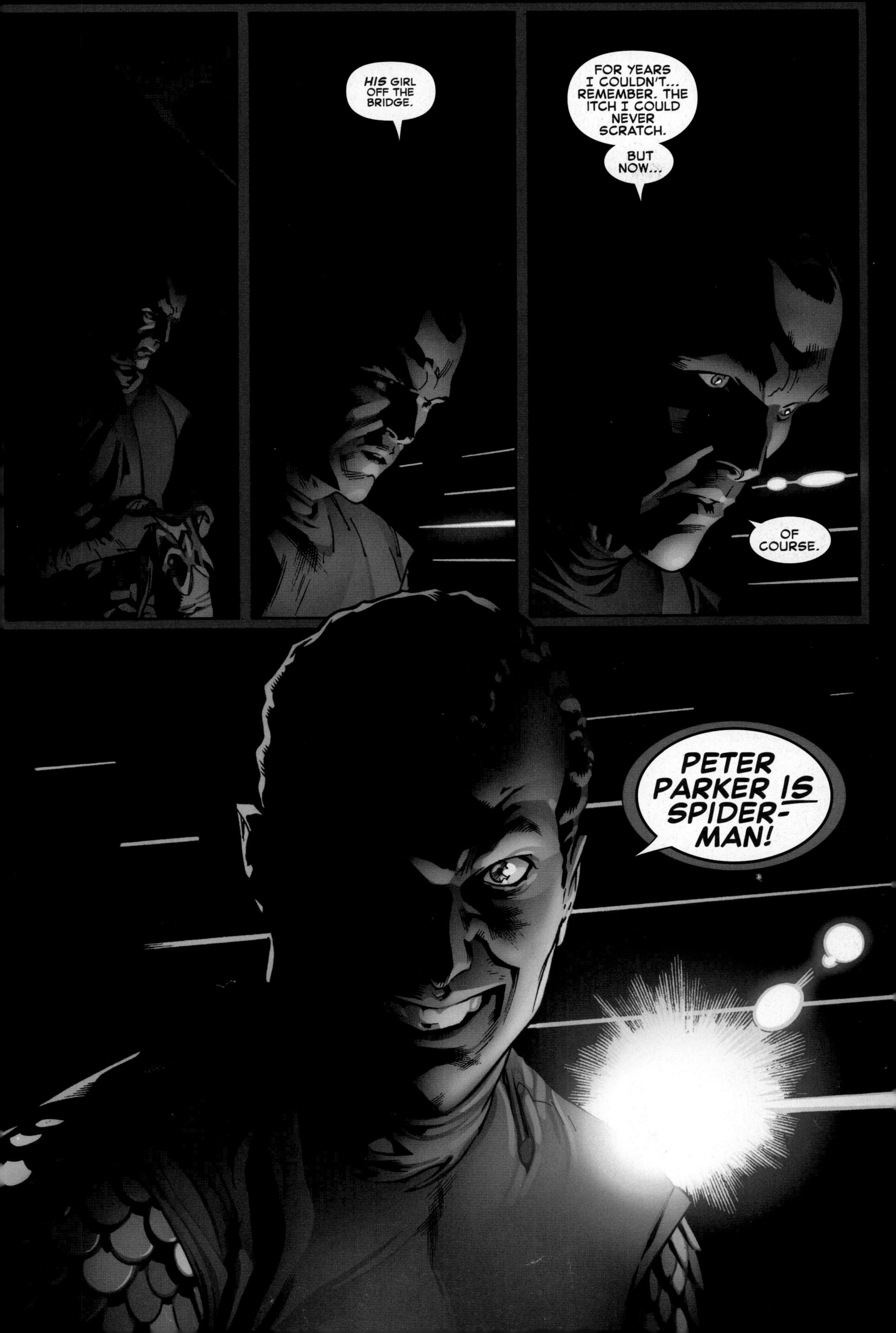

HIS GIRL OFF THE BRIDGE.
FOR YEARS I COULDN'T... REMEMBER. THE ITCH I COULD NEVER SCRATCH.
BUT NOW...
OF COURSE.
PETER PARKER IS SPIDER-MAN!

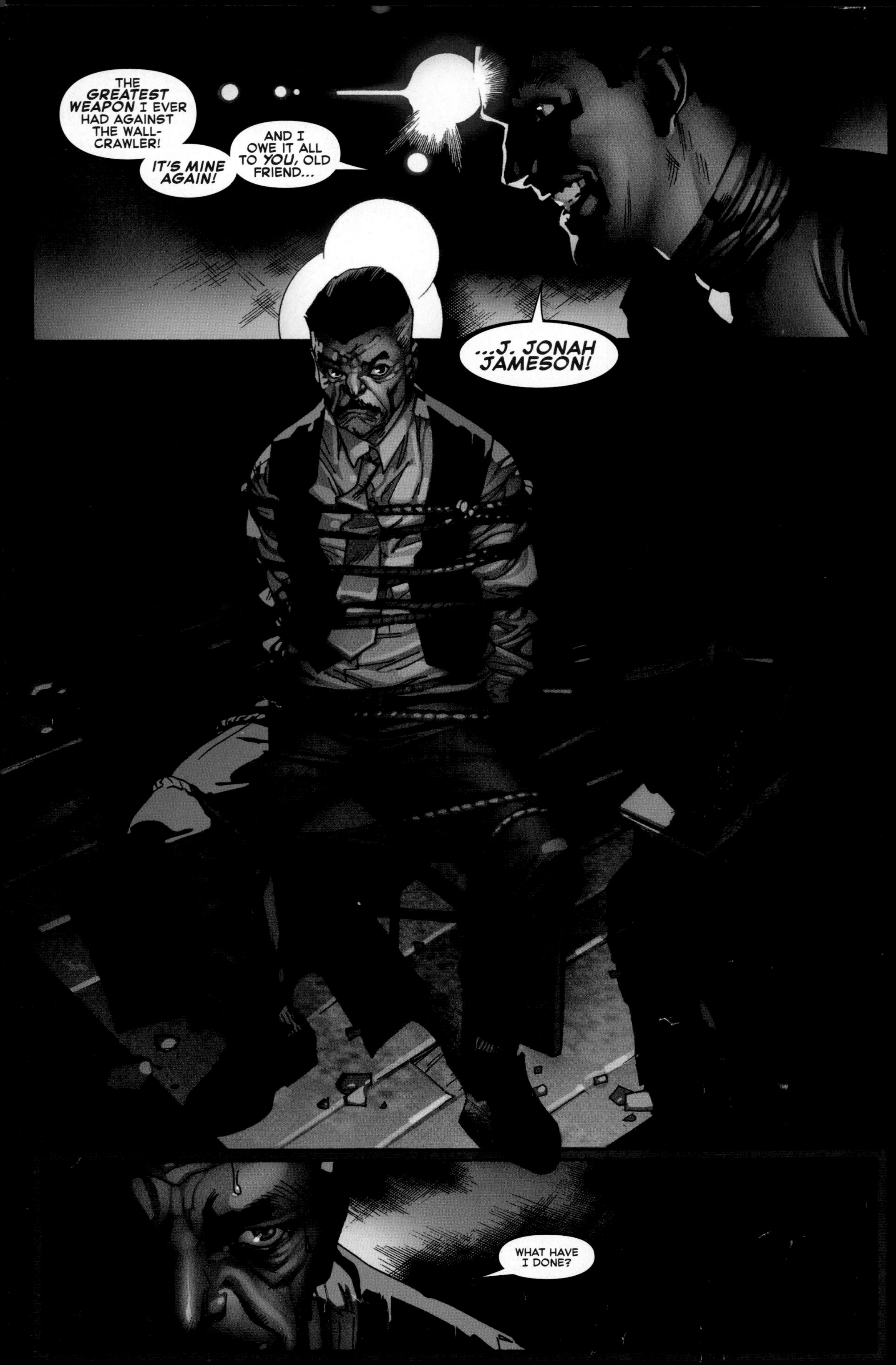

THE GREATEST WEAPON I EVER HAD AGAINST THE WALL-CRAWLER!
IT'S MINE AGAIN!
AND I OWE IT ALL TO YOU, OLD FRIEND...
...J. JONAH JAMESON!
WHAT HAVE I DONE?

798

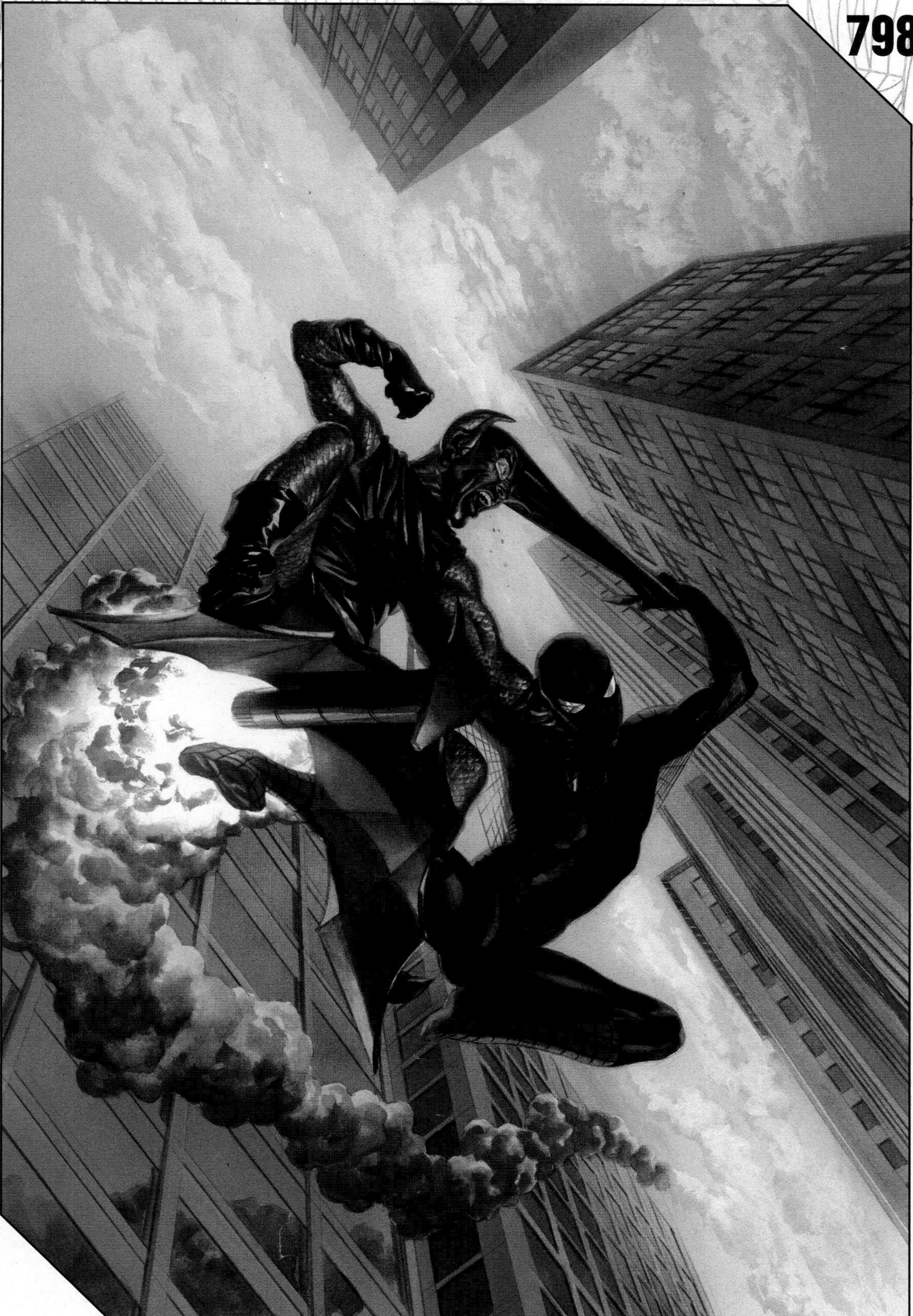

GO DOWN SWINGING PART TWO "THE ROPE-A-DOPE"

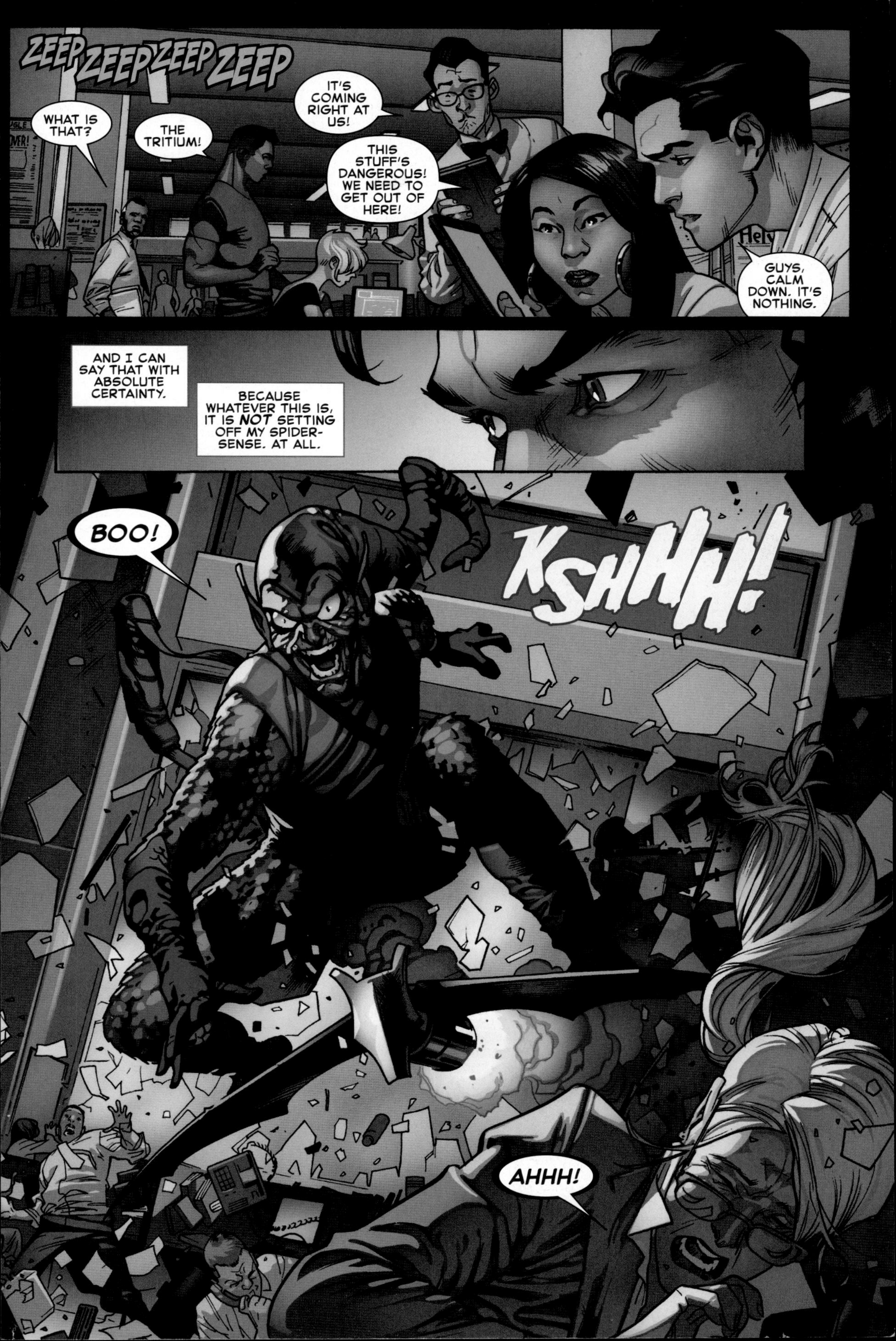
ZEEP ZEEP ZEEP ZEEP
WHAT IS THAT?
THE TRITIUM!
IT'S COMING RIGHT AT US!
THIS STUFF'S DANGEROUS! WE NEED TO GET OUT OF HERE!
GUYS, CALM DOWN. IT'S NOTHING.
AND I CAN SAY THAT WITH ABSOLUTE CERTAINTY.
BECAUSE WHATEVER THIS IS, IT IS NOT SETTING OFF MY SPIDER-SENSE. AT ALL.
BOO!
KSHHH!
AHHH!

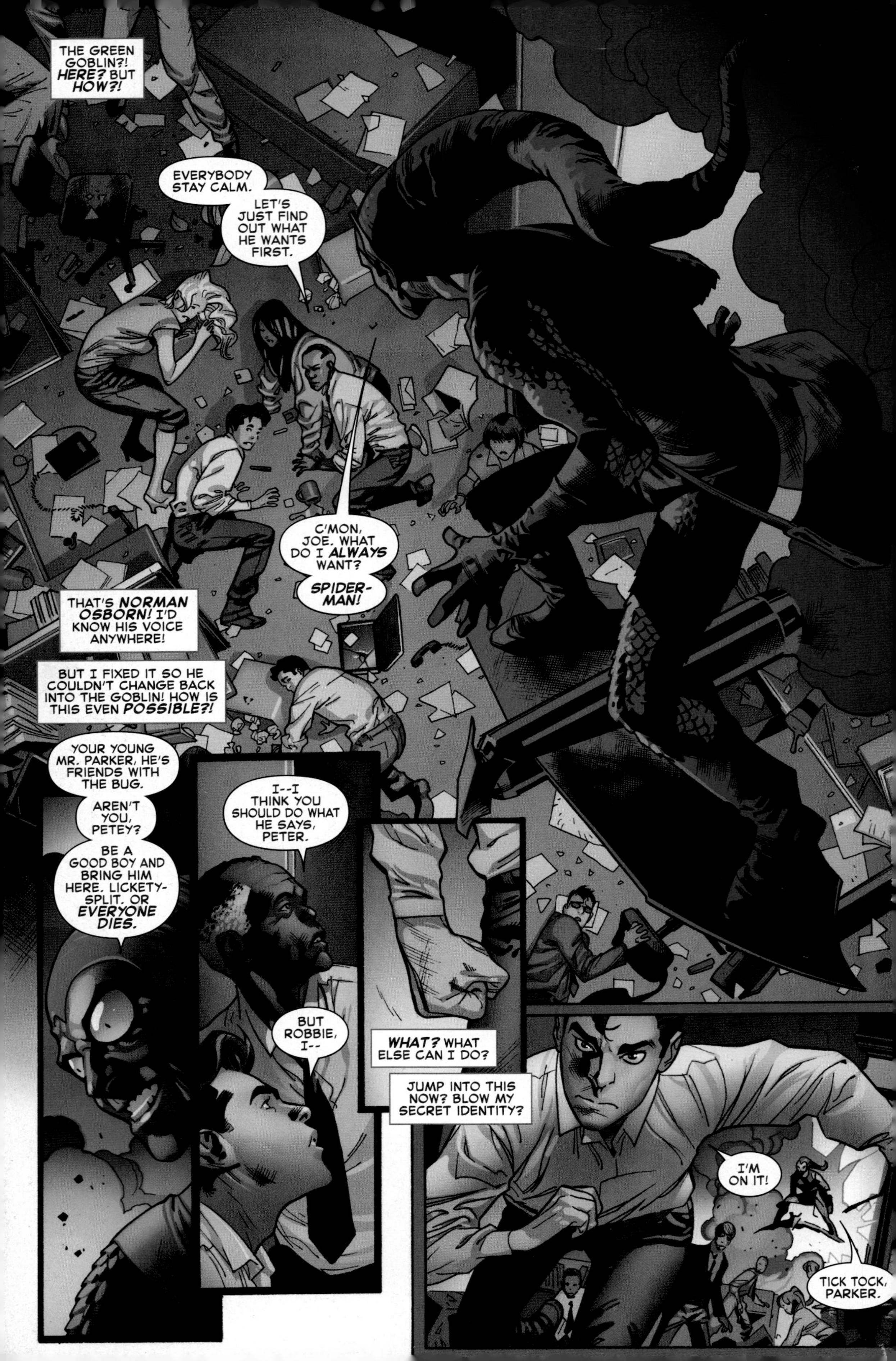
THE GREEN GOBLIN?! *HERE?* BUT *HOW?!*
EVERYBODY STAY CALM.
LET'S JUST FIND OUT WHAT HE WANTS FIRST.
C'MON, JOE. WHAT DO I *ALWAYS* WANT?
SPIDER-MAN!
THAT'S *NORMAN OSBORN!* I'D KNOW HIS VOICE ANYWHERE!
BUT I FIXED IT SO HE COULDN'T CHANGE BACK INTO THE GOBLIN! HOW IS THIS EVEN *POSSIBLE?!*
YOUR YOUNG MR. PARKER, HE'S FRIENDS WITH THE BUG.
AREN'T YOU, PETEY?
BE A GOOD BOY AND BRING HIM HERE. LICKETY-SPLIT. OR *EVERYONE DIES.*
I--I THINK YOU SHOULD DO WHAT HE SAYS, PETER.
BUT ROBBIE, I--
WHAT? WHAT ELSE CAN I DO?
JUMP INTO THIS NOW? BLOW MY SECRET IDENTITY?
I'M ON IT!
TICK TOCK, PARKER.

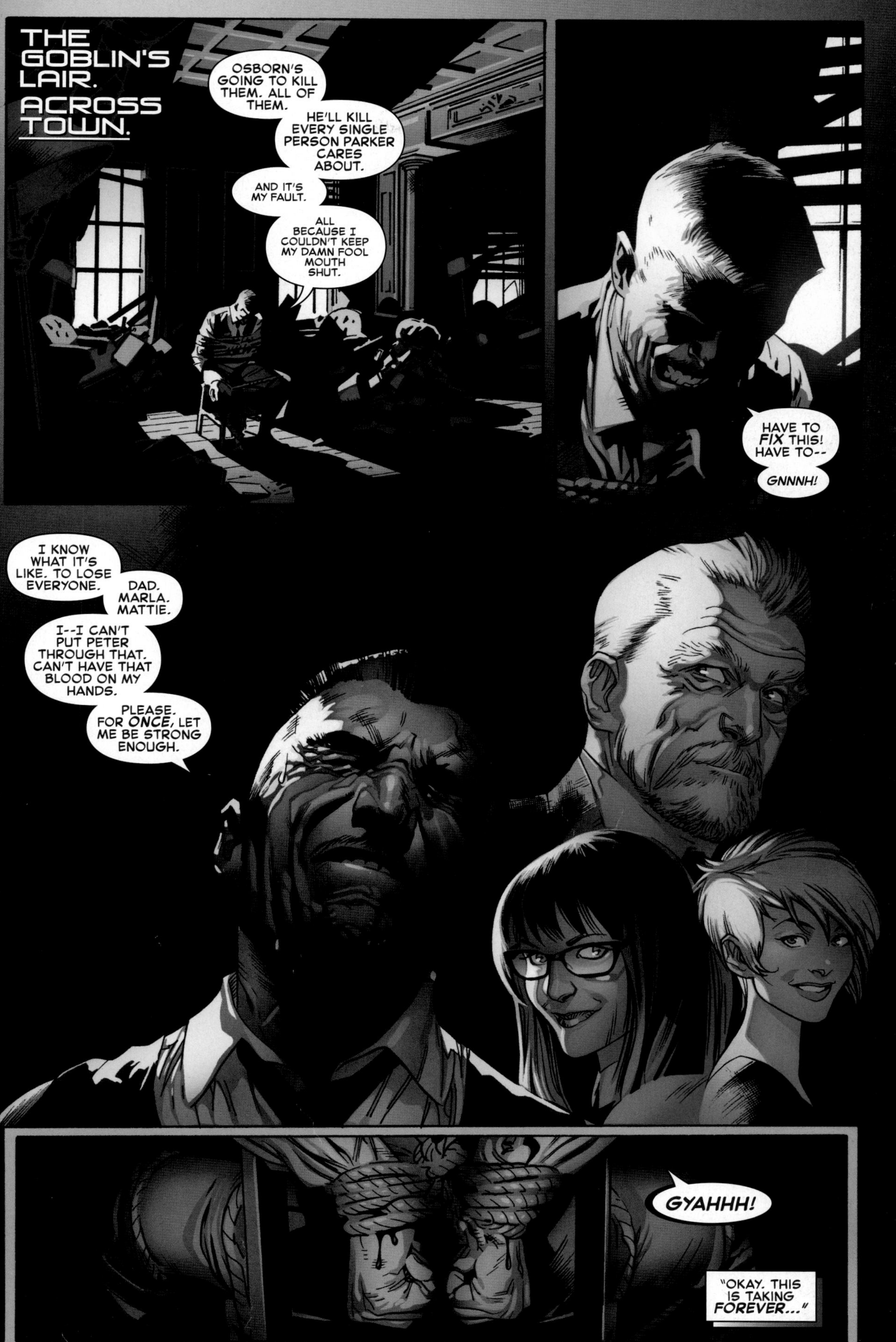
THE GOBLIN'S LAIR.
ACROSS TOWN.
OSBORN'S GOING TO KILL THEM. ALL OF THEM.
HE'LL KILL EVERY SINGLE PERSON PARKER CARES ABOUT.
AND IT'S MY FAULT.
ALL BECAUSE I COULDN'T KEEP MY DAMN FOOL MOUTH SHUT.
HAVE TO FIX THIS! HAVE TO--
GNNNH!
I KNOW WHAT IT'S LIKE. TO LOSE EVERYONE.
DAD. MARLA. MATTIE.
I--I CAN'T PUT PETER THROUGH THAT. CAN'T HAVE THAT BLOOD ON MY HANDS.
PLEASE. FOR ONCE, LET ME BE STRONG ENOUGH.
GYAHHH!
"OKAY. THIS IS TAKING FOREVER..."

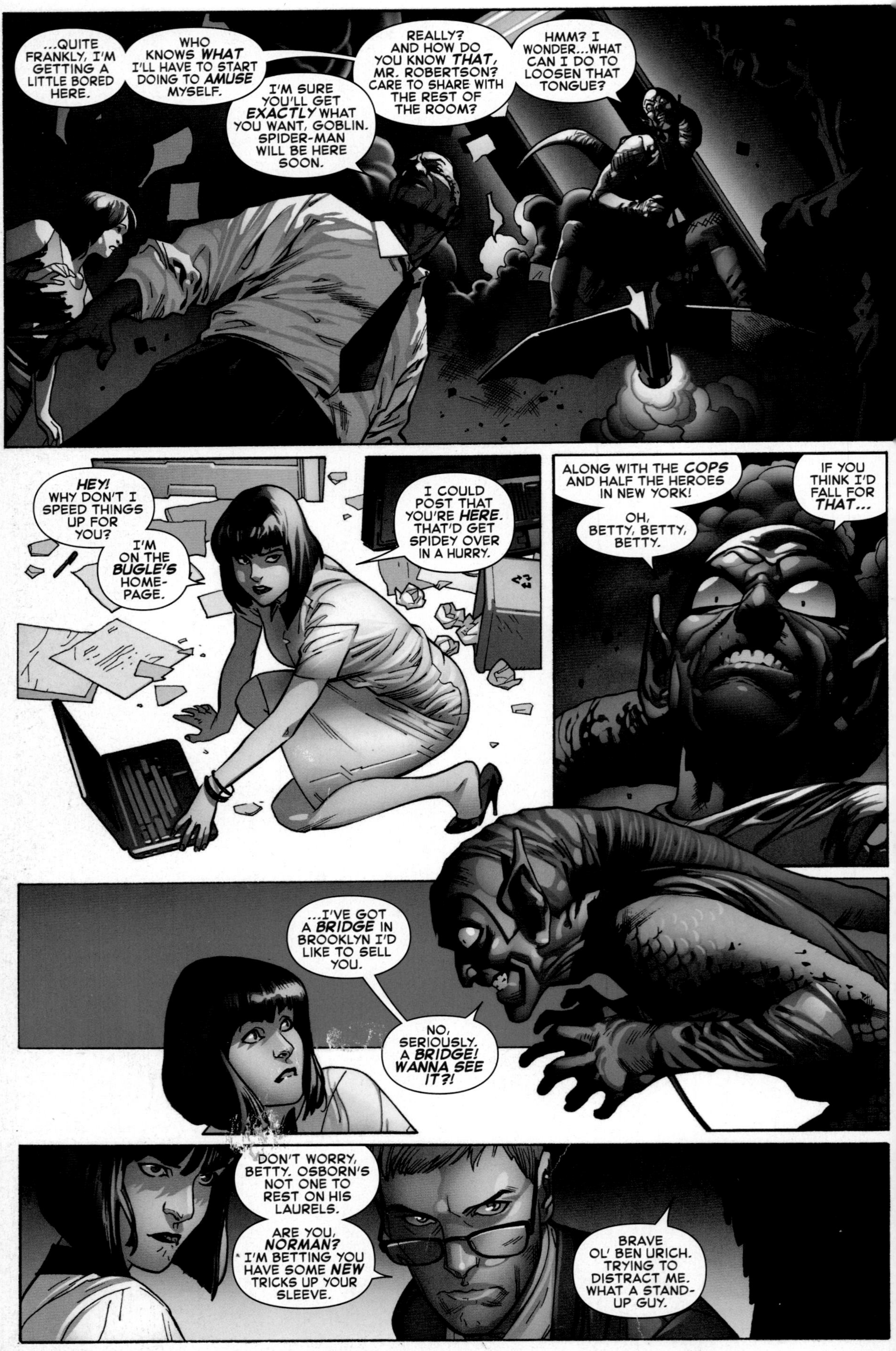
...QUITE FRANKLY, I'M GETTING A LITTLE BORED HERE.
WHO KNOWS *WHAT* I'LL HAVE TO START DOING TO *AMUSE* MYSELF.
I'M SURE YOU'LL GET *EXACTLY* WHAT YOU WANT, GOBLIN. SPIDER-MAN WILL BE HERE SOON.
REALLY? AND HOW DO YOU KNOW *THAT*, MR. ROBERTSON? CARE TO SHARE WITH THE REST OF THE ROOM?
HMM? I WONDER...WHAT CAN I DO TO LOOSEN THAT TONGUE?
HEY! WHY DON'T I SPEED THINGS UP FOR YOU?
I'M ON THE *BUGLE'S* HOME-PAGE.
I COULD POST THAT YOU'RE *HERE*. THAT'D GET SPIDEY OVER IN A HURRY.
ALONG WITH THE *COPS* AND HALF THE HEROES IN NEW YORK!
OH, BETTY, BETTY, BETTY.
IF YOU THINK I'D FALL FOR *THAT...*
...I'VE GOT A *BRIDGE* IN BROOKLYN I'D LIKE TO SELL YOU.
NO, SERIOUSLY. A *BRIDGE! WANNA SEE IT?!*
DON'T WORRY, BETTY. OSBORN'S NOT ONE TO REST ON HIS LAURELS.
ARE YOU, *NORMAN?* I'M BETTING YOU HAVE SOME *NEW* TRICKS UP YOUR SLEEVE.
BRAVE OL' BEN URICH. TRYING TO DISTRACT ME. WHAT A STAND-UP GUY.

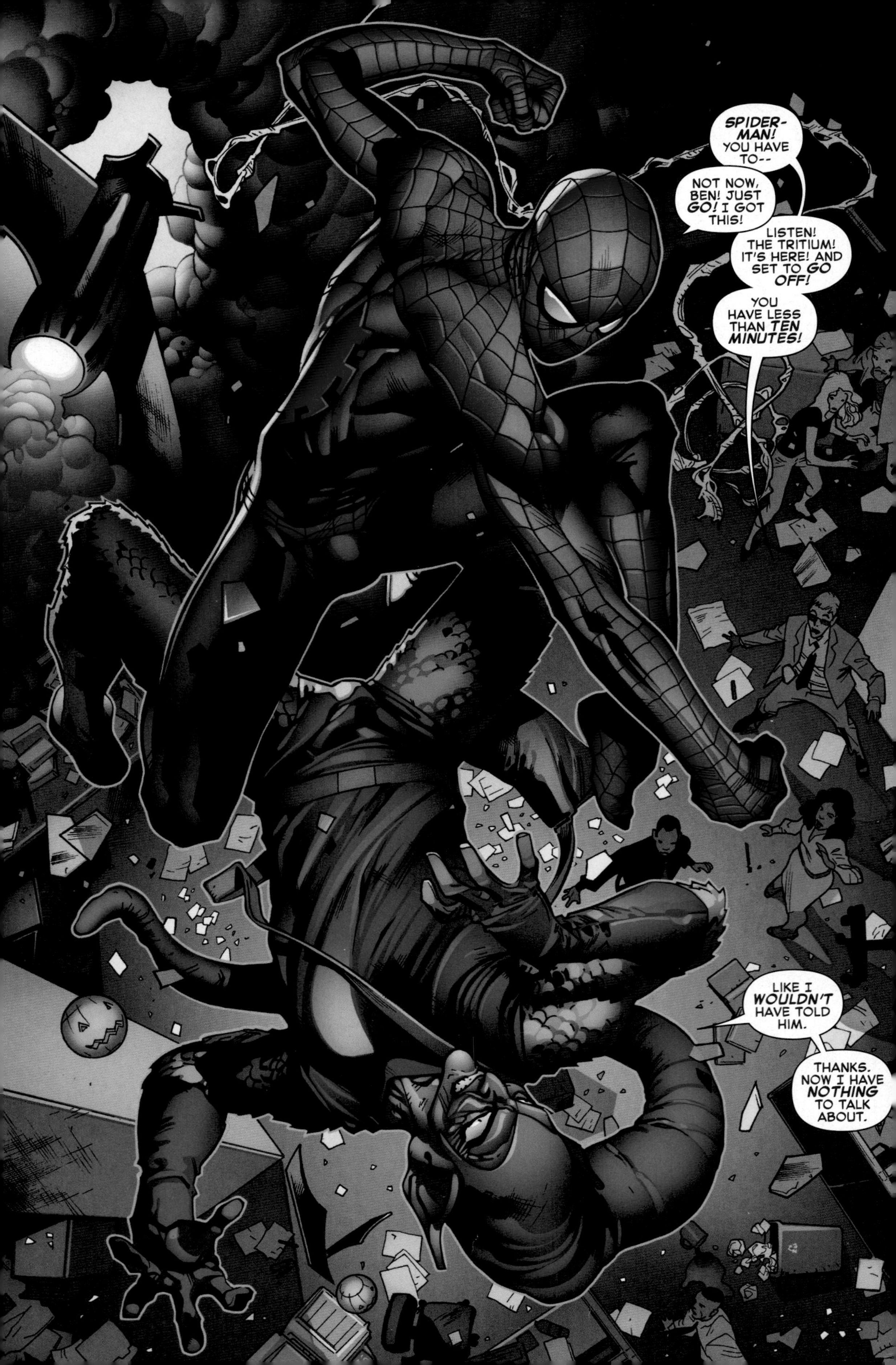
SPIDER-MAN! YOU HAVE TO--
NOT NOW, BEN! JUST GO! I GOT THIS!
LISTEN! THE TRITIUM! IT'S HERE! AND SET TO GO OFF!
YOU HAVE LESS THAN TEN MINUTES!
LIKE I WOULDN'T HAVE TOLD HIM.
THANKS. NOW I HAVE NOTHING TO TALK ABOUT.

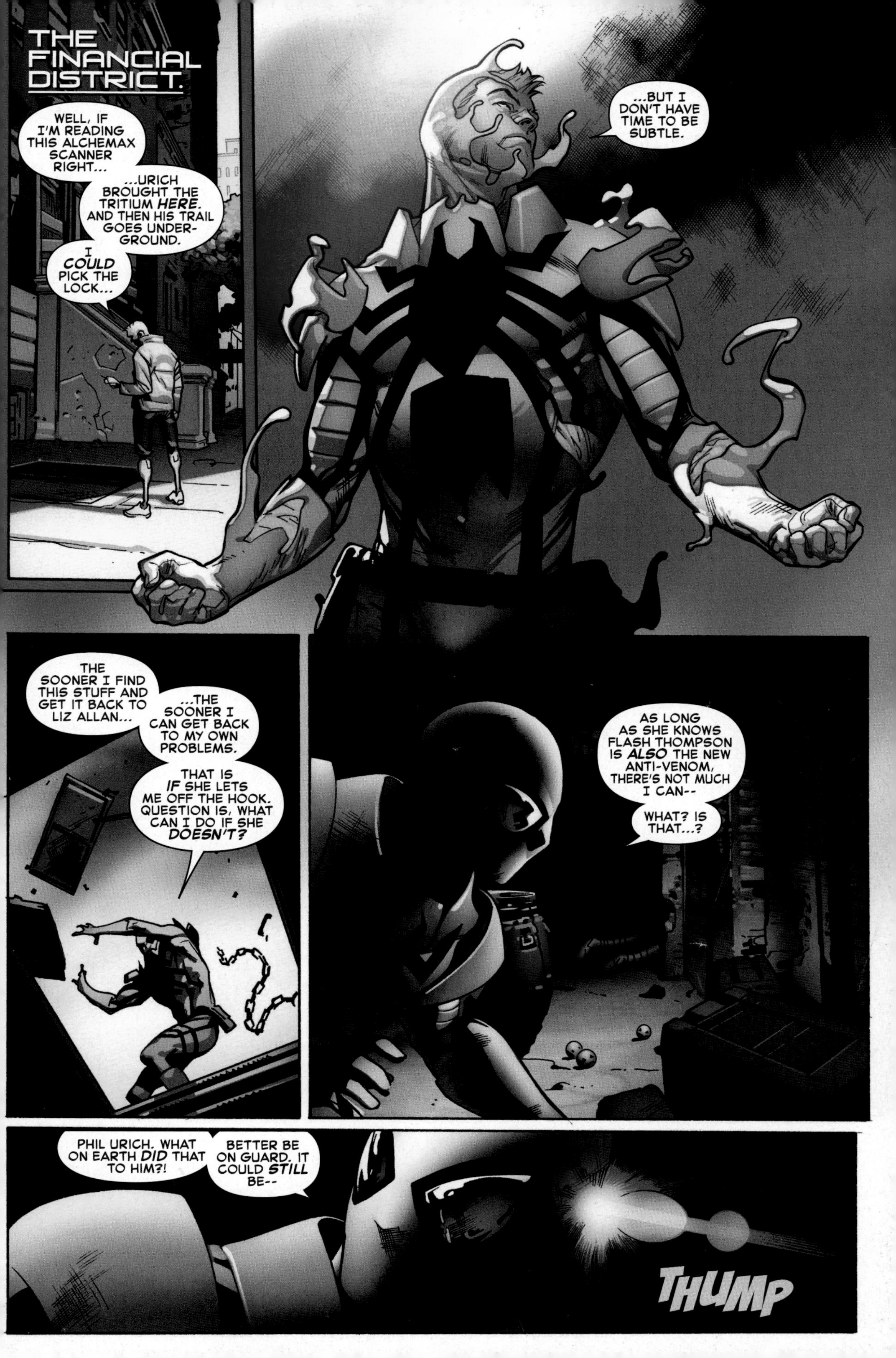
THE FINANCIAL DISTRICT.
WELL, IF I'M READING THIS ALCHEMAX SCANNER RIGHT...
...URICH BROUGHT THE TRITIUM HERE. AND THEN HIS TRAIL GOES UNDER-GROUND.
I COULD PICK THE LOCK...
...BUT I DON'T HAVE TIME TO BE SUBTLE.
THE SOONER I FIND THIS STUFF AND GET IT BACK TO LIZ ALLAN...
...THE SOONER I CAN GET BACK TO MY OWN PROBLEMS.
THAT IS IF SHE LETS ME OFF THE HOOK. QUESTION IS, WHAT CAN I DO IF SHE DOESN'T?
AS LONG AS SHE KNOWS FLASH THOMPSON IS ALSO THE NEW ANTI-VENOM, THERE'S NOT MUCH I CAN--
WHAT? IS THAT...?
PHIL URICH. WHAT ON EARTH DID THAT TO HIM?!
BETTER BE ON GUARD. IT COULD STILL BE--
THUMP

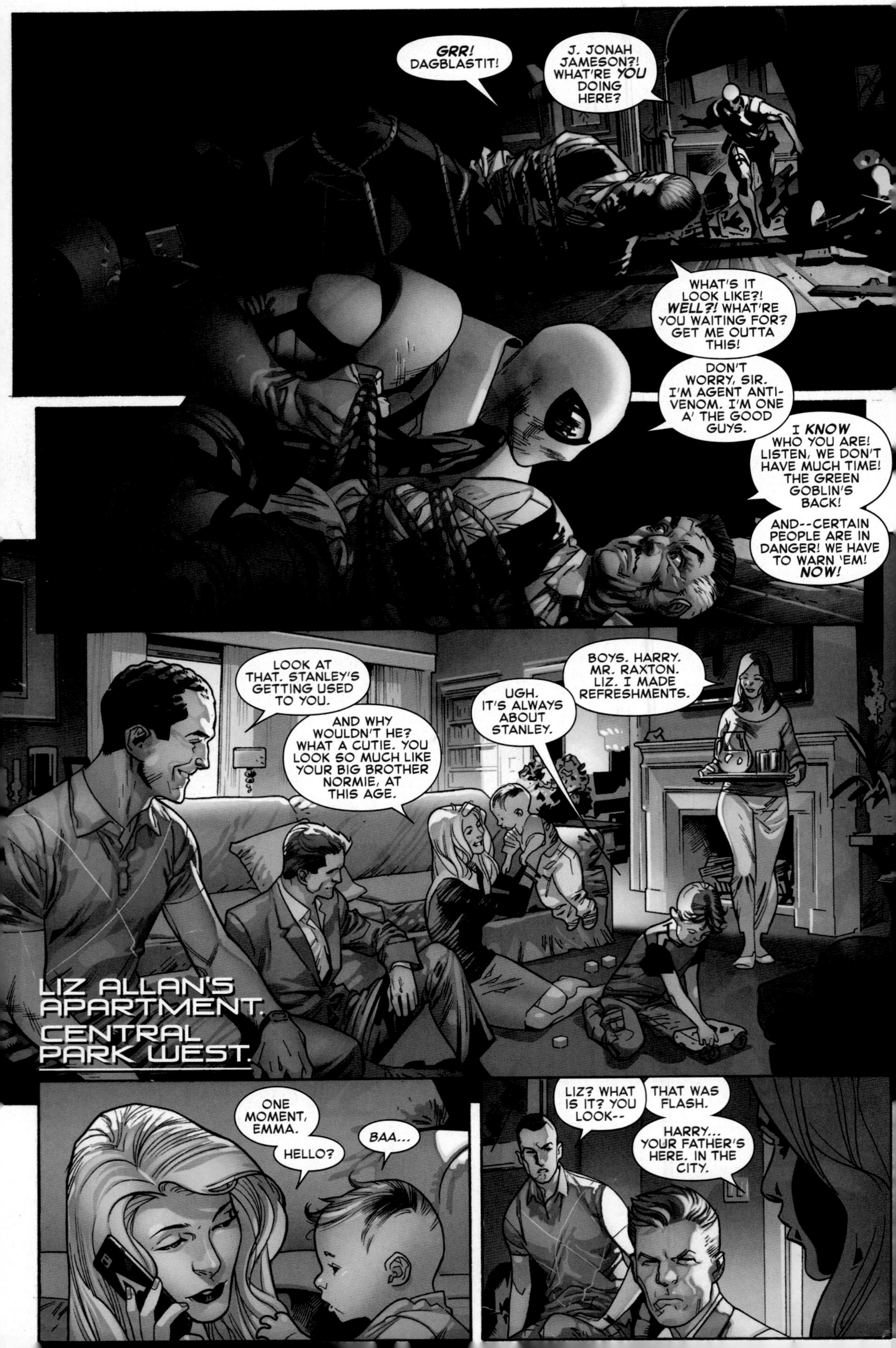
GRR! DAGBLASTIT!
J. JONAH JAMESON?! WHAT'RE YOU DOING HERE?
WHAT'S IT LOOK LIKE?! WELL?! WHAT'RE YOU WAITING FOR? GET ME OUTTA THIS!
DON'T WORRY, SIR. I'M AGENT ANTI-VENOM. I'M ONE A' THE GOOD GUYS.
I KNOW WHO YOU ARE! LISTEN, WE DON'T HAVE MUCH TIME! THE GREEN GOBLIN'S BACK!
AND--CERTAIN PEOPLE ARE IN DANGER! WE HAVE TO WARN 'EM! NOW!
LIZ ALLAN'S APARTMENT. CENTRAL PARK WEST.
LOOK AT THAT. STANLEY'S GETTING USED TO YOU.
AND WHY WOULDN'T HE? WHAT A CUTIE. YOU LOOK SO MUCH LIKE YOUR BIG BROTHER NORMIE, AT THIS AGE.
UGH. IT'S ALWAYS ABOUT STANLEY.
BOYS. HARRY. MR. RAXTON. LIZ. I MADE REFRESHMENTS.
ONE MOMENT, EMMA.
HELLO?
BAA...
LIZ? WHAT IS IT? YOU LOOK--
THAT WAS FLASH.
HARRY... YOUR FATHER'S HERE. IN THE CITY.

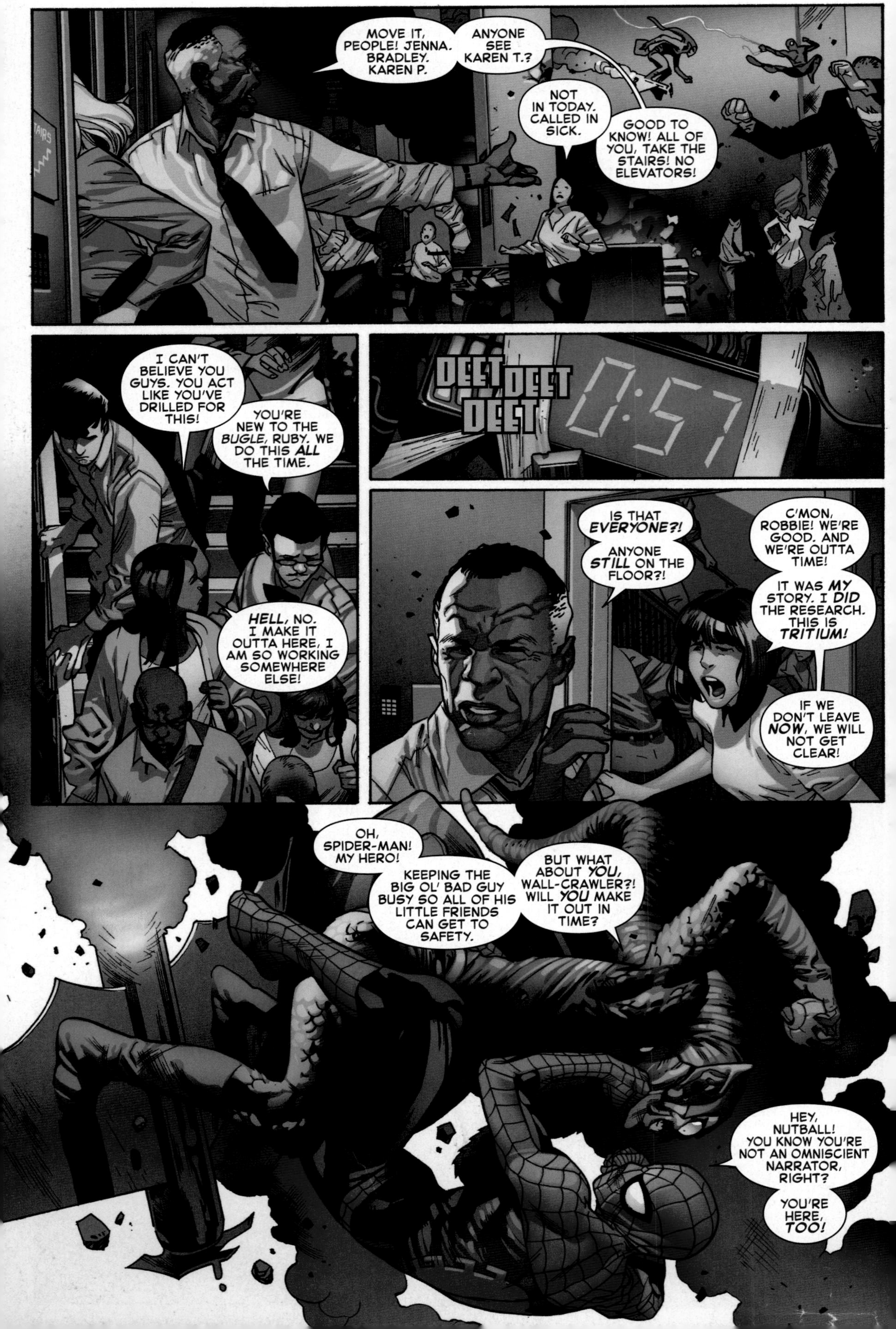
MOVE IT, PEOPLE! JENNA. BRADLEY. KAREN P.
ANYONE SEE KAREN T.?
NOT IN TODAY. CALLED IN SICK.
GOOD TO KNOW! ALL OF YOU, TAKE THE STAIRS! NO ELEVATORS!
STAIRS
I CAN'T BELIEVE YOU GUYS. YOU ACT LIKE YOU'VE DRILLED FOR THIS!
YOU'RE NEW TO THE *BUGLE*, RUBY. WE DO THIS *ALL* THE TIME.
HELL, NO. I MAKE IT OUTTA HERE, I AM SO WORKING SOMEWHERE ELSE!
DEET DEET DEET
0:57
IS THAT *EVERYONE?!*
ANYONE *STILL* ON THE FLOOR?!
C'MON, ROBBIE! WE'RE GOOD. AND WE'RE OUTTA TIME!
IT WAS *MY* STORY. I *DID* THE RESEARCH. THIS IS *TRITIUM!*
IF WE DON'T LEAVE *NOW*, WE WILL NOT GET CLEAR!
OH, SPIDER-MAN! MY HERO!
KEEPING THE BIG OL' BAD GUY BUSY SO ALL OF HIS LITTLE FRIENDS CAN GET TO SAFETY.
BUT WHAT ABOUT *YOU*, WALL-CRAWLER?! WILL *YOU* MAKE IT OUT IN TIME?
HEY, NUTBALL! YOU KNOW YOU'RE NOT AN OMNISCIENT NARRATOR, RIGHT?
YOU'RE HERE, *TOO!*

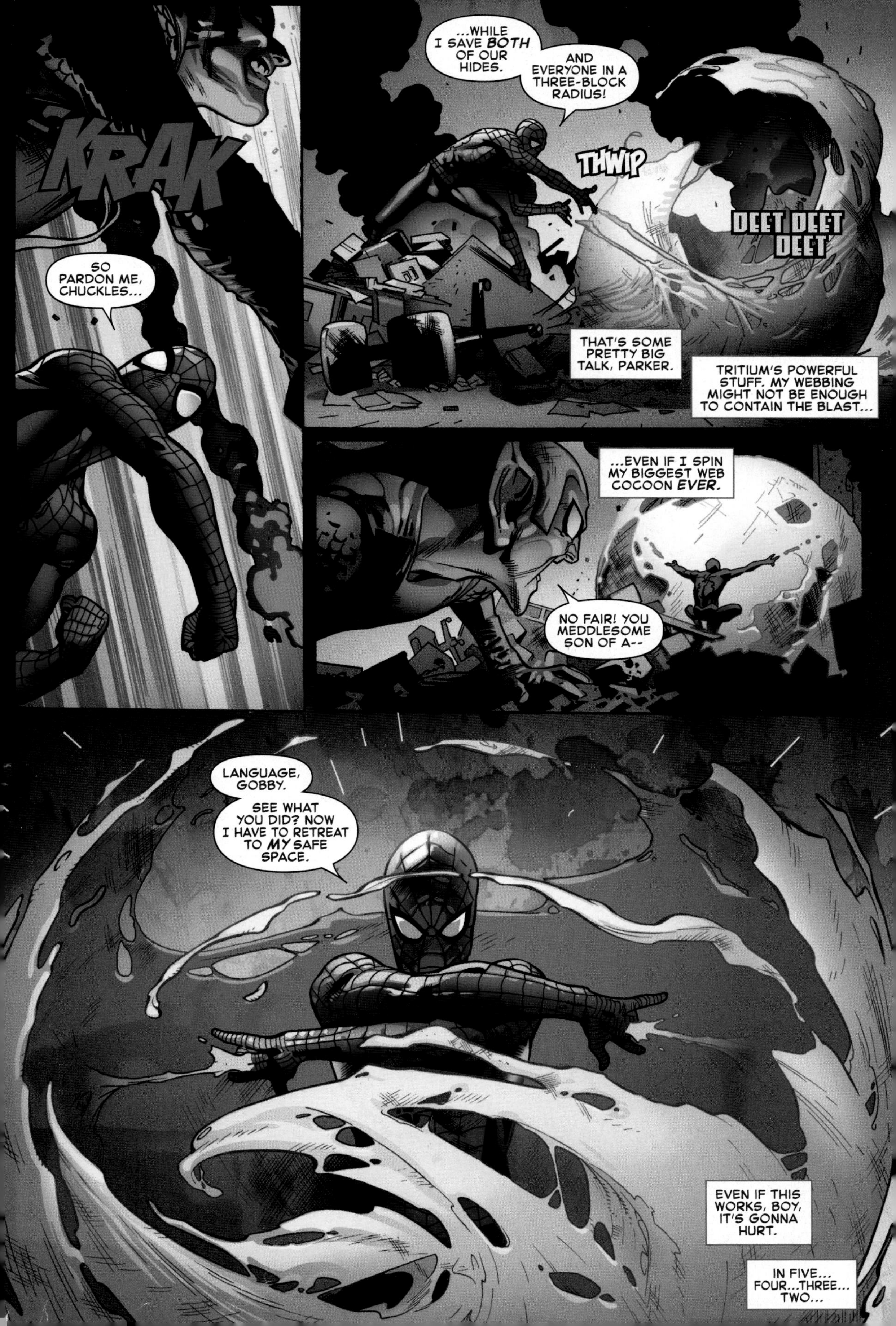
KRAK
SO PARDON ME, CHUCKLES...
...WHILE I SAVE BOTH OF OUR HIDES.
AND EVERYONE IN A THREE-BLOCK RADIUS!
THWIP
DEET DEET DEET
THAT'S SOME PRETTY BIG TALK, PARKER.
TRITIUM'S POWERFUL STUFF. MY WEBBING MIGHT NOT BE ENOUGH TO CONTAIN THE BLAST...
...EVEN IF I SPIN MY BIGGEST WEB COCOON EVER.
NO FAIR! YOU MEDDLESOME SON OF A--
LANGUAGE, GOBBY.
SEE WHAT YOU DID? NOW I HAVE TO RETREAT TO MY SAFE SPACE.
EVEN IF THIS WORKS, BOY, IT'S GONNA HURT.
IN FIVE... FOUR...THREE... TWO...

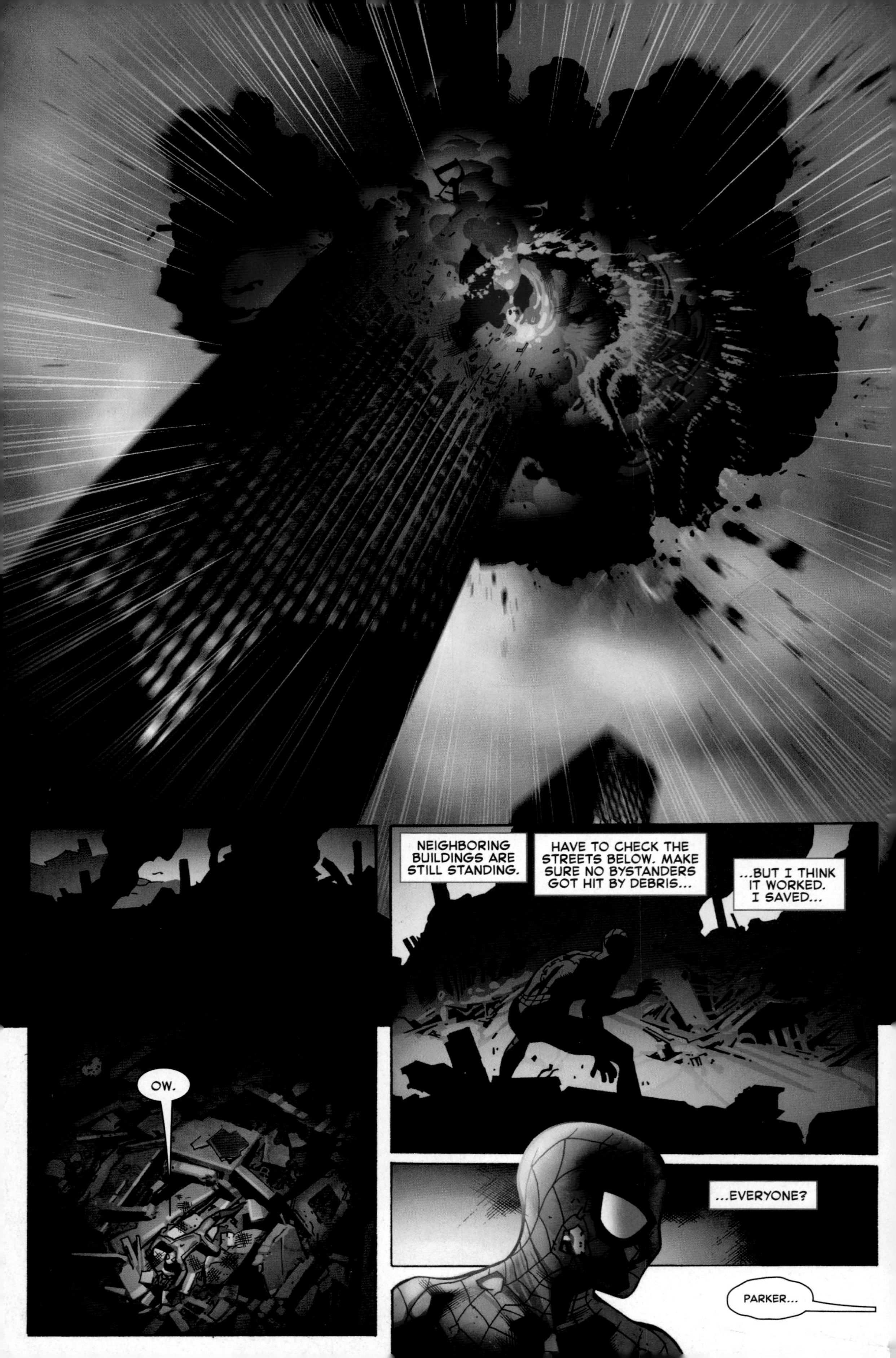
NEIGHBORING BUILDINGS ARE STILL STANDING.
HAVE TO CHECK THE STREETS BELOW. MAKE SURE NO BYSTANDERS GOT HIT BY DEBRIS...
...BUT I THINK IT WORKED. I SAVED...
OW.
...EVERYONE?
PARKER...

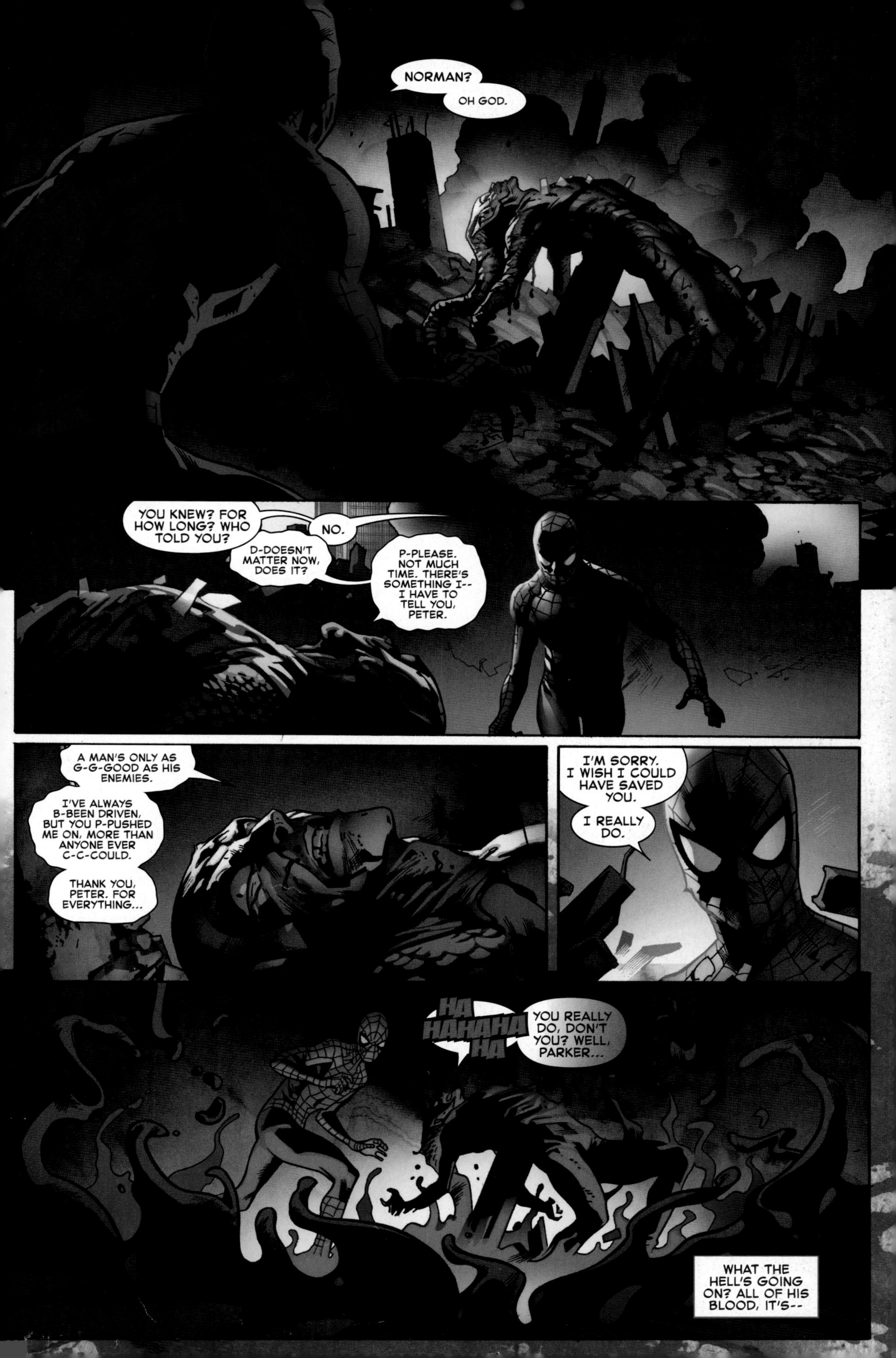
NORMAN?
OH GOD.
YOU KNEW? FOR HOW LONG? WHO TOLD YOU?
NO.
D-DOESN'T MATTER NOW, DOES IT?
P-PLEASE. NOT MUCH TIME. THERE'S SOMETHING I-- I HAVE TO TELL YOU, PETER.
A MAN'S ONLY AS G-G-GOOD AS HIS ENEMIES.
I'VE ALWAYS B-BEEN DRIVEN, BUT YOU P-PUSHED ME ON, MORE THAN ANYONE EVER C-C-COULD.
THANK YOU, PETER. FOR EVERYTHING...
I'M SORRY. I WISH I COULD HAVE SAVED YOU.
I REALLY DO.
HA HAHAHA HA
YOU REALLY DO, DON'T YOU? WELL, PARKER...
WHAT THE HELL'S GOING ON? ALL OF HIS BLOOD, IT'S--

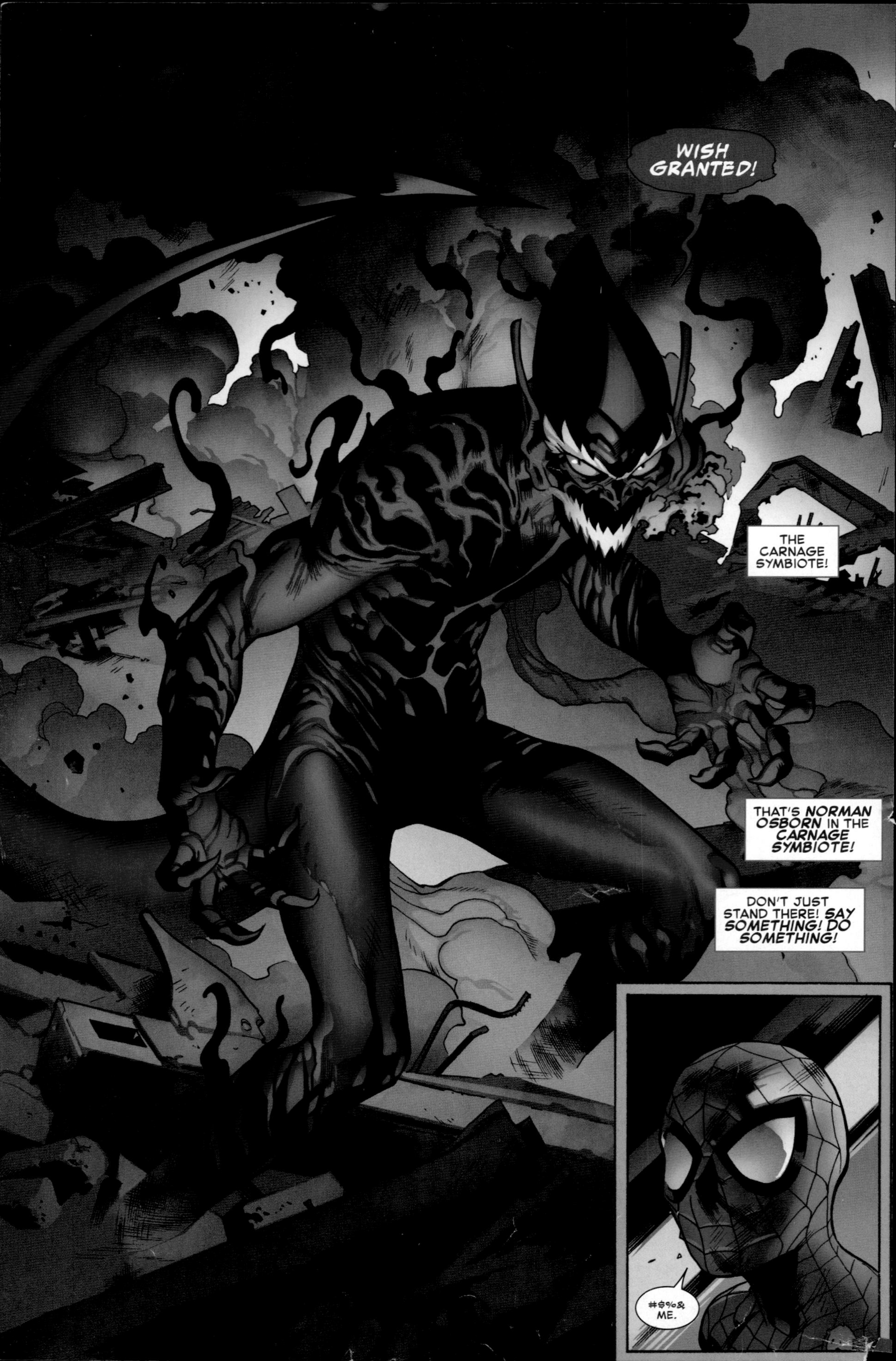
WISH GRANTED!
THE CARNAGE SYMBIOTE!
THAT'S NORMAN OSBORN IN THE CARNAGE SYMBIOTE!
DON'T JUST STAND THERE! SAY SOMETHING! DO SOMETHING!
#$%& ME.

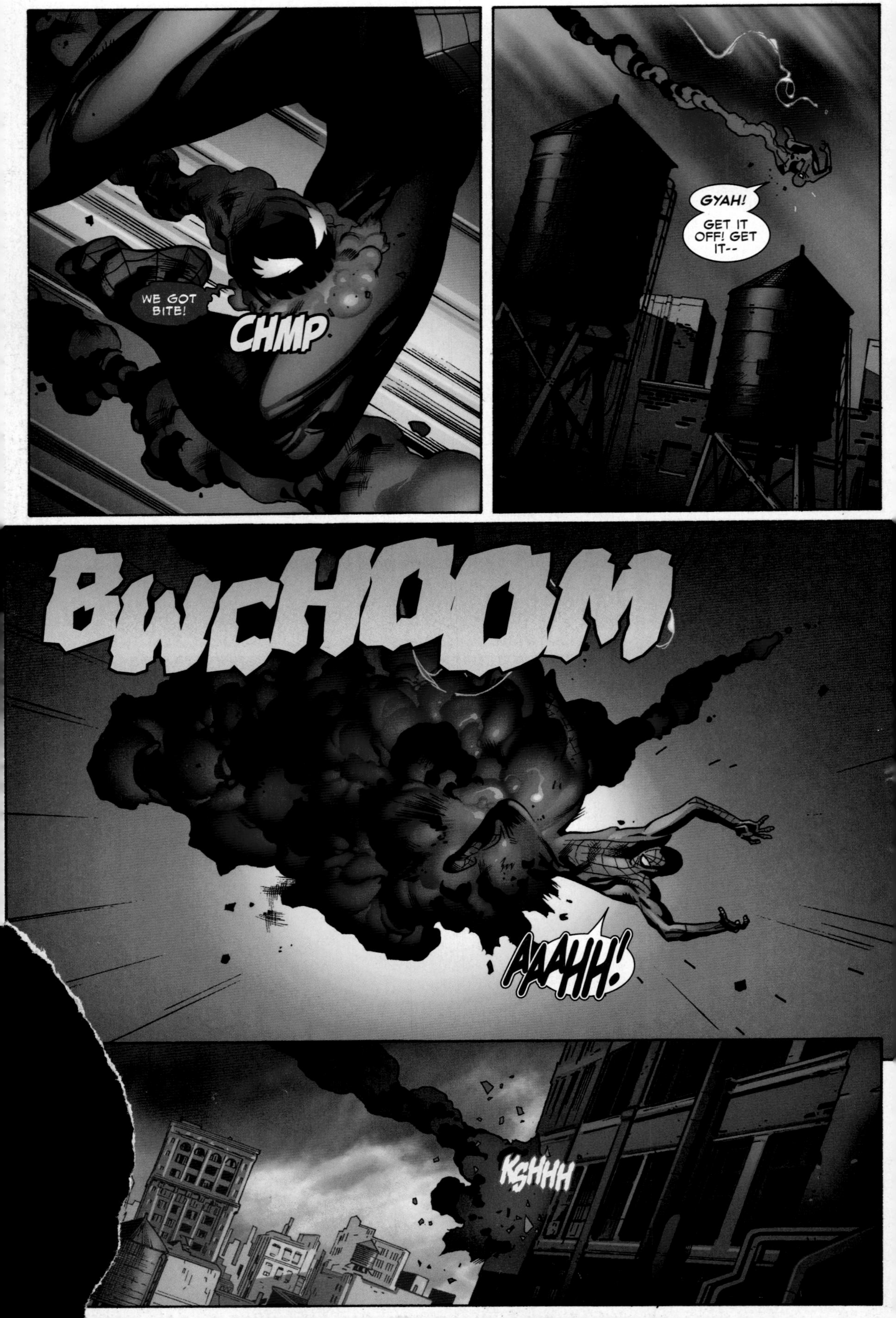

WE GOT BITE!
CHMP
GYAH!
GET IT OFF! GET IT--
BWCHOOM
AAAHH!
KSHHH

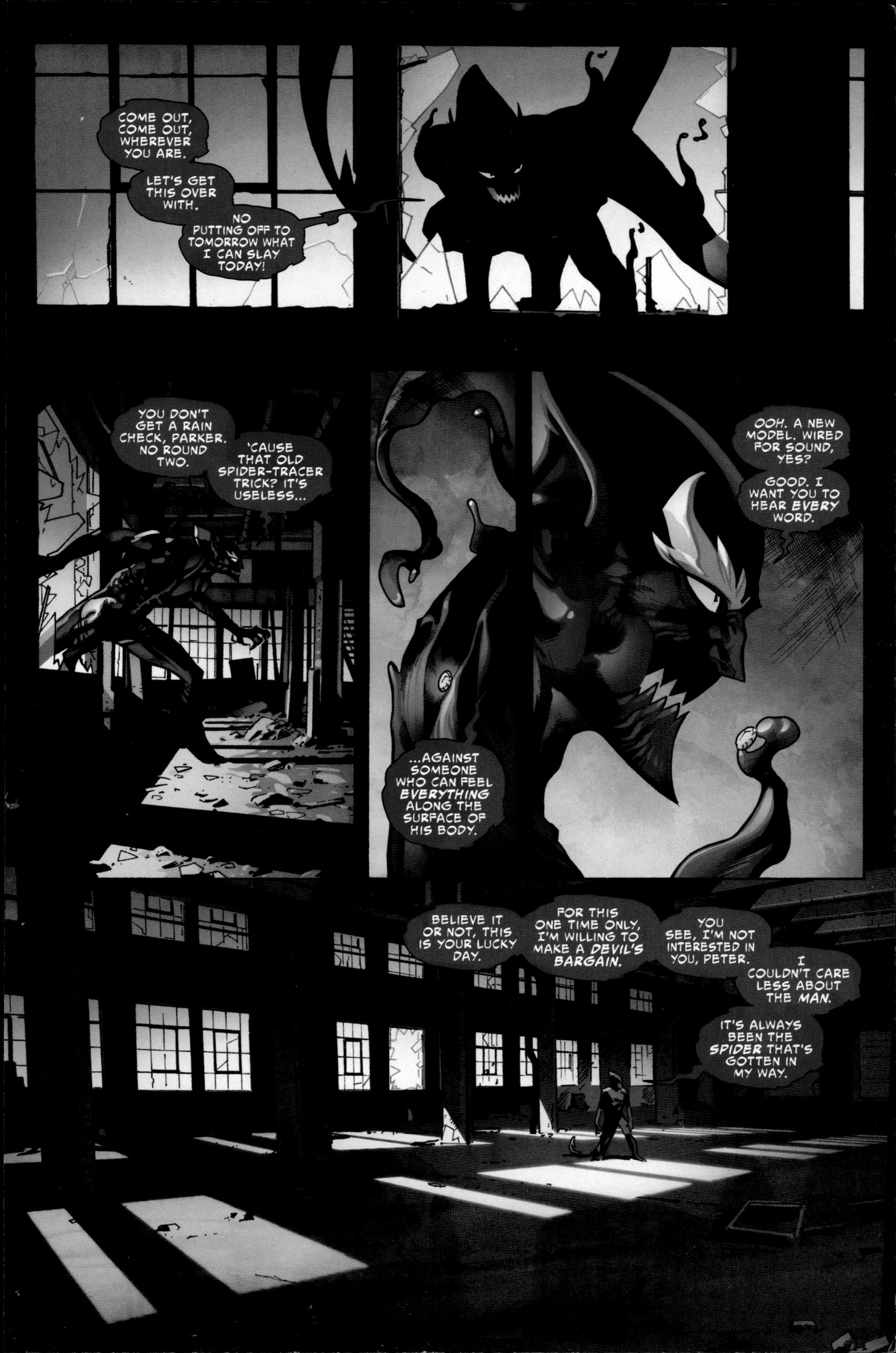
COME OUT, COME OUT, WHEREVER YOU ARE.
LET'S GET THIS OVER WITH.
NO PUTTING OFF TO TOMORROW WHAT I CAN SLAY TODAY!
YOU DON'T GET A RAIN CHECK, PARKER. NO ROUND TWO.
'CAUSE THAT OLD SPIDER-TRACER TRICK? IT'S USELESS...
...AGAINST SOMEONE WHO CAN FEEL EVERYTHING ALONG THE SURFACE OF HIS BODY.
OOH. A NEW MODEL. WIRED FOR SOUND, YES?
GOOD. I WANT YOU TO HEAR EVERY WORD.
BELIEVE IT OR NOT, THIS IS YOUR LUCKY DAY.
FOR THIS ONE TIME ONLY, I'M WILLING TO MAKE A DEVIL'S BARGAIN.
YOU SEE, I'M NOT INTERESTED IN YOU, PETER.
I COULDN'T CARE LESS ABOUT THE MAN.
IT'S ALWAYS BEEN THE SPIDER THAT'S GOTTEN IN MY WAY.

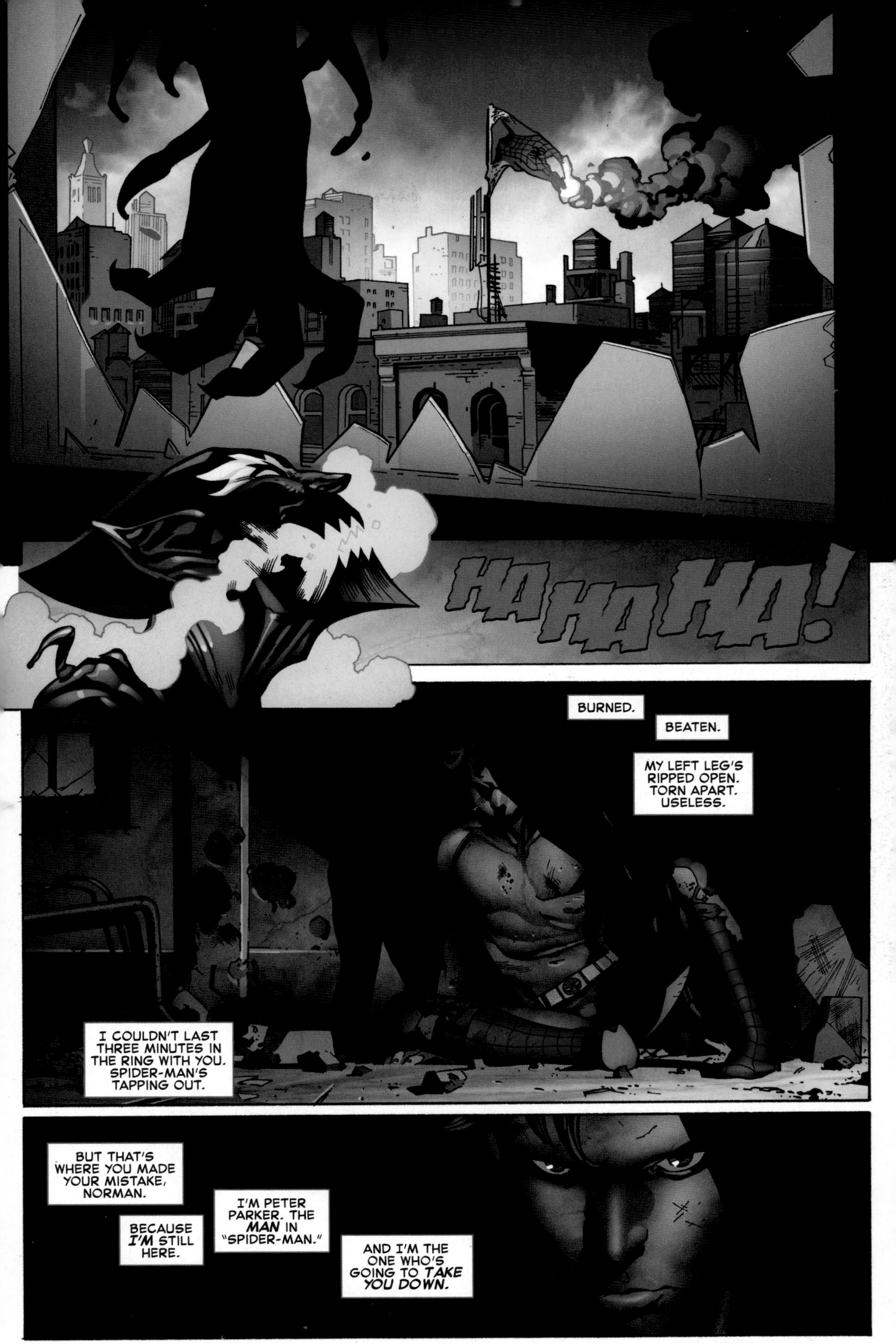
HA HA HA HA!
BURNED.
BEATEN.
MY LEFT LEG'S RIPPED OPEN. TORN APART. USELESS.
I COULDN'T LAST THREE MINUTES IN THE RING WITH YOU. SPIDER-MAN'S TAPPING OUT.
BUT THAT'S WHERE YOU MADE YOUR MISTAKE, NORMAN.
BECAUSE *I'M* STILL HERE.
I'M PETER PARKER. THE *MAN* IN "SPIDER-MAN."
AND I'M THE ONE WHO'S GOING TO *TAKE YOU DOWN.*

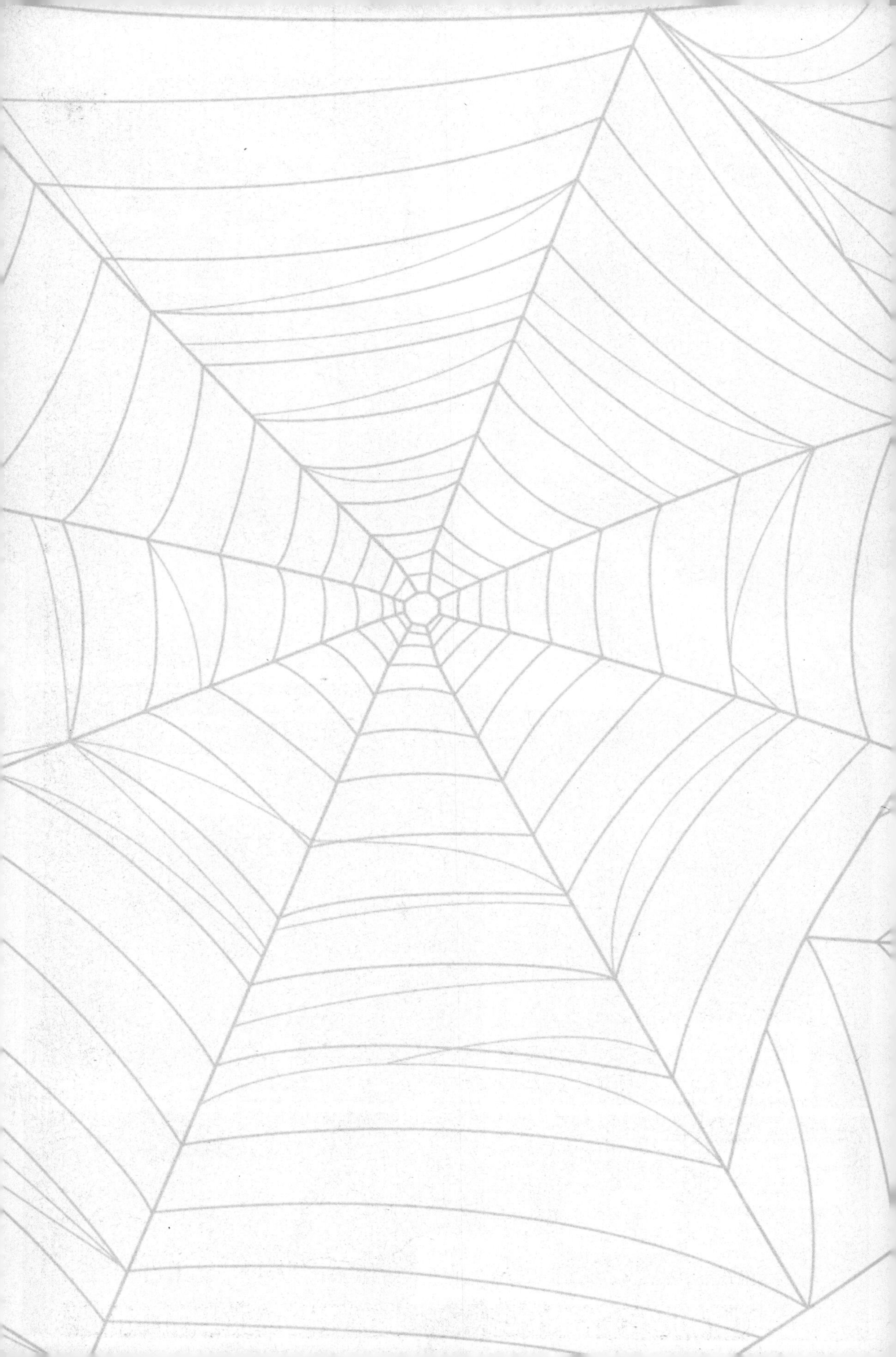

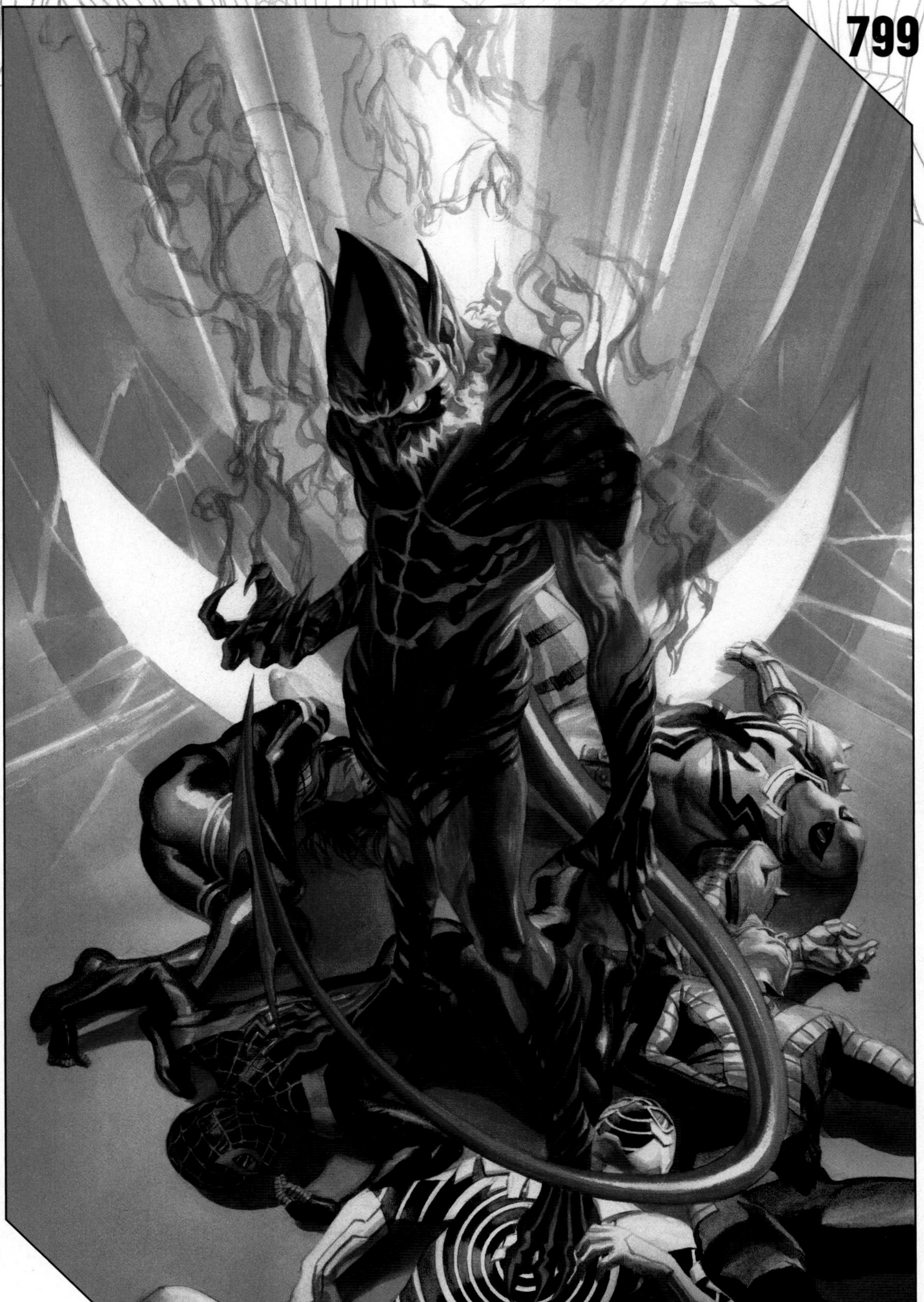
799

GO DOWN SWINGING PART THREE "THE TIES THAT BIND"

EXACTLY. A SYMBIOTE. AND I'VE GOT *FLAME* POWERS. ONE ZAP AND HE'S TOAST.

I PROMISE, I WON'T LET YOU DOWN.

DON'T WORRY, KID. I *TRUST* YOU.

HMM.

OR GET THEM ALL OUT OF THE CITY?

NO. PUTTING EVERYONE TOGETHER WOULD JUST CREATE ONE BIG, EASY TARGET.

AND IT WOULD TIP OUR HAND. WITH WHAT HE DID TO MY *LEG*, THE GOBLIN THINKS I'M INJURED AND OUT OF THE PICTURE.

WHICH IS KINDA TRUE.

BUT RIGHT NOW, I'M IN ONE OF THE LAST PLACES HE'D EVER THINK TO LOOK FOR ME...

...AND I'VE GOT THE GREATEST ASSET OF ALL--SOME PRETTY *AMAZING* FRIENDS.

ALL OF YOU, YOU'RE MY *WEB*. THE *SECOND* HE STRIKES, WE'LL PULL THAT THREAD, I'LL BRING THE *REST* OF YOU IN. AND WE'LL TAKE HIM DOWN-- *TOGETHER*.

QUICK HEADS-UP, THIS IS A PARTY LINE. SO NO MORE CALLING ME "PETE"...

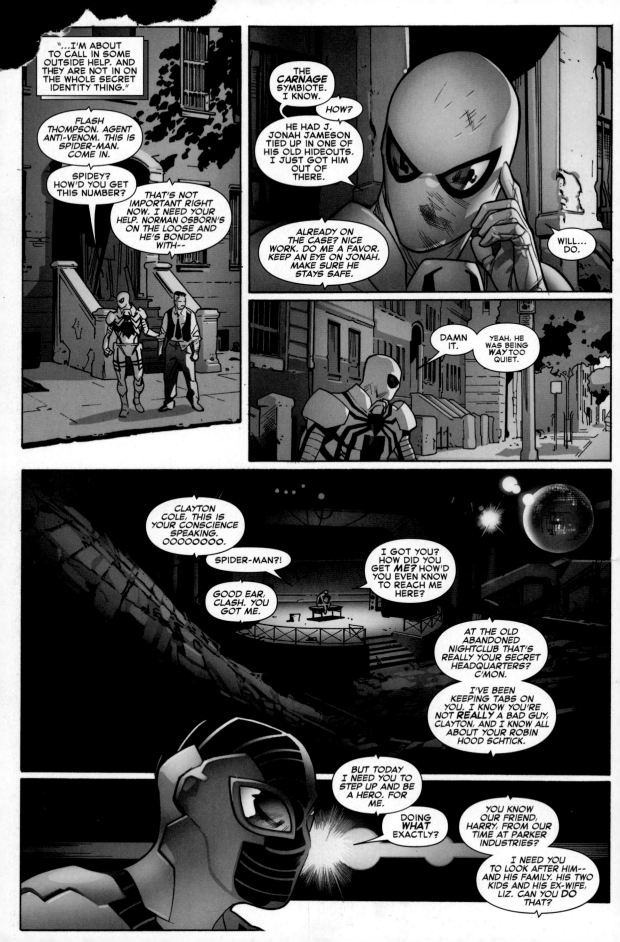

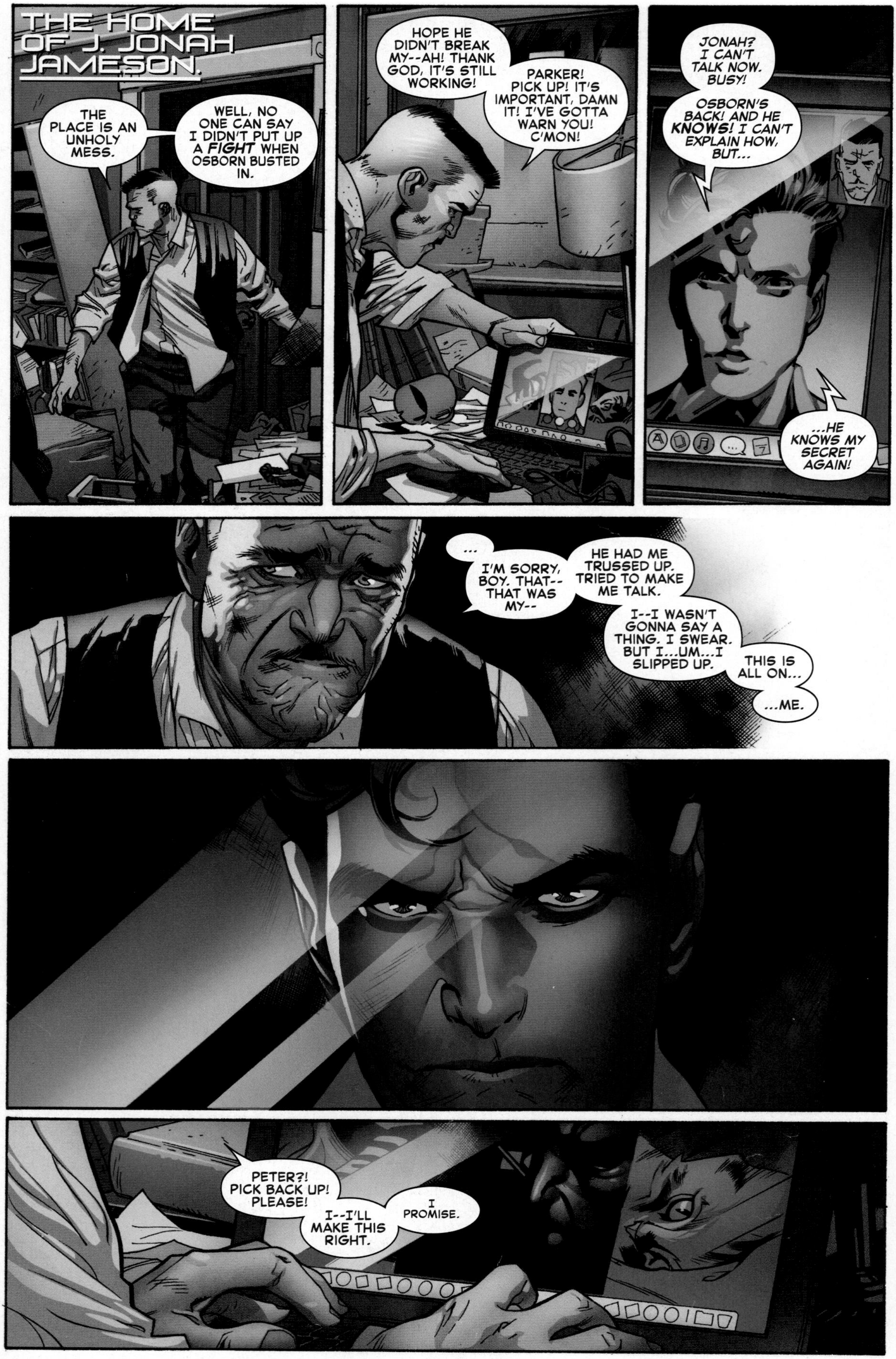
THE HOME OF J. JONAH JAMESON.
THE PLACE IS AN UNHOLY MESS.
WELL, NO ONE CAN SAY I DIDN'T PUT UP A FIGHT WHEN OSBORN BUSTED IN.
HOPE HE DIDN'T BREAK MY--AH! THANK GOD, IT'S STILL WORKING!
PARKER! PICK UP! IT'S IMPORTANT, DAMN IT! I'VE GOTTA WARN YOU! C'MON!
JONAH? I CAN'T TALK NOW. BUSY!
OSBORN'S BACK! AND HE KNOWS! I CAN'T EXPLAIN HOW, BUT...
...HE KNOWS MY SECRET AGAIN!
...
I'M SORRY, BOY. THAT--THAT WAS MY--
HE HAD ME TRUSSED UP. TRIED TO MAKE ME TALK.
I--I WASN'T GONNA SAY A THING. I SWEAR. BUT I...UM...I SLIPPED UP.
THIS IS ALL ON...
...ME.
PETER?! PICK BACK UP! PLEASE!
I--I'LL MAKE THIS RIGHT.
I PROMISE.

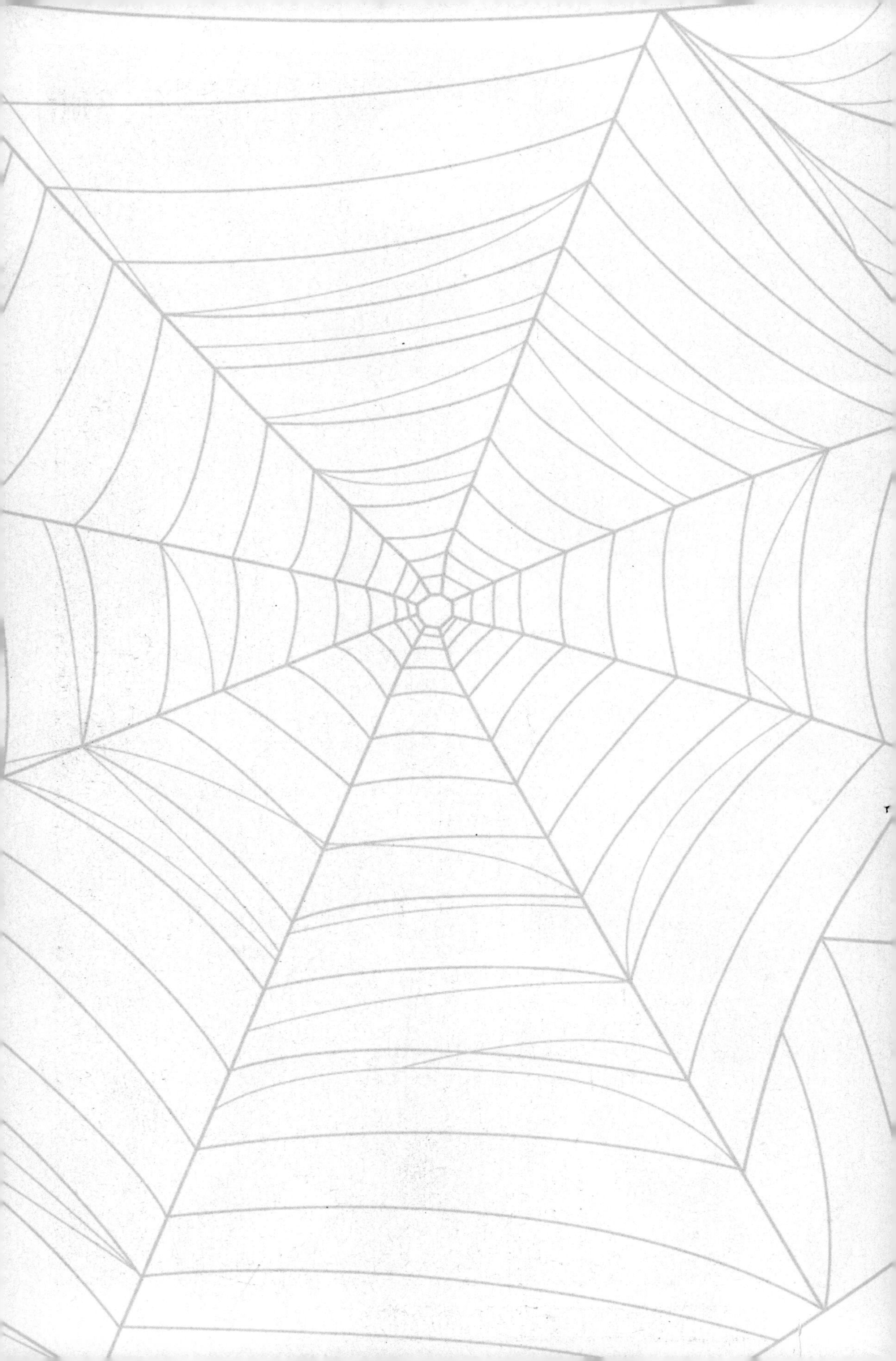

800

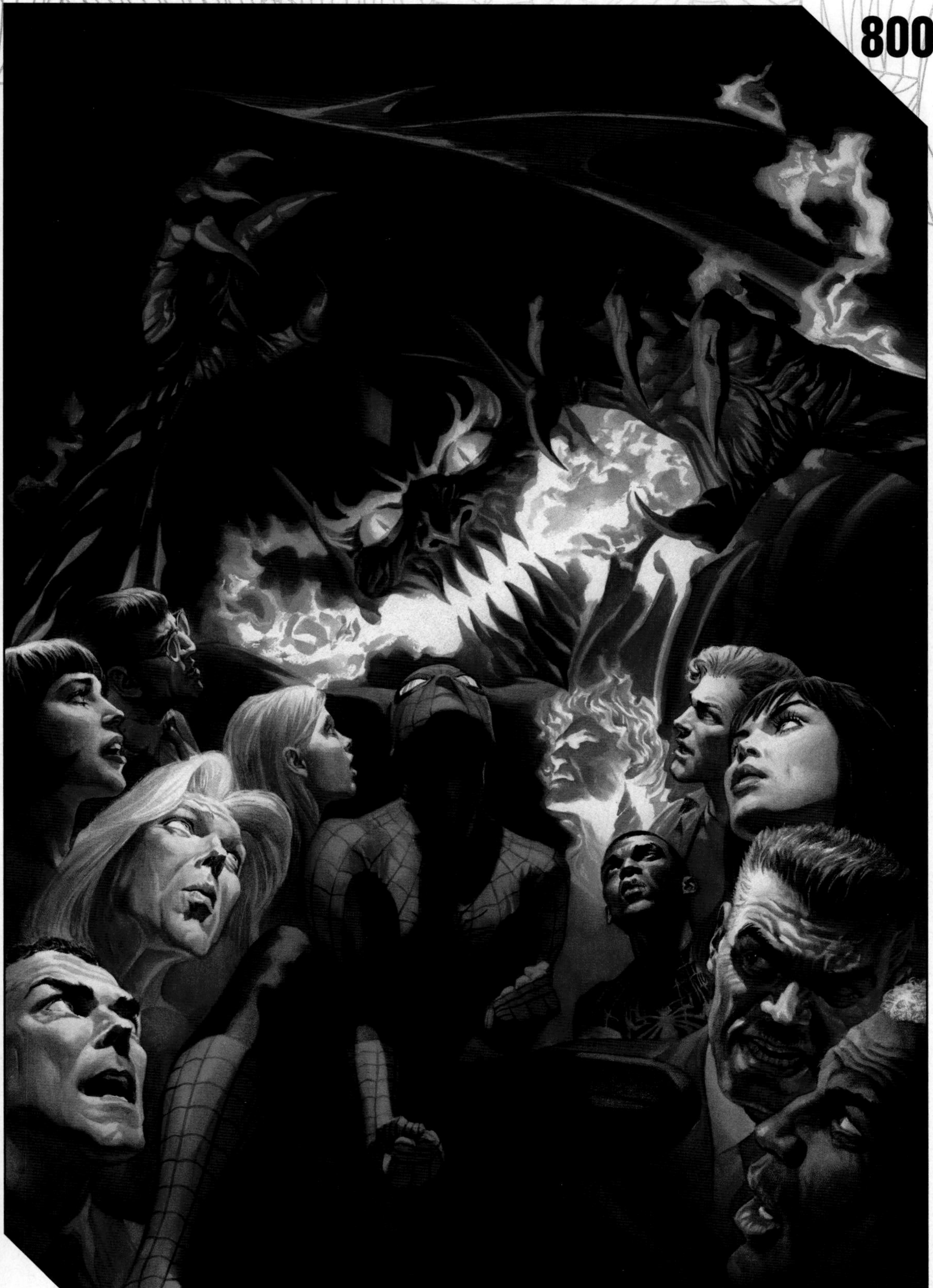

GO DOWN SWINGING CONCLUSION

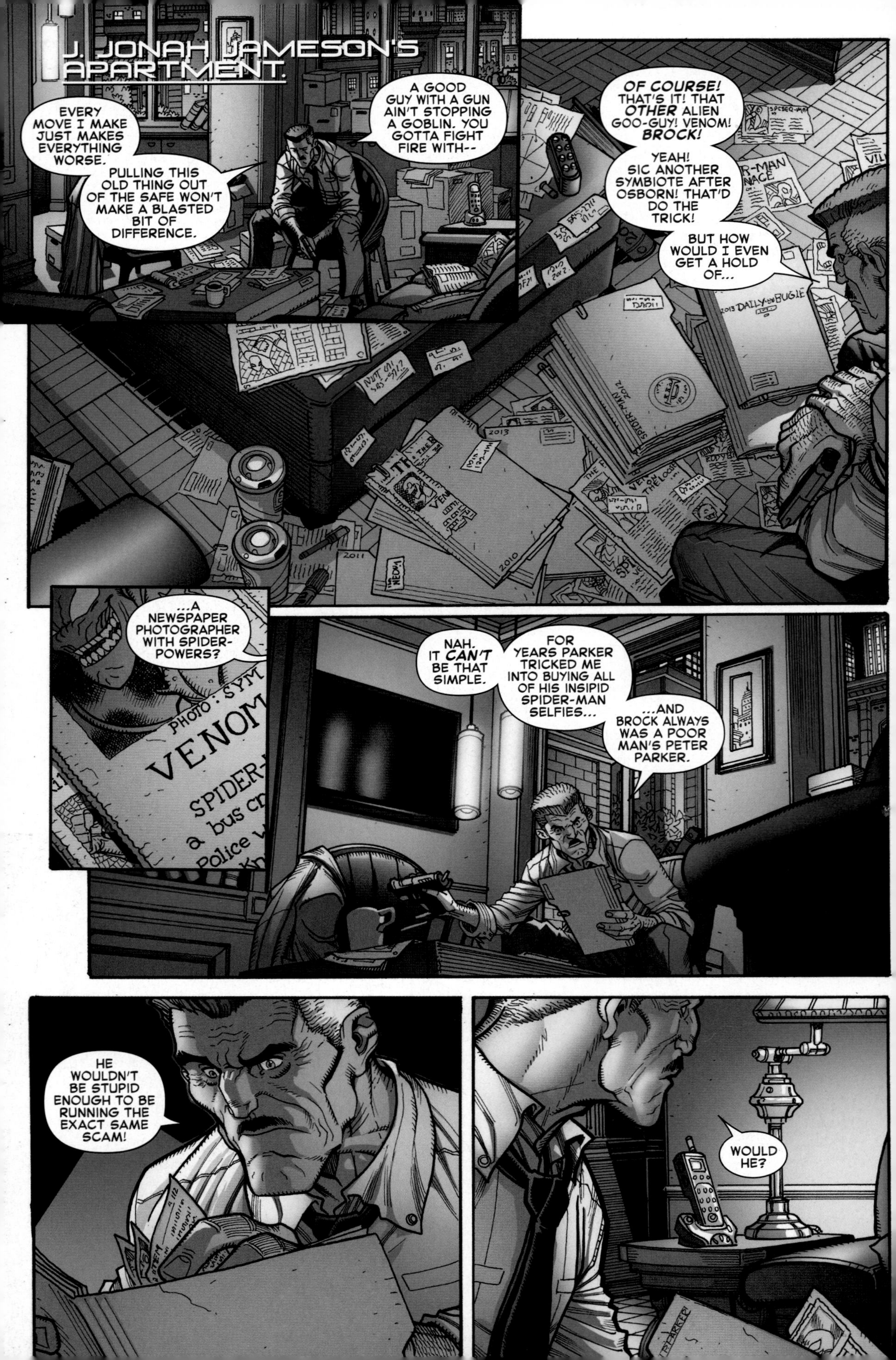
J. JONAH JAMESON'S APARTMENT.
EVERY MOVE I MAKE JUST MAKES EVERYTHING WORSE.
PULLING THIS OLD THING OUT OF THE SAFE WON'T MAKE A BLASTED BIT OF DIFFERENCE.
A GOOD GUY WITH A GUN AIN'T STOPPING A GOBLIN. YOU GOTTA FIGHT FIRE WITH--
OF COURSE! THAT'S IT! THAT OTHER ALIEN GOO-GUY! VENOM! BROCK!
YEAH! SIC ANOTHER SYMBIOTE AFTER OSBORN! THAT'D DO THE TRICK!
BUT HOW WOULD I EVEN GET A HOLD OF...
...A NEWSPAPER PHOTOGRAPHER WITH SPIDER-POWERS?
PHOTO: SYM
VENOM
NAH. IT CAN'T BE THAT SIMPLE.
FOR YEARS PARKER TRICKED ME INTO BUYING ALL OF HIS INSIPID SPIDER-MAN SELFIES...
...AND BROCK ALWAYS WAS A POOR MAN'S PETER PARKER.
HE WOULDN'T BE STUPID ENOUGH TO BE RUNNING THE EXACT SAME SCAM!
WOULD HE?

Chapter 2
Too Many Targets

THIS TAKES ME BACK. IT'S ALL BEEN REBUILT, AND THE LOGO'S CHANGED...

...BUT IT FEELS LIKE *HORIZON LABS*. AND THE FOUNDATIONS ARE THE SAME...

...INCLUDING THE SECRET TUNNELS MICHAEL MORBIUS USED TO GET IN AND OUT OF THIS PLACE.

BEST IF I STAY OUT OF SIGHT AS LONG AS POSSIBLE.

AT LEAST UNTIL I'VE MIXED ALCHEMAX'S ANTI-VENOM INTO MY NEXT BATCH OF WEB-FLUID.

NOT A BAD PLAN AT ALL. I MEAN, FOR ONCE I'M...

...ONE STEP *AHEAD?*

SECURITY GUARDS. ALL DEAD. THERE WAS NO *NEED* TO DO THAT. THE GREEN GOBLIN WOULDN'T--

HAVE TO STOP THINKING THAT WAY. THIS IS THE *RED* GOBLIN...

...AND HE PLAYS BY A DIFFERENT SET OF RULES.

YEAH. IT'S EMPTY. HE GOT ME. SO MUCH FOR MORE ANTI-VENOM.

WAIT. SOMETHING'S MOVING IN THERE. WHAT...?

PEEKABOO...

OHHH NO!

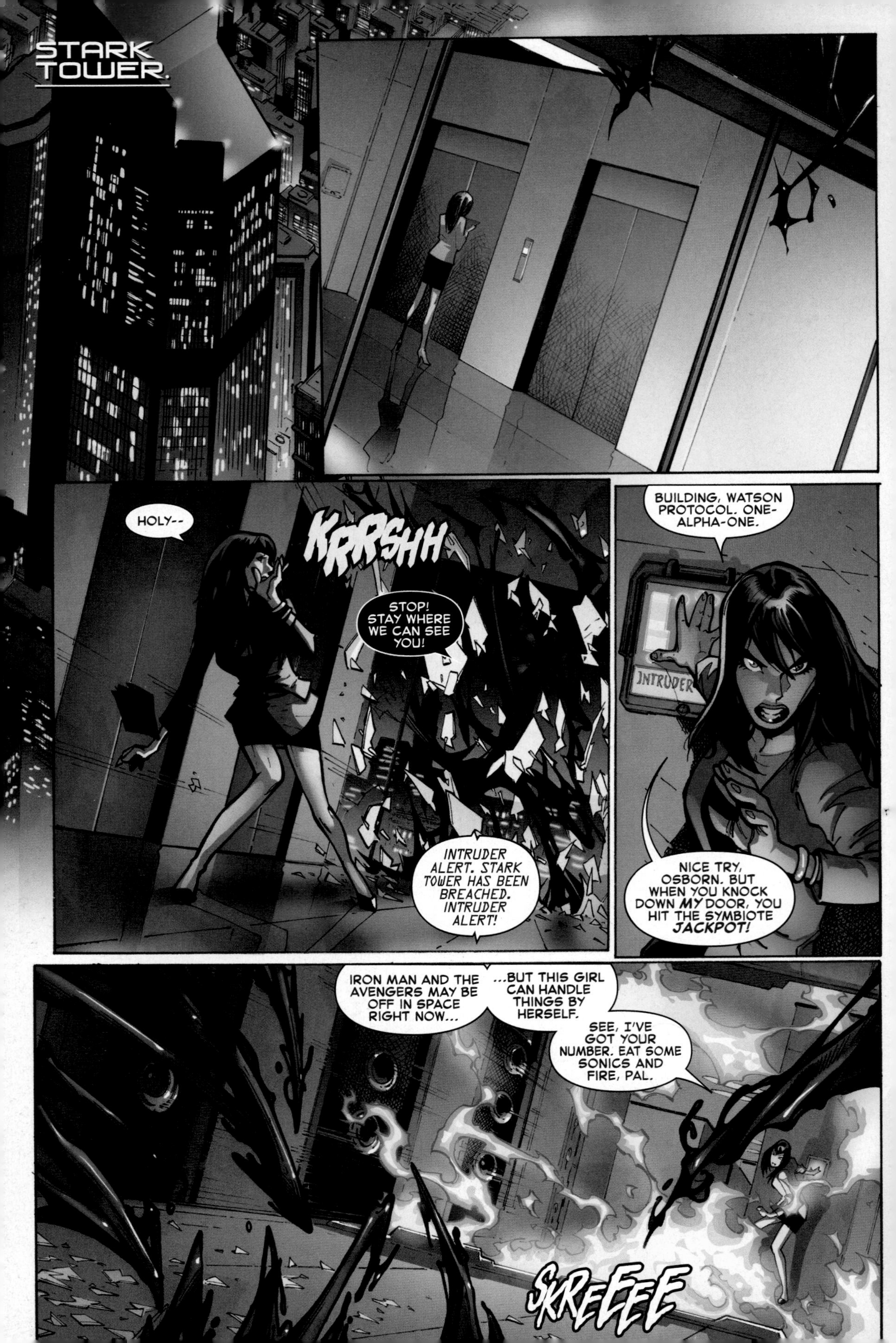
STARK TOWER.
HOLY--
KRRSHH
STOP! STAY WHERE WE CAN SEE YOU!
INTRUDER ALERT. STARK TOWER HAS BEEN BREACHED. INTRUDER ALERT!
BUILDING, WATSON PROTOCOL. ONE-ALPHA-ONE.
INTRUDER
NICE TRY, OSBORN. BUT WHEN YOU KNOCK DOWN MY DOOR, YOU HIT THE SYMBIOTE JACKPOT!
IRON MAN AND THE AVENGERS MAY BE OFF IN SPACE RIGHT NOW...
...BUT THIS GIRL CAN HANDLE THINGS BY HERSELF.
SEE, I'VE GOT YOUR NUMBER. EAT SOME SONICS AND FIRE, PAL.
SKREEEEE

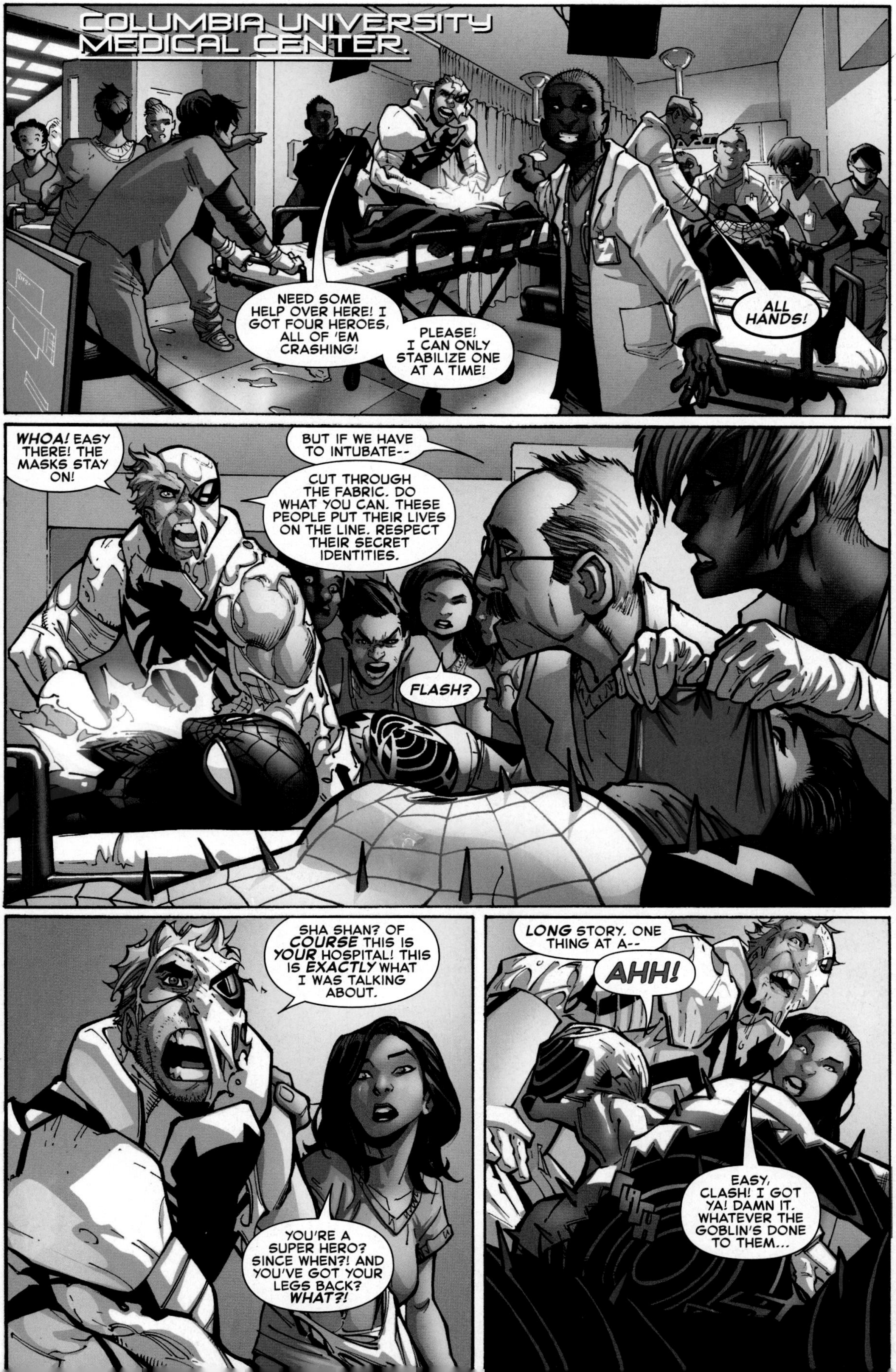
COLUMBIA UNIVERSITY MEDICAL CENTER.
NEED SOME HELP OVER HERE! I GOT FOUR HEROES, ALL OF 'EM CRASHING!
PLEASE! I CAN ONLY STABILIZE ONE AT A TIME!
ALL HANDS!
WHOA! EASY THERE! THE MASKS STAY ON!
BUT IF WE HAVE TO INTUBATE--
CUT THROUGH THE FABRIC. DO WHAT YOU CAN. THESE PEOPLE PUT THEIR LIVES ON THE LINE. RESPECT THEIR SECRET IDENTITIES.
FLASH?
SHA SHAN? OF COURSE THIS IS YOUR HOSPITAL! THIS IS EXACTLY WHAT I WAS TALKING ABOUT.
YOU'RE A SUPER HERO? SINCE WHEN?! AND YOU'VE GOT YOUR LEGS BACK? WHAT?!
LONG STORY. ONE THING AT A--
AHH!
EASY, CLASH! I GOT YA! DAMN IT. WHATEVER THE GOBLIN'S DONE TO THEM...

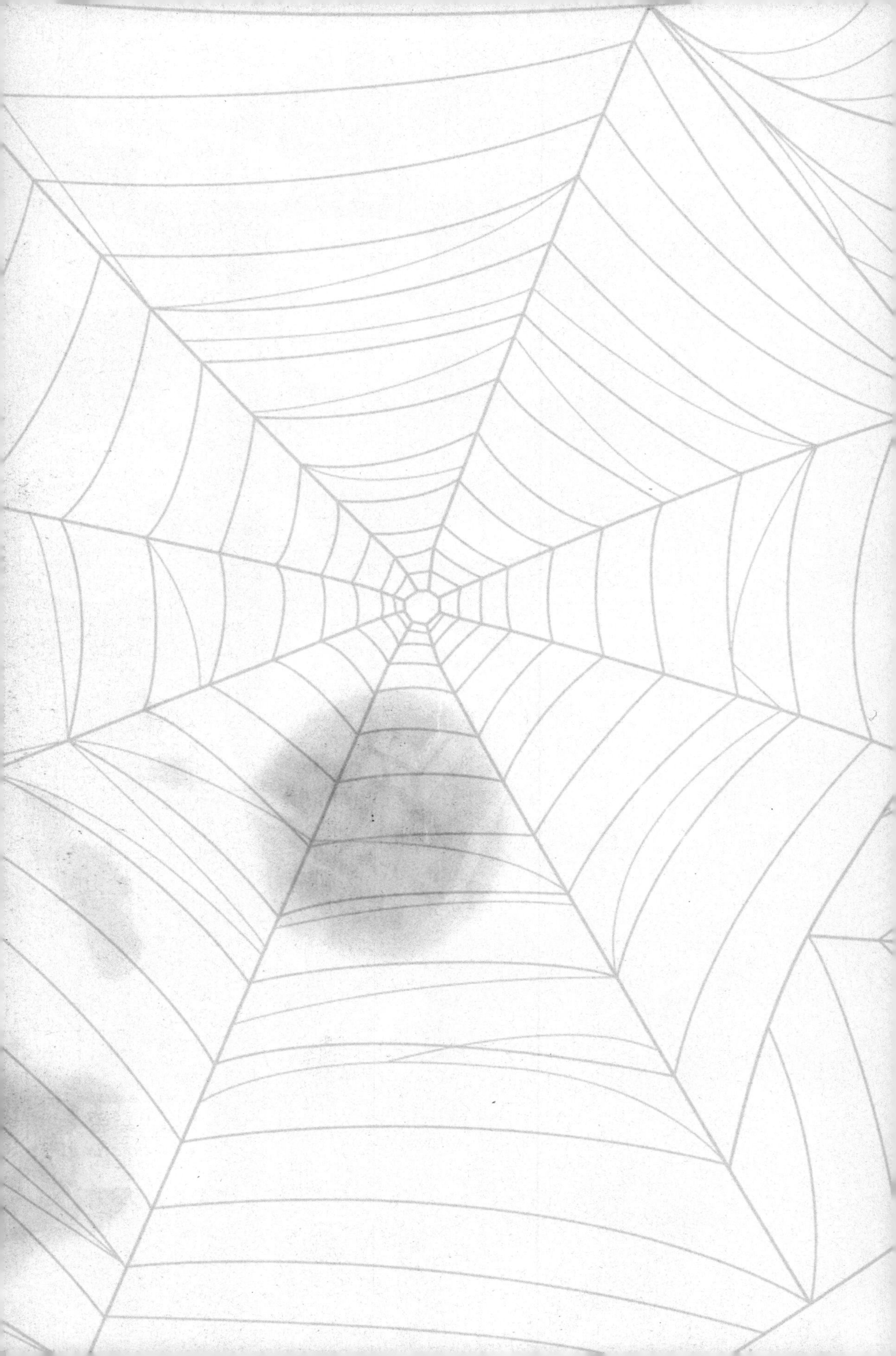

Chapter 3
Family Infighting

CHAPTER 4
THE GOBLIN TRIUMPHANT

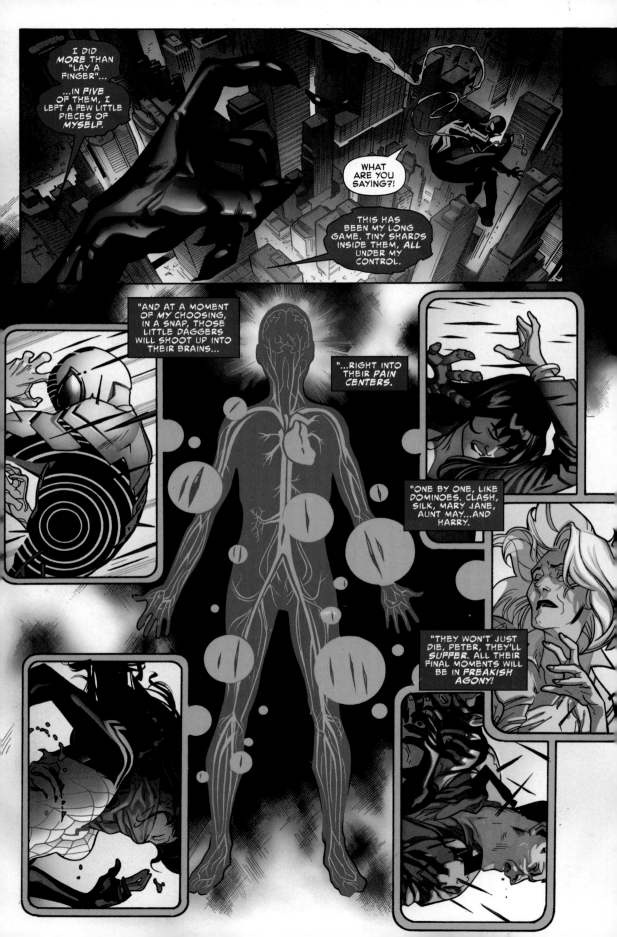

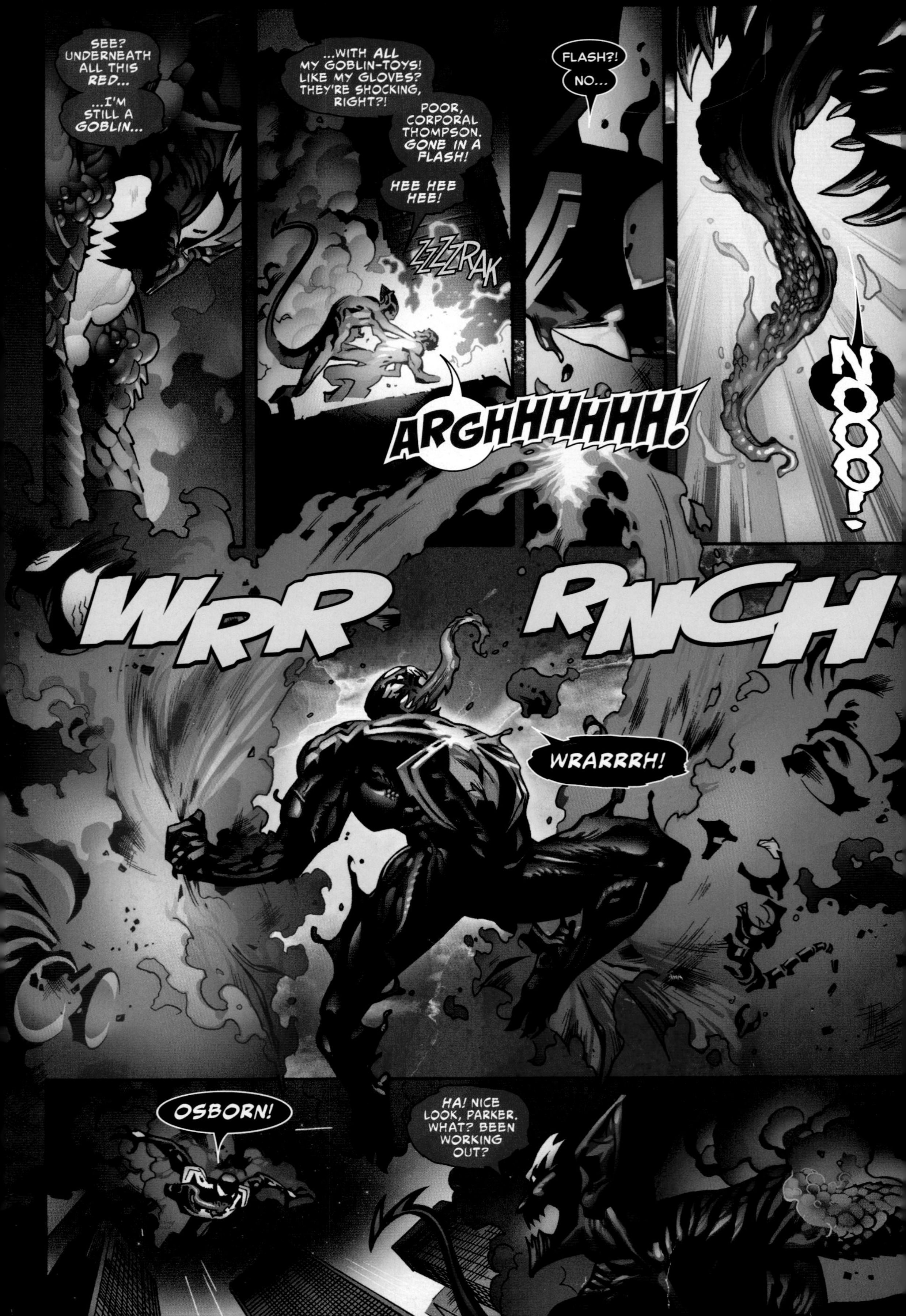
SEE? UNDERNEATH ALL THIS RED...
...I'M STILL A GOBLIN...
...WITH ALL MY GOBLIN-TOYS! LIKE MY GLOVES? THEY'RE SHOCKING, RIGHT?!
POOR, CORPORAL THOMPSON. GONE IN A FLASH!
HEE HEE HEE!
ZZZZRAK
ARGHHHHHH!
FLASH?!
NO...
NOOO!
WRR
RNCH
WRARRRH!
OSBORN!
HA! NICE LOOK, PARKER. WHAT? BEEN WORKING OUT?

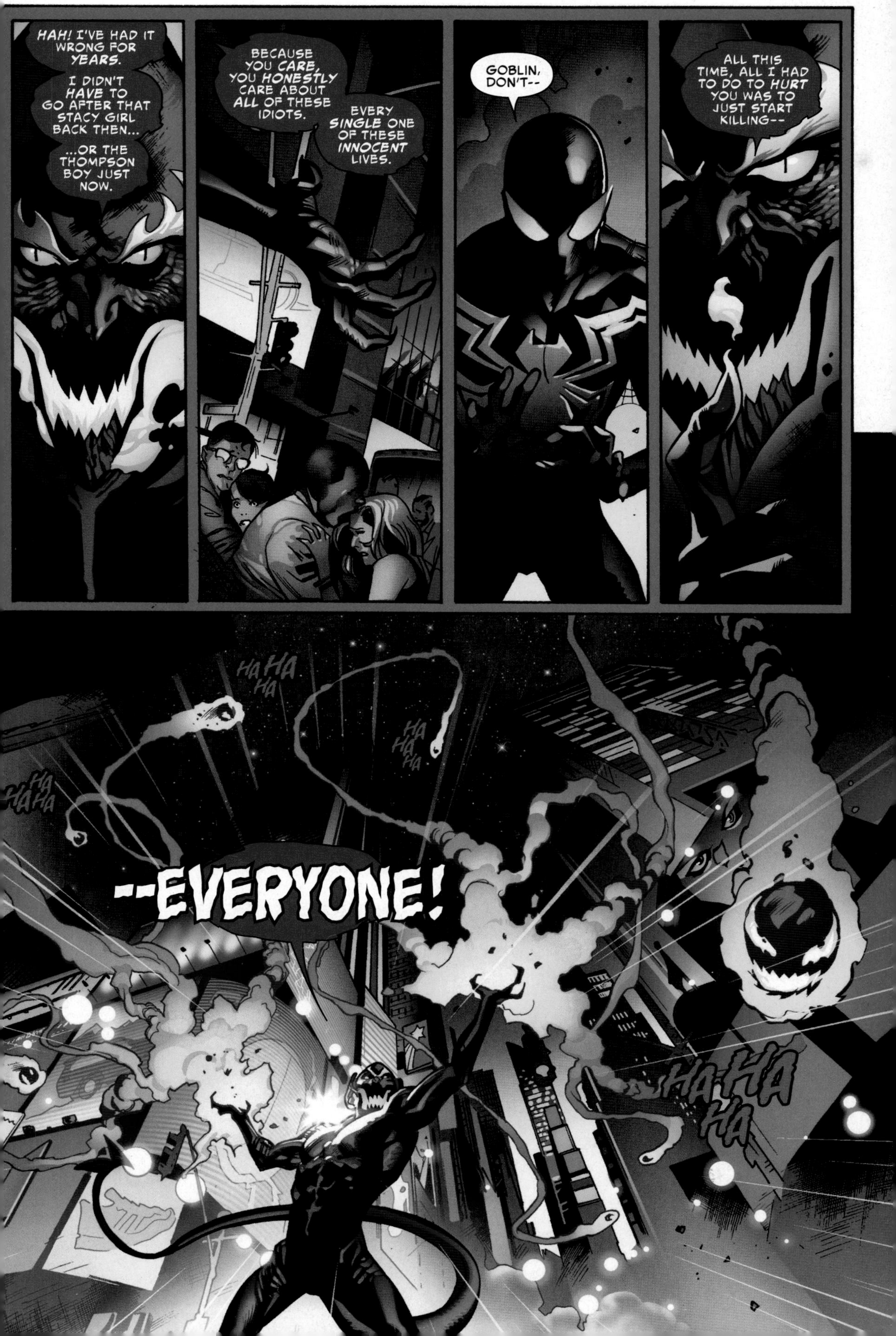
HAH! I'VE HAD IT WRONG FOR YEARS.
I DIDN'T HAVE TO GO AFTER THAT STACY GIRL BACK THEN...
...OR THE THOMPSON BOY JUST NOW.
BECAUSE YOU CARE, YOU HONESTLY CARE ABOUT ALL OF THESE IDIOTS.
EVERY SINGLE ONE OF THESE INNOCENT LIVES.
GOBLIN, DON'T--
ALL THIS TIME, ALL I HAD TO DO TO HURT YOU WAS TO JUST START KILLING--
HA HA HA
HA HA HA HA
HA HA HA
--EVERYONE!
HA HA HA

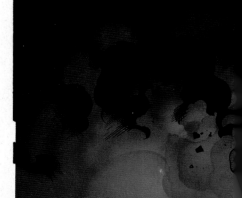

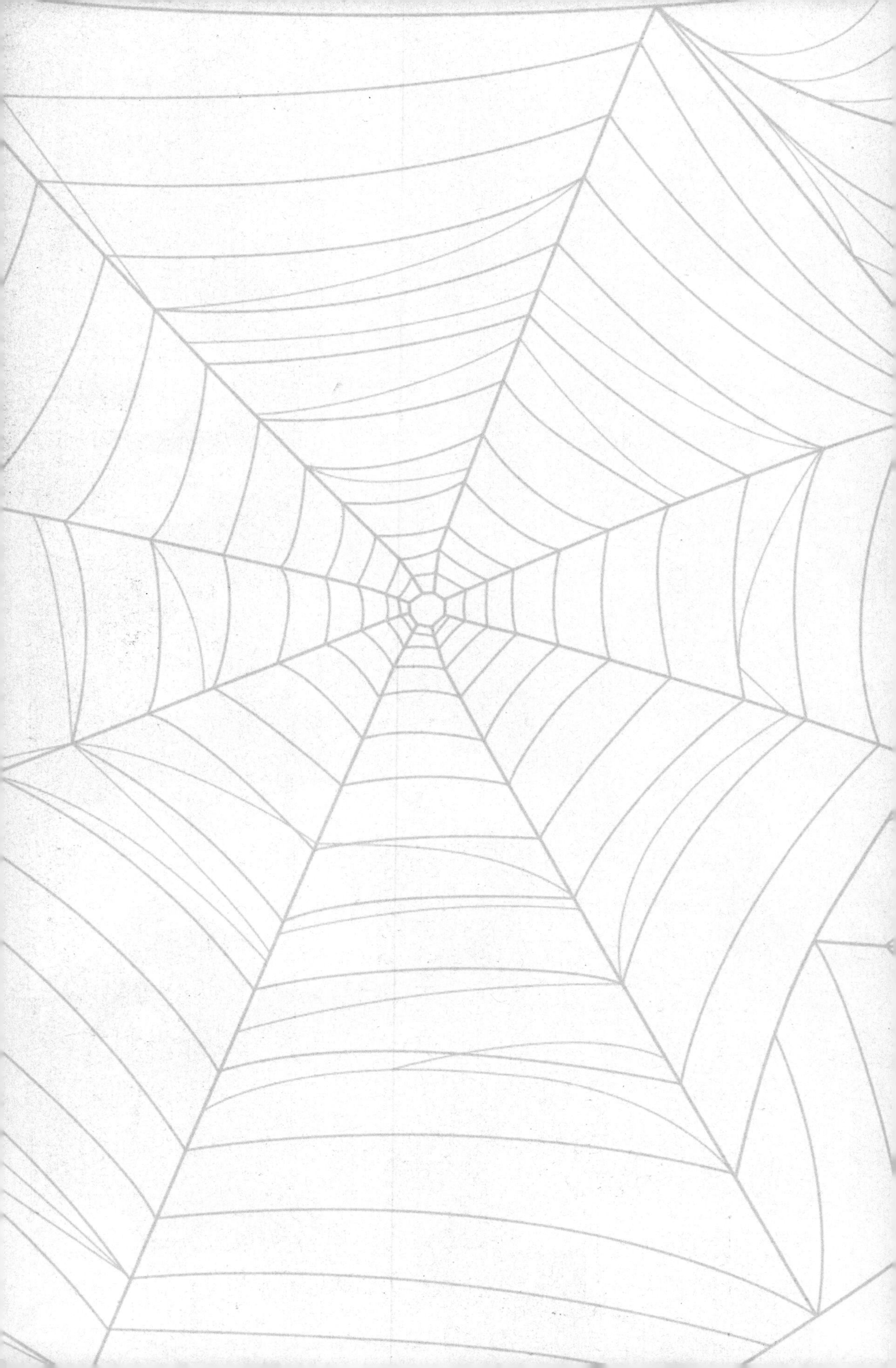

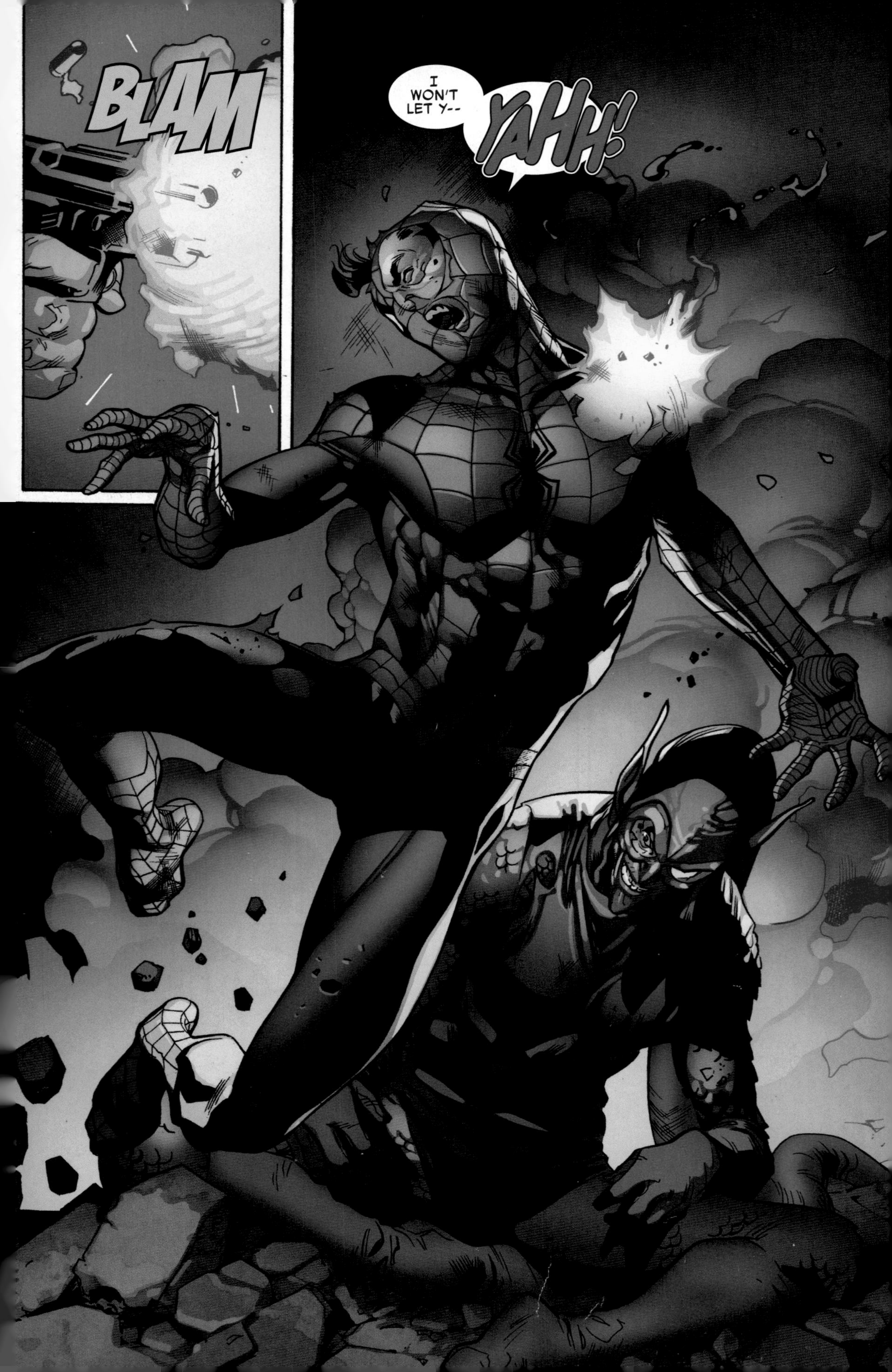
BLAM
I WON'T LET Y--
YAHH!

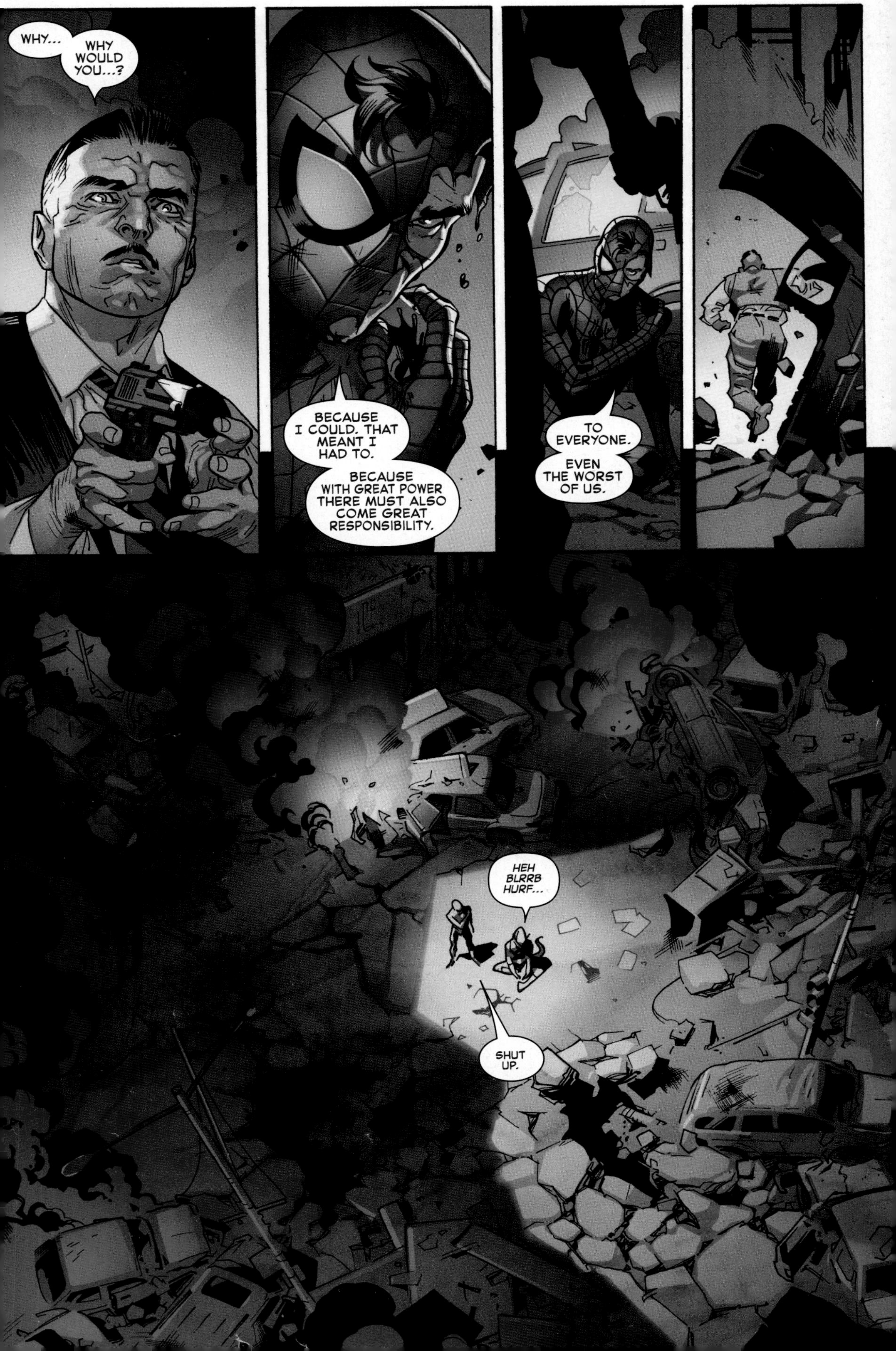
WHY...
WHY WOULD YOU...?
BECAUSE I COULD. THAT MEANT I HAD TO.
BECAUSE WITH GREAT POWER THERE MUST ALSO COME GREAT RESPONSIBILITY.
TO EVERYONE.
EVEN THE WORST OF US.
HEH BLRRB HURF...
SHUT UP.

ALMOST SOLITARY CONFINEMENT

THE RETURN OF
HARRY OSBORN

GOODBYE

the AMAZING SPIDER-MAN #800

DAN SLOTT writer **VC's JOE CARAMAGNA** letterer

chapter one: **CRAWLING THROUGH THE WRECKAGE**
NICK BRADSHAW artist **EDGAR DELGADO** color artist

chapter two: **TOO MANY TARGETS**
HUMBERTO RAMOS penciler **VICTOR OLAZABA** inker **EDGAR DELGADO** color artist

chapter three: **FAMILY INFIGHTING**
GIUSEPPE CAMUNCOLI penciler **CAM SMITH** inker **JAVA TARTAGLIA** color artist

chapter four: **THE GOBLIN TRIUMPHANT**
STUART IMMONEN penciler **WADE von GRAWBADGER** inker **MARTE GRACIA** color artist

ALMOST SOLITARY CONFINEMENT
and *THE RETURN OF HARRY OSBORN*
GIUSEPPE CAMUNCOLI penciler **CAM SMITH** inker **JAVA TARTAGLIA** color artist

GOODBYE
MARCOS MARTÍN artist **MUNTSA VICENTE** color artist

ANTHONY GAMBINO production designer **KATHLEEN WISNESKI** assistant editor **NICK LOWE** with **DEVIN LEWIS** editor

C.B. CEBULSKI editor in chief **JOE QUESADA** chief creative officer **DAN BUCKLEY** president **ALAN FINE** executive produce

Spider-Man created by **STAN LEE** and **STEVE DITKO**

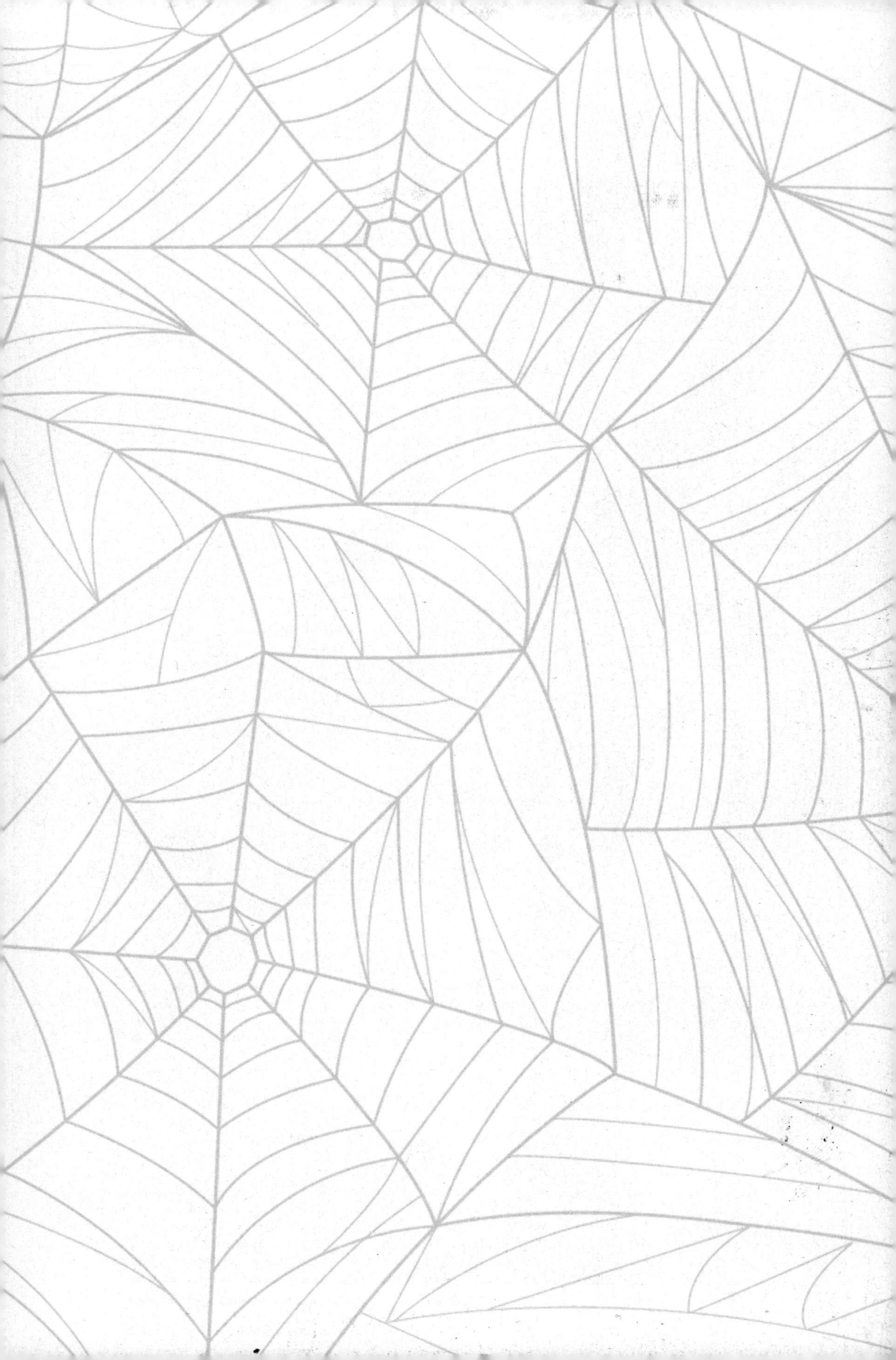

801

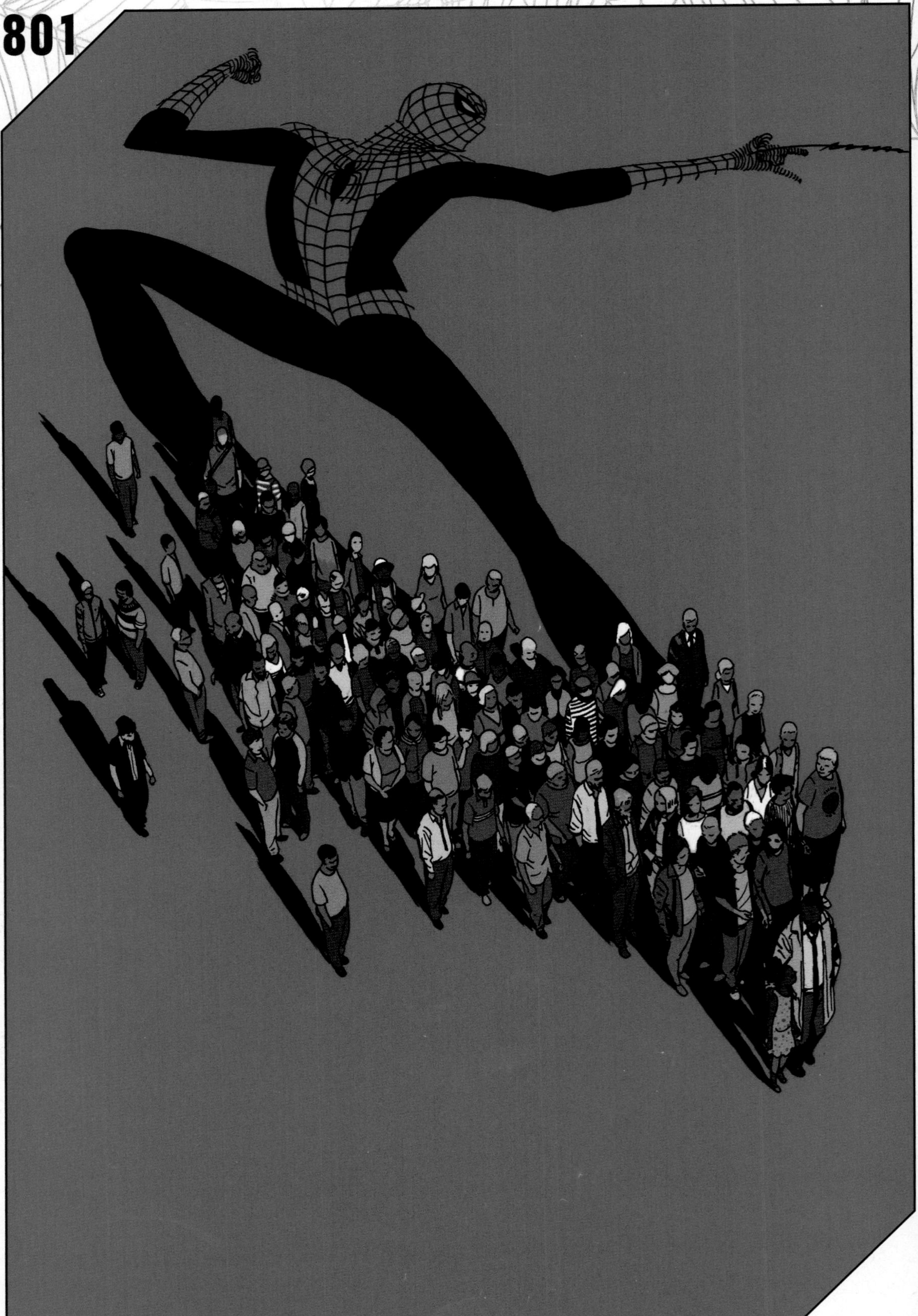

"THERE FOR YOU"

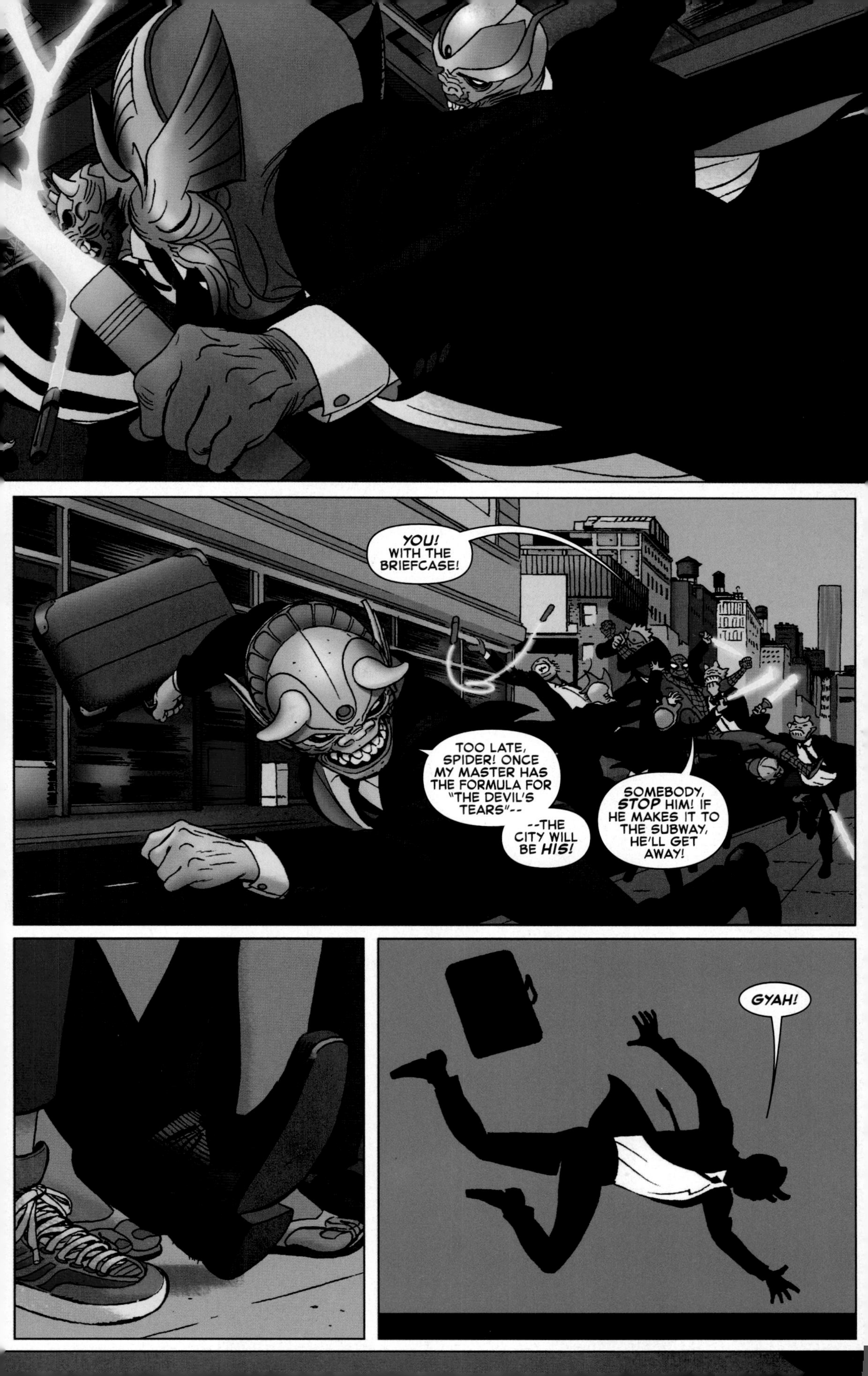
YOU! WITH THE BRIEFCASE!
TOO LATE, SPIDER! ONCE MY MASTER HAS THE FORMULA FOR "THE DEVIL'S TEARS"--
--THE CITY WILL BE HIS!
SOMEBODY, STOP HIM! IF HE MAKES IT TO THE SUBWAY, HE'LL GET AWAY!
GYAH!

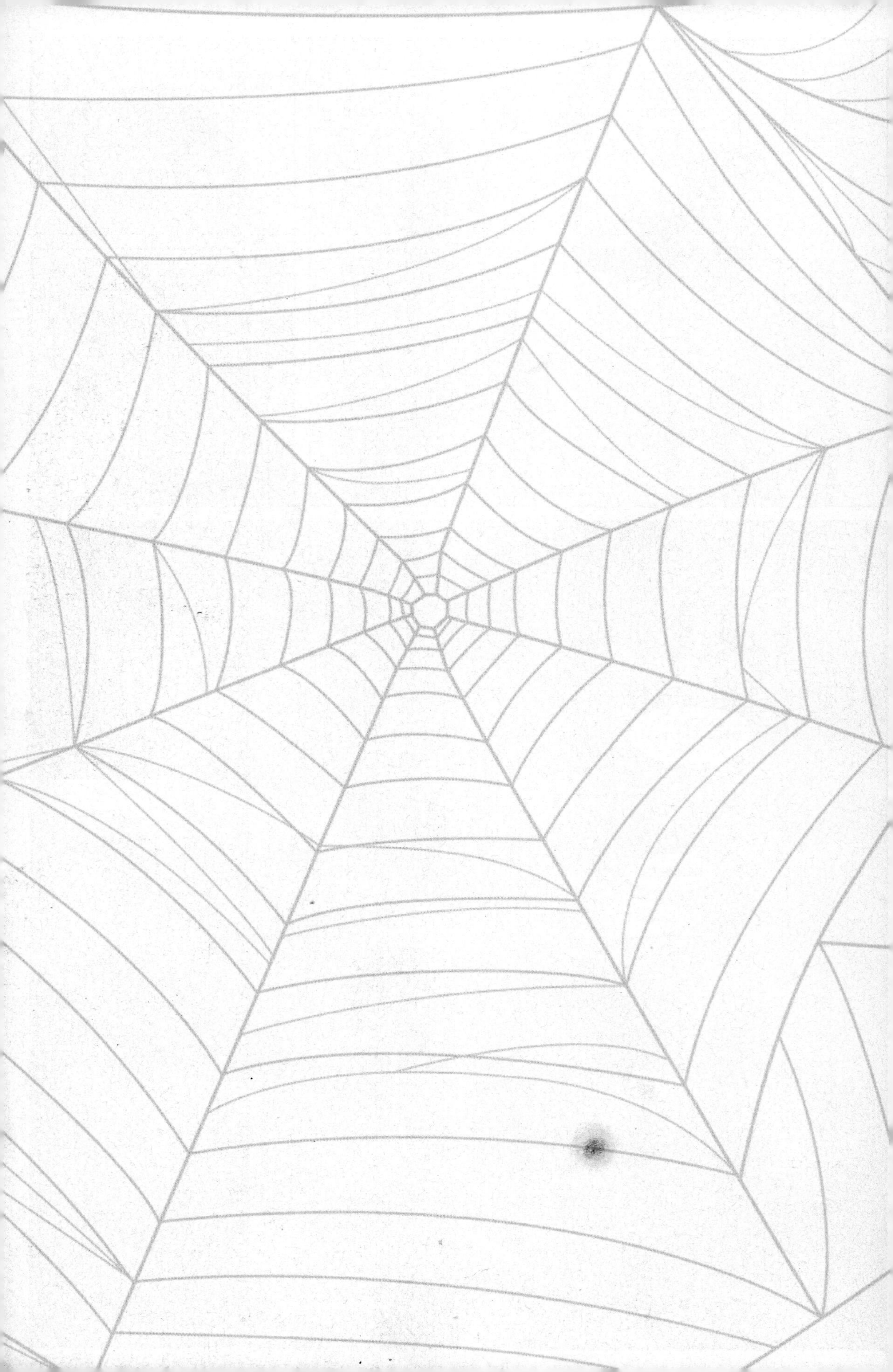

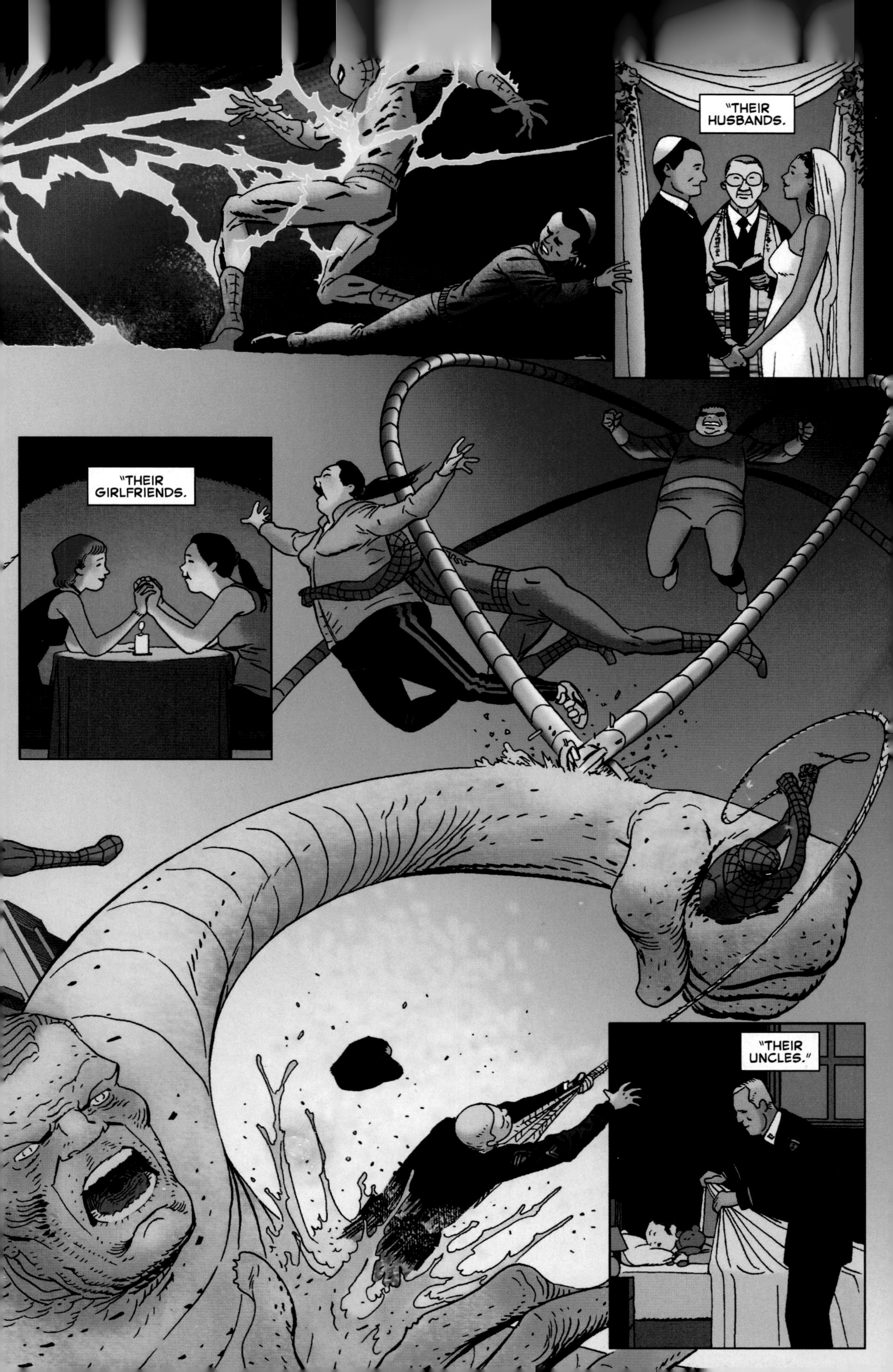
"THEIR HUSBANDS.
"THEIR GIRLFRIENDS.
"THEIR UNCLES."

the AMAZING SPIDER-MAIL

KATHLEEN WISNESKI
ASSISTANT EDITOR

NICK LOWE
with
DEVIN LEWIS
EDITORS

Send e-mail to **SPIDEYOFFICE@MARVEL.COM** (please mark "OKAY TO PRI

How about that? Hope you had a hanky with you. I read this lettering earlier this week on the subway heading to work and cried, so I'm with you. Let's talk about Marcos Martin and Muntsa Vicente. If you don't know who they are, go immediately to www.PanelSyndicate.com and check out Private Eye and Barrier or run back to your comic shop to get their work together years ago on AMAZING SPIDER-MAN or DOCTOR STRANGE: THE OATH. You back? HOW AWESOME ARE MUNTSA AND MARCOS?!?!?! They haven't done print comics in several years, so you know it had to be a special occasion to get them back here. And what an occasion this is…

In case this is your first issue of AMAZING SPIDER-MAN, or first in a very, very long time, you should know that this is Dan Slott's last issue as writer. Dan came onto the book about ten years ago and has written more issues of AMAZING SPIDER-MAN than any writer ever. With those issues he, along with some of the best artists in the world, created some of the best Spider-Man stories EVER, to which we can add THIS issue. But before you close the book, Dan wanted to say a few words…

Since I was eight years old, writing SPIDER-MAN has been my dream job. Why would I ever let it go?

When I meet people at signings, there are some readers who say they've started with my run. Maybe with "New Ways to Die," "Big Time," "Spider-Verse" or you name it. But since people heard I was leaving, there've been fans telling me, "Your run is the only Spider-Man I've known my whole life." I have a hard time processing that.

That's when it hits me. It really has been ten years. At a signing for #797, one young reader asked me not to go, because it was like a security blanket to him, knowing my next ASM would always be on the rack waiting for him. Hey, wherever you are, I hope you're reading this. Trust me. Spidey's gonna be in the best of webbed-hands. I've heard Nick Spencer's plans and they're brilliant, funny, surprising and, in every way, amazing.

Meanwhile, me and all the other ASM writers, we're still here for you. All crammed together in your long boxes. We're here whenever you wanna visit, and we'd just love it if you would. We'll always be here for you. And I want to thank you for being there for me these ten years. You guys, you let me have my dream job. Thank you.

Now, I've got a ton of people to thank. I promise I'll be quick! I'm eternally grateful to…

Editor Stephen Wacker, for bringing me on board and having my back. Editor Nick Lowe, who kept me on and kept everything fun. Every assistant editor ever, for EVERYTHING. Senior VP Tom Brevoort, for sage-like wisdom and guidance. My three editor in chiefs: Quesada, Alonso and Cebulski, for trusting me with your flagship character, even when I wrote about brain-swaps and giant spiders.

Every penciler, inker, colorist and letterer in all 180 issues. Special thanks to the hardworking crew who came back for the quadruple-sized ASM #800, especially longtime collaborators Humberto and Giuseppe. I miss you both so much!

The stellar creative team on the last year of my run--Stuart, Wade and Marte, you're not just the finest artists working in the industry, you're also the most professional and dedicated people I've ever worked with. I am in awe of you.

My good friend Marcos Martin, for promising ages ago you'd come back for my last story, and then pulling it off (as I knew you would) perfectly.

My two real-life super heroes: Christos Gage, who'd parachute in at a moment's notice to co-write issues while everything was on fire. And Joe Caramagna, who'd letter entire books in ludicrous amounts of time while even the fire was on fire. I'd be dead without you two.

But most of all, Stan Lee, Steve Ditko and John Romita Sr., for creating the world of Spider-Man, my favorite place in all of fiction. I've had so much fun living there--and I can't imagine my life without it. Thank you.

Dan

About four years ago, I took the editorial reins of the Spider-Books and had my first of many long phone calls with Dan Slott. We'd only worked together on a short story while I was X-Editor, so I wasn't quite sure how we'd work together. While there have been times that Dan has driven me crazy, it was always in service to the book and to Spider-Man himself. At the expense of his personal life and often his personal health, Dan devoted 100 percent of himself to making this book the best it could possibly be. Dan bled for this book, and for that, all of us at Marvel will be forever grateful. I count myself very lucky to have been along for some of the ride, and lucky to consider myself Dan's friend.

But you're not off the hook. You have to come back in two weeks for AMAZING SPIDER-MAN #1 where Nick Spencer and Ryan Ottley (along with Cliff Rathburn and Laura Martin) kick off the next era for the web-slinger. And if you glance over on the stands a little further down, you should see the first issue of TONY STARK: IRON MAN, written by our dear friend Dan. He'll add FANTASTIC FOUR to his docket soon as well, so don't miss it.

Happy trails, Dan, and keep swinging!
Nick

#797-801 CONNECTING VARIANTS BY **HUMBERTO RAMOS & EDGAR DELGADO**

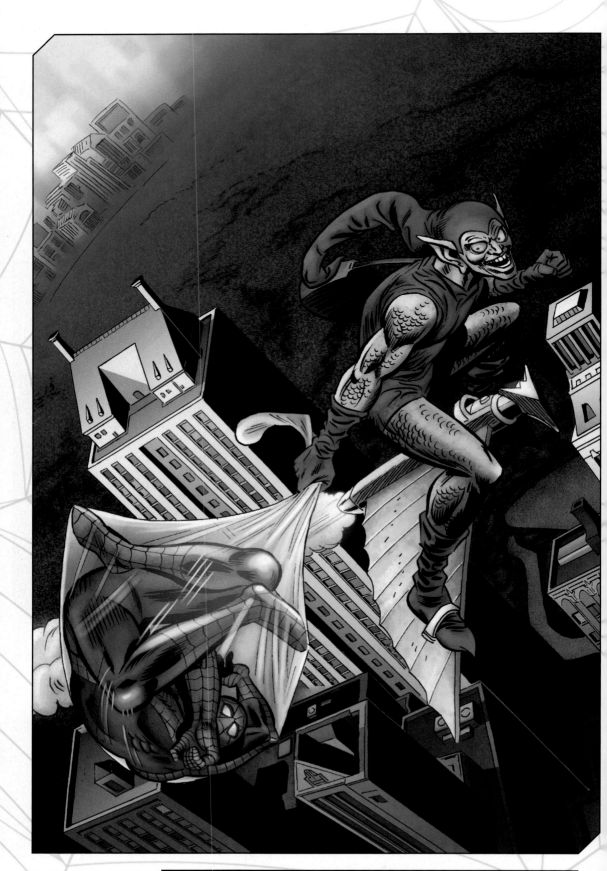

#797 REMASTERED VARIANT BY **ROSS ANDRU, MIKE ESPOSITO & MORRY HOLLOWELL** WITH **MICHAEL KELLEHER**

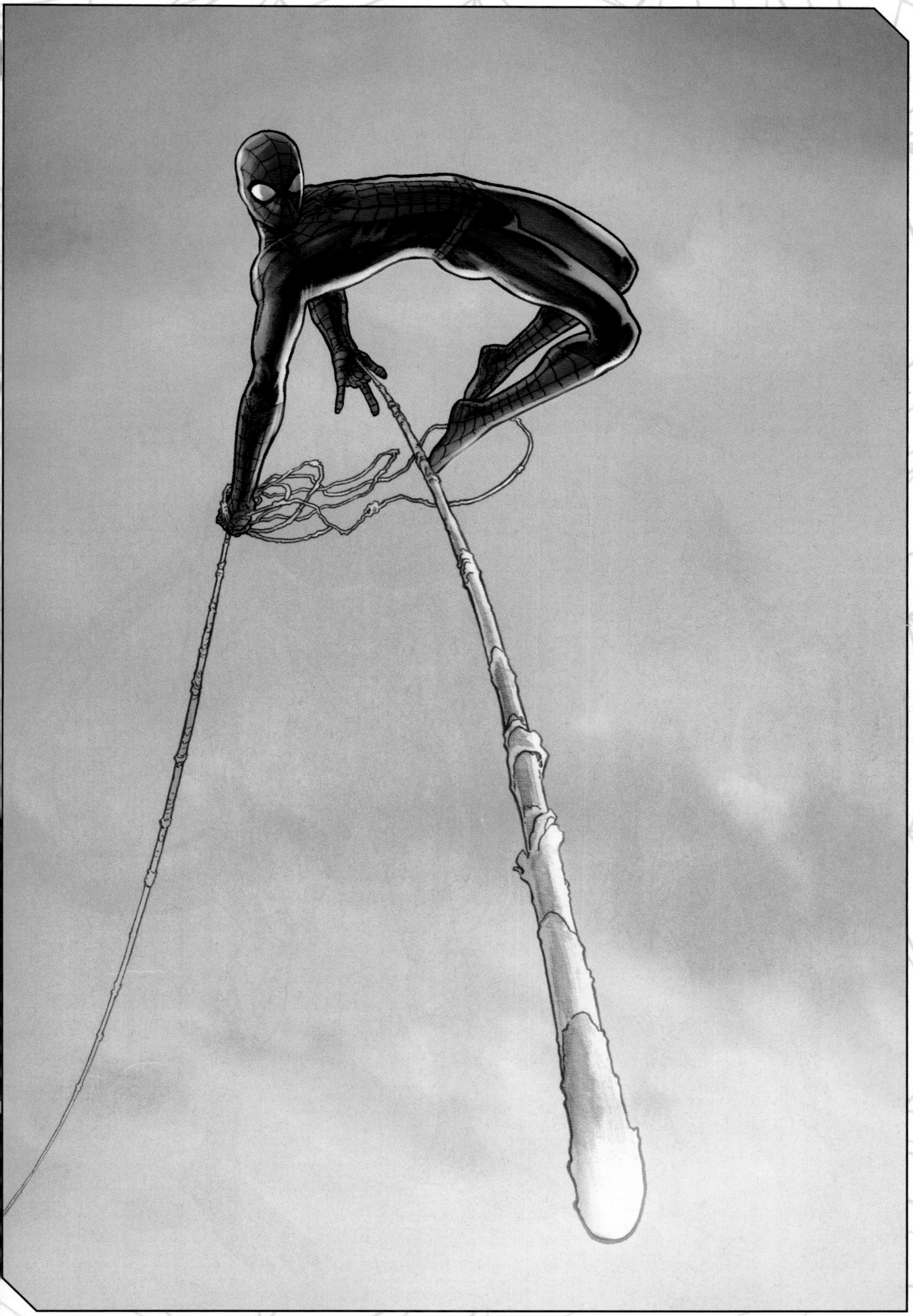

#797 YOUNG GUNS VARIANT BY AARON KUDER & JASON KEITH

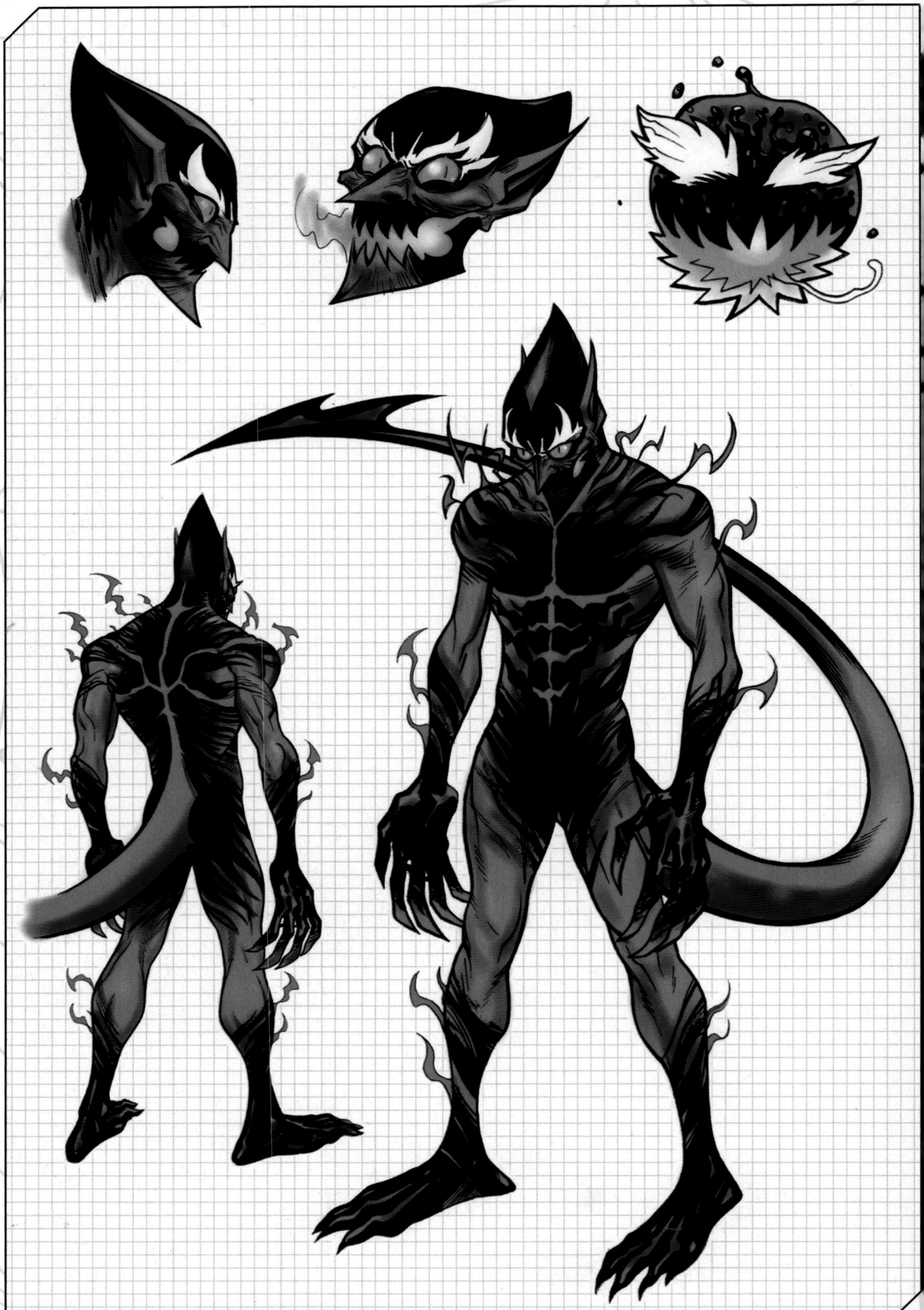

#797 DESIGN VARIANT BY **ED McGUINNESS**

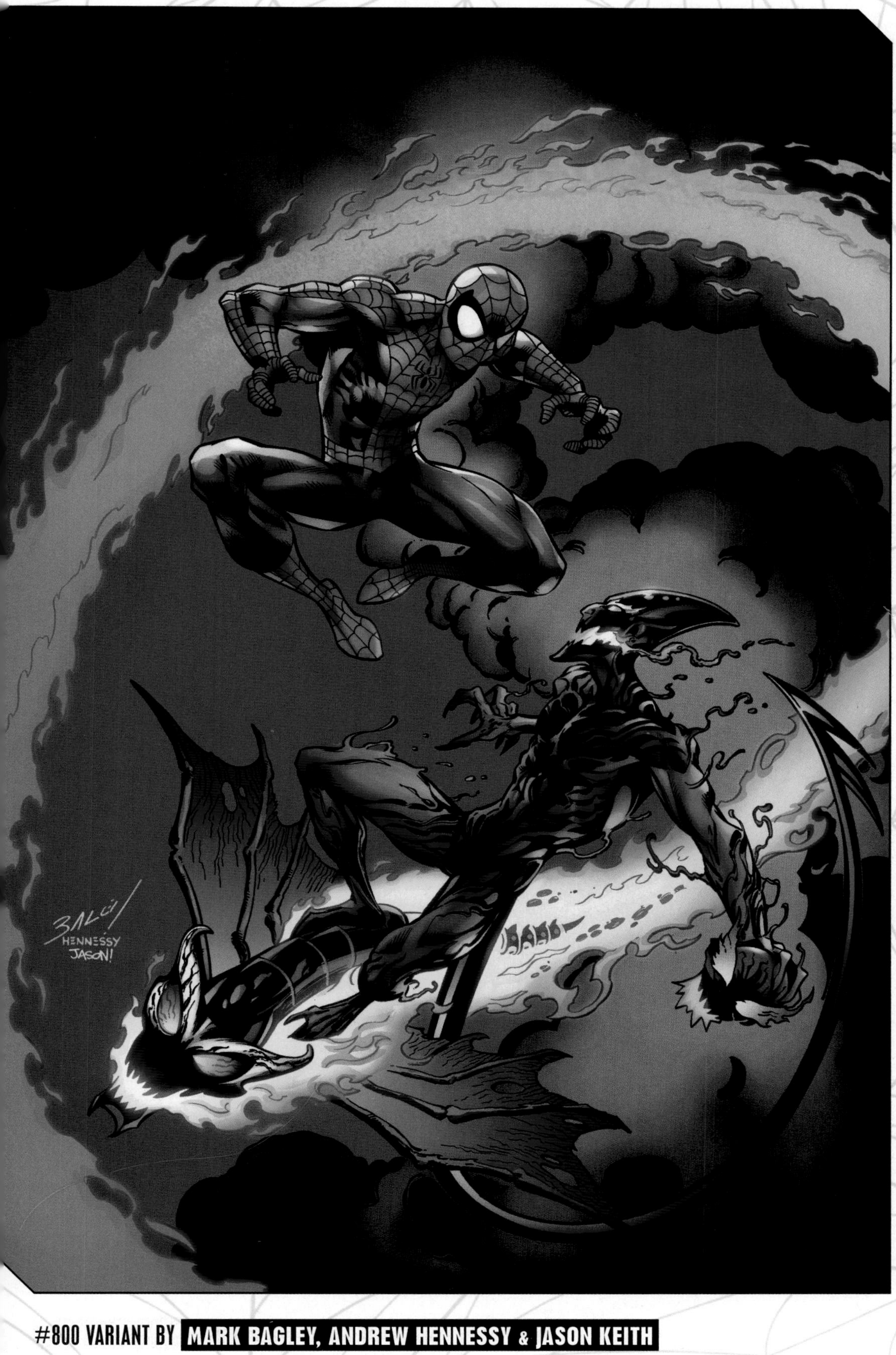
HENNESSY
JASON!

#800 VARIANT BY **MARK BAGLEY, ANDREW HENNESSY & JASON KEITH**

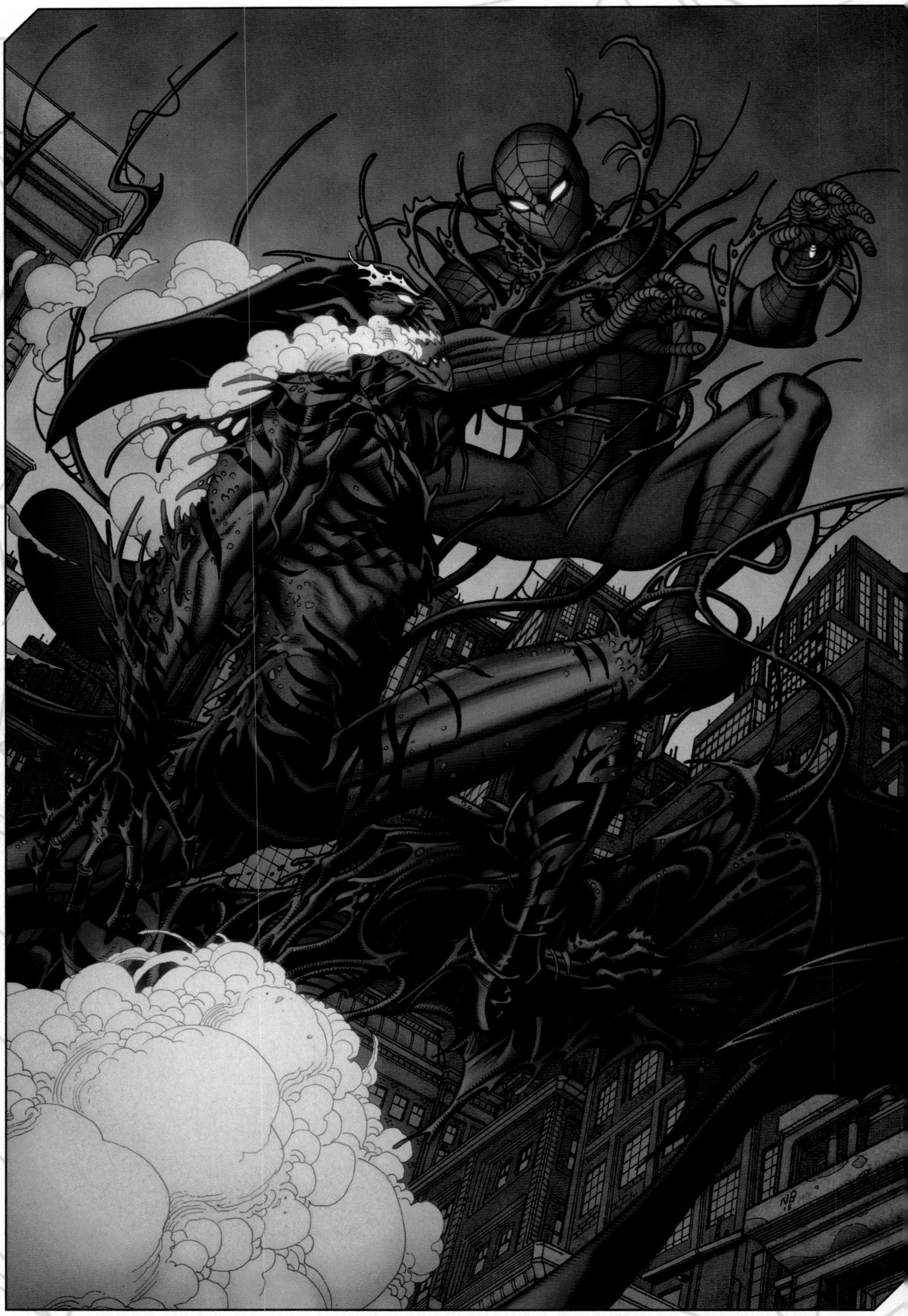

#800 VARIANT BY **NICK BRADSHAW & MORRY HOLLOWELL**

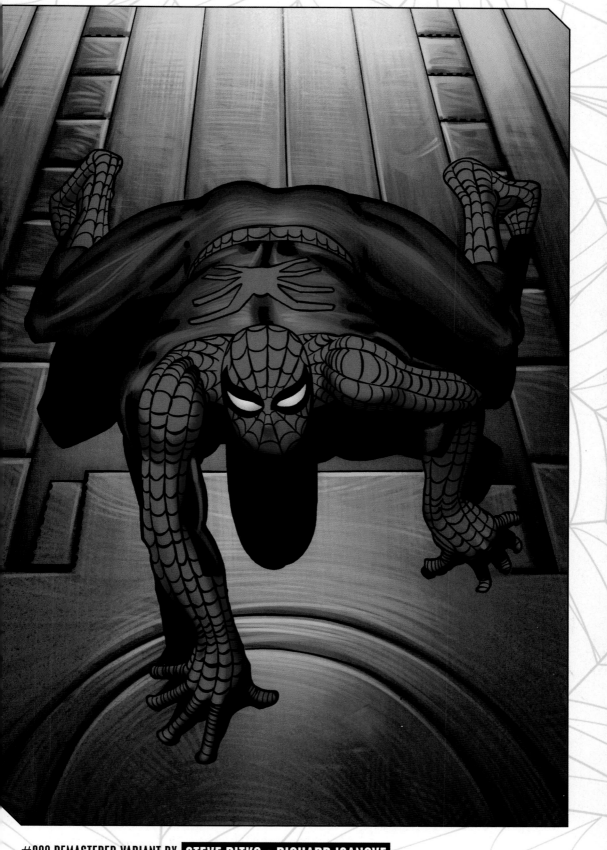

#800 REMASTERED VARIANT BY **STEVE DITKO & RICHARD ISANOVE**

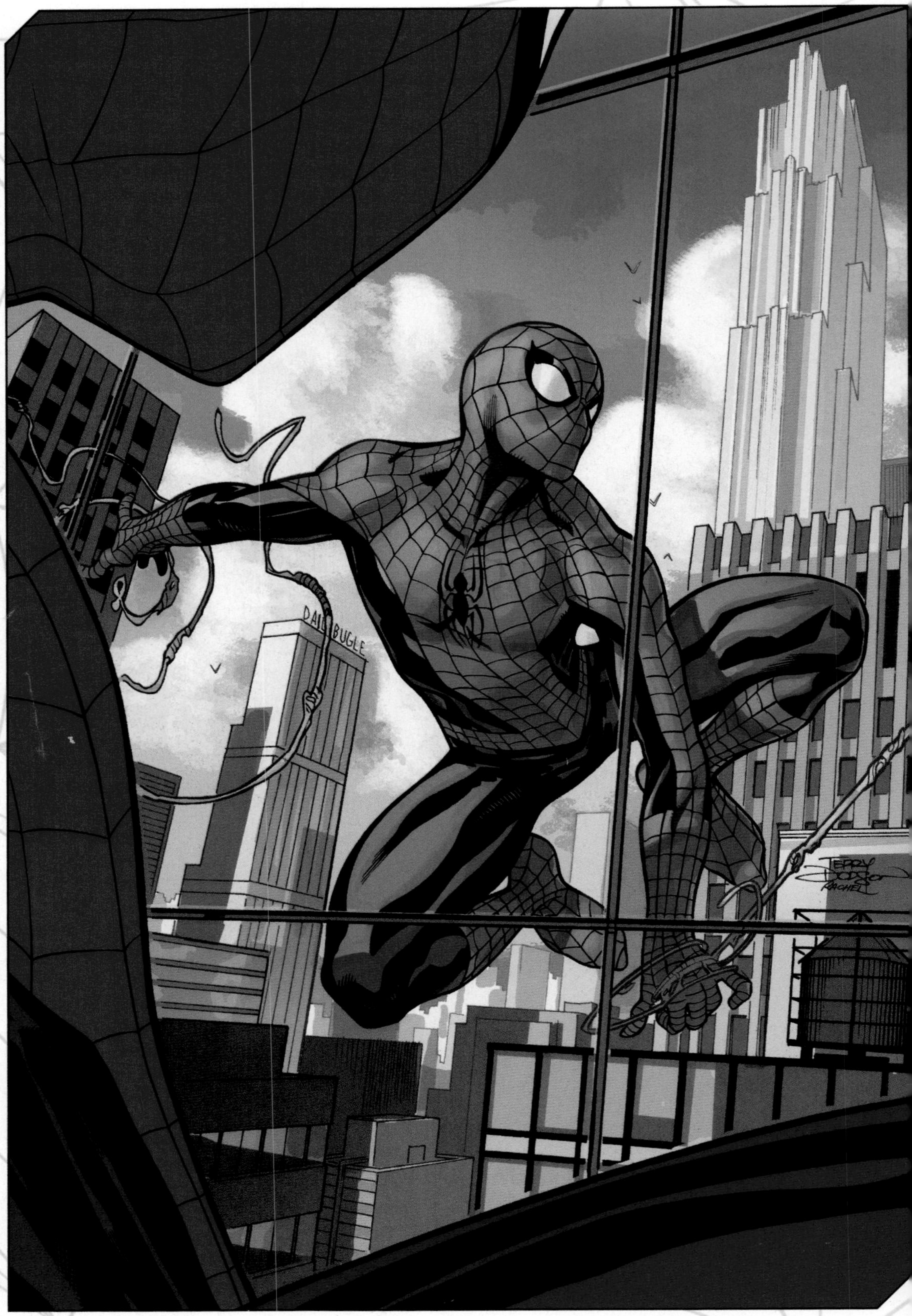
DAILY BUGLE

#800 VARIANT BY **TERRY DODSON & RACHEL DODSON**

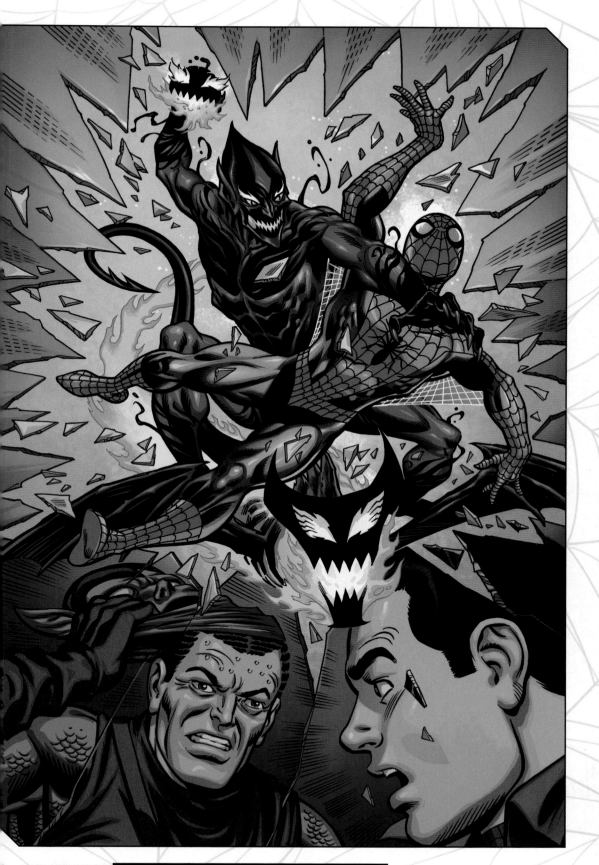

#800 VARIANT BY **RON FRENZ, BRETT BREEDING & DAVE McCAIG**

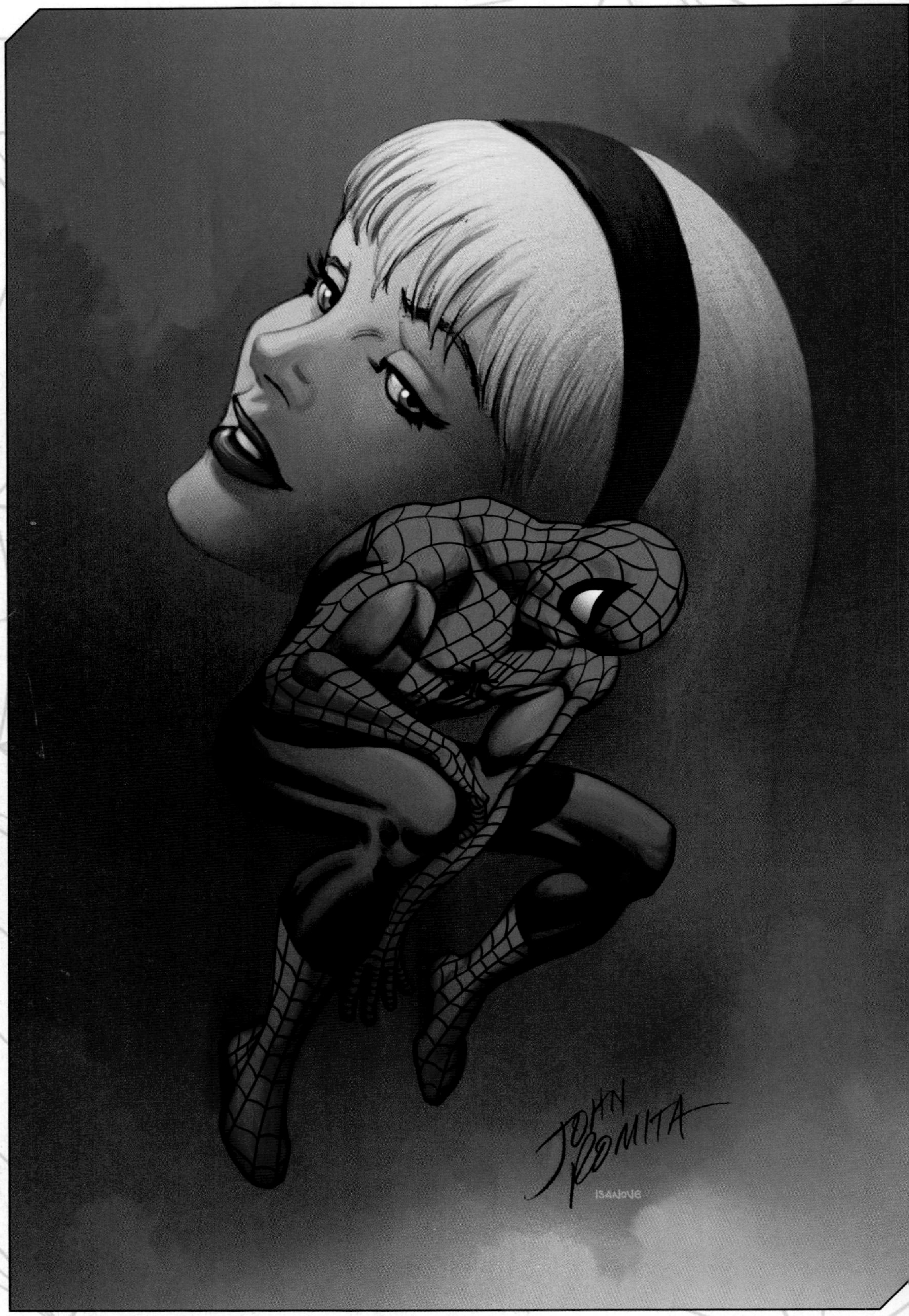
JOHN ROMITA
ISANOVE

#800 VARIANT BY JOHN ROMITA SR. & RICHARD ISANOVE

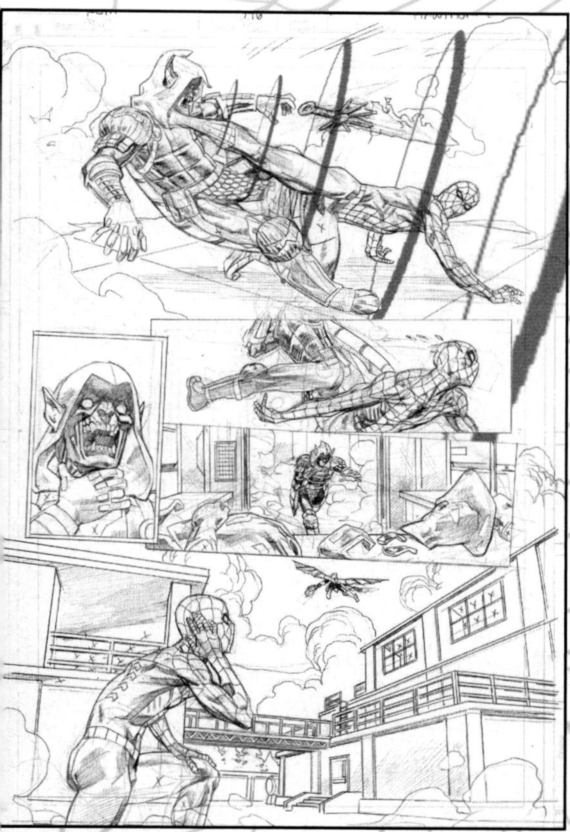

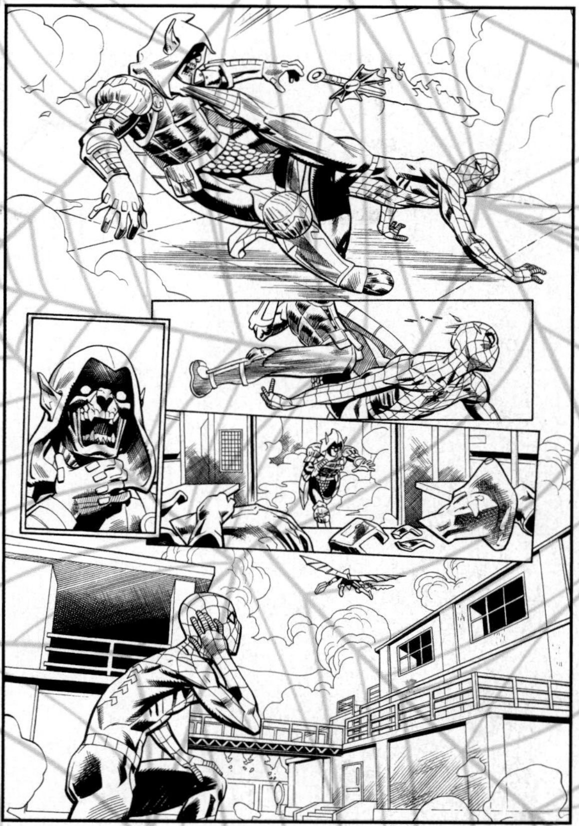

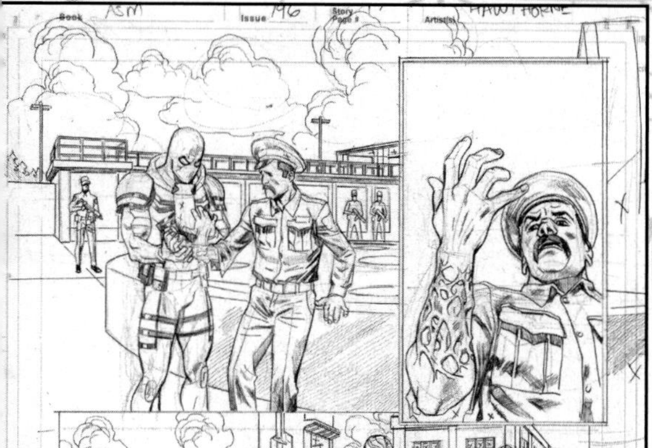

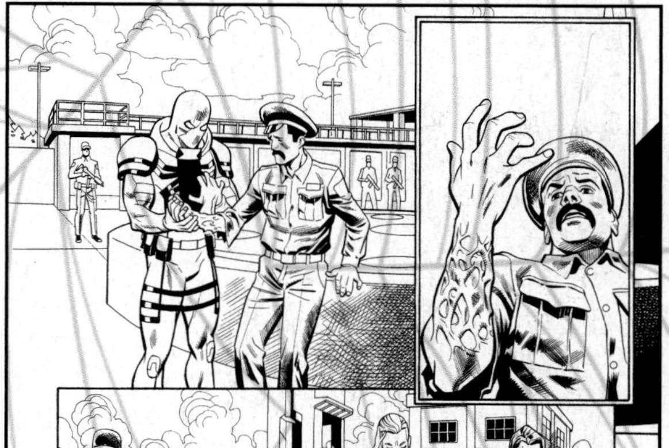

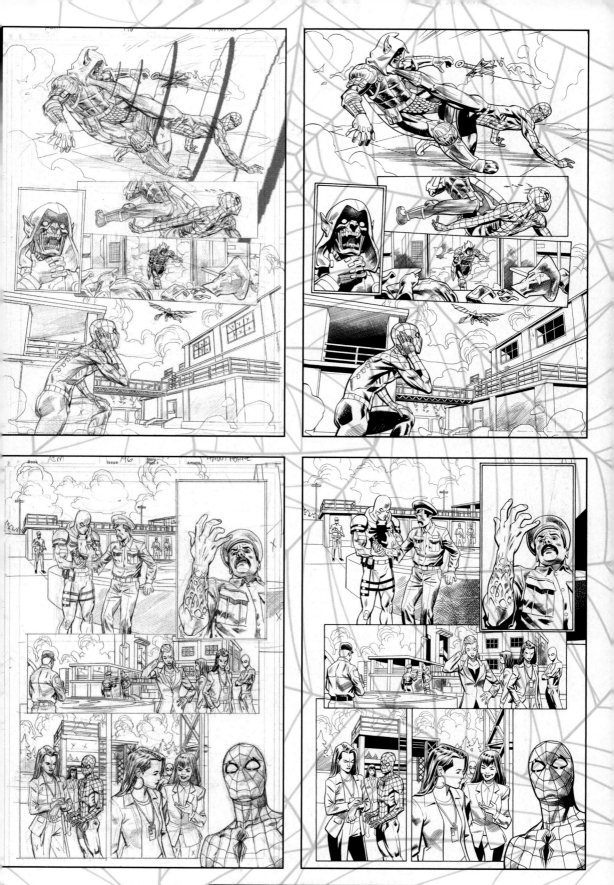

#796, PAGES 16-17 ART PROCESS BY **MIKE HAWTHORNE & TERRY PALLOT**

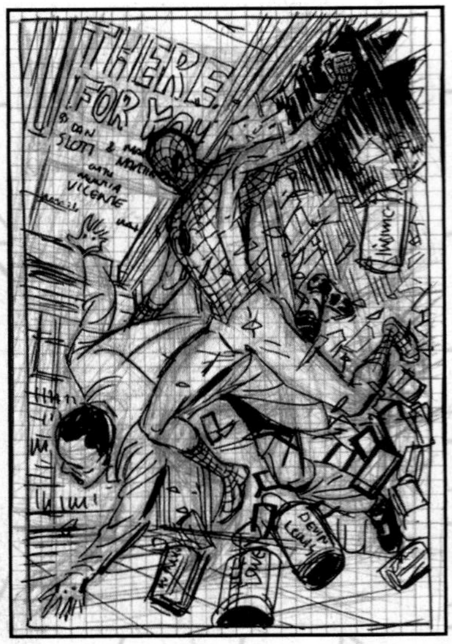
THERE FOR YOU

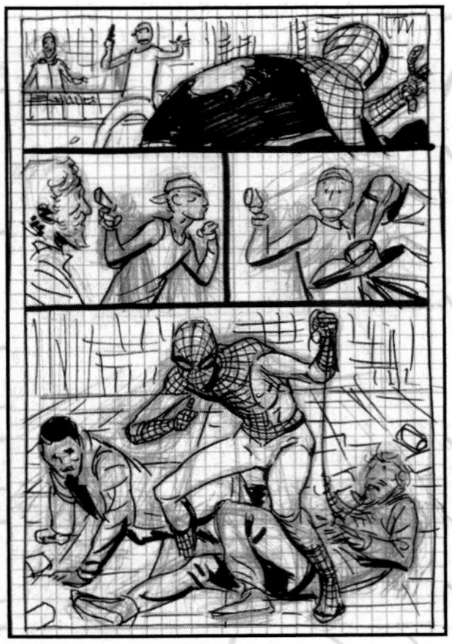

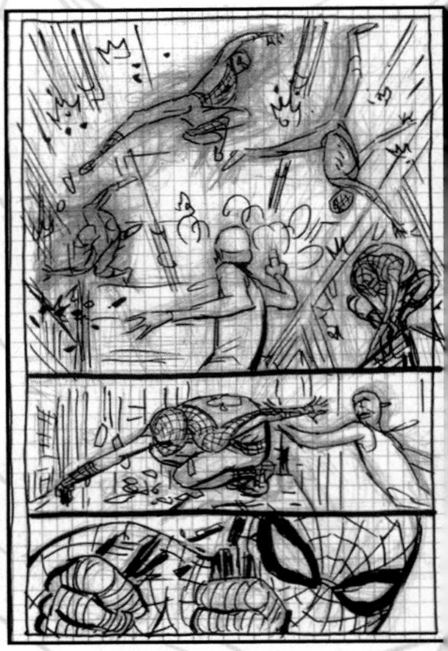

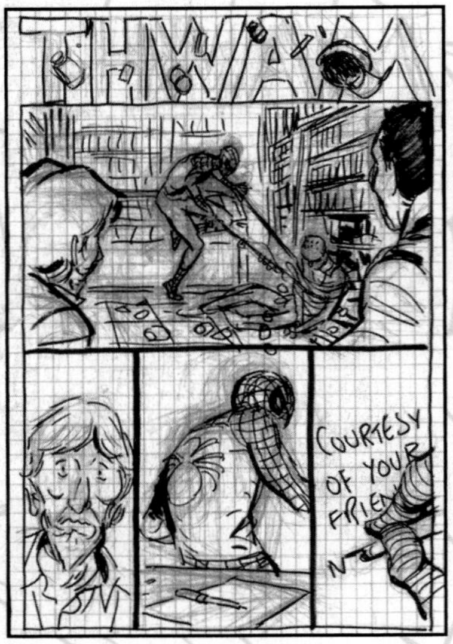
THWAM
COURTESY OF YOUR FRIEN

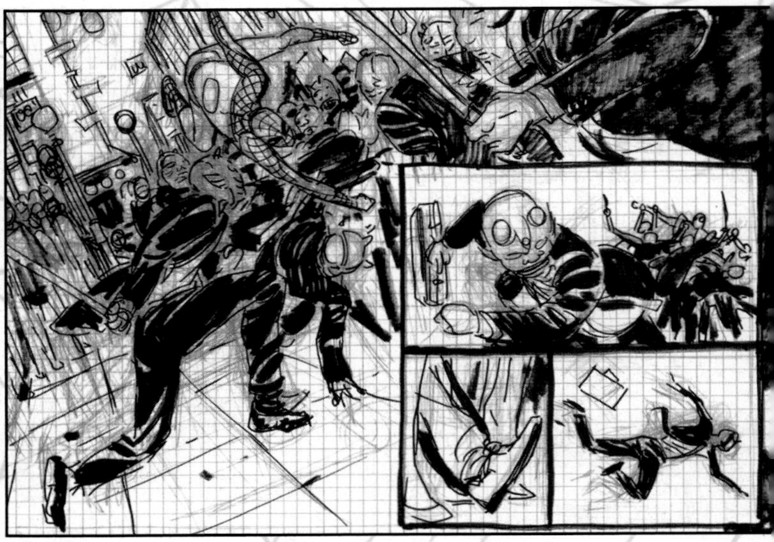

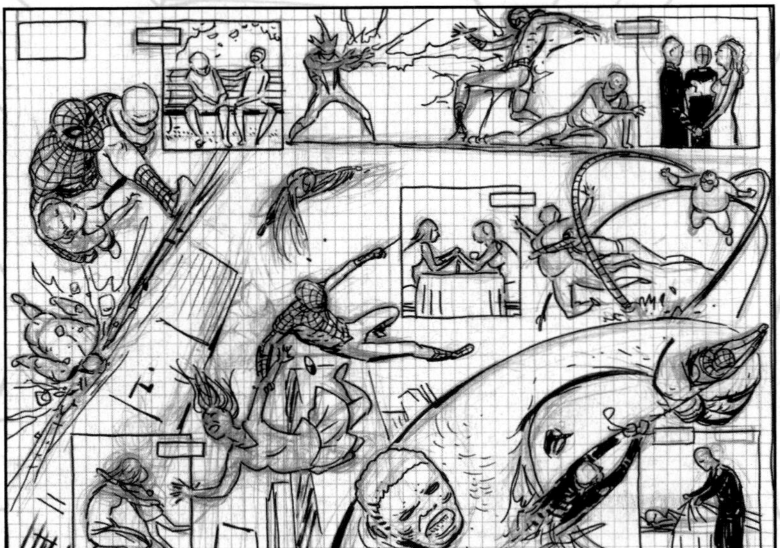

#801, PAGES 5-8, 12-13 & 17-18 LAYOUTS BY **MARCOS MARTIN**

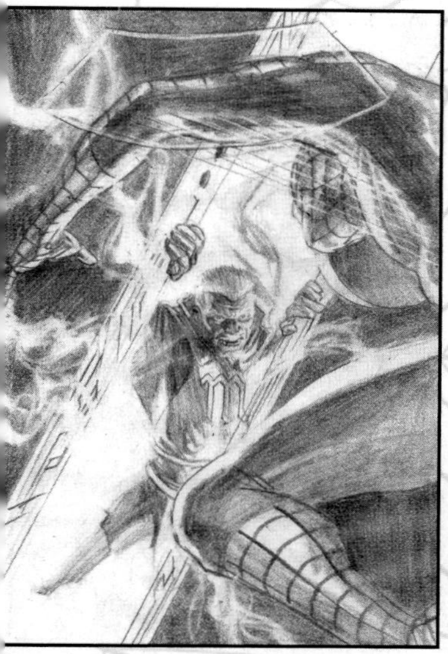
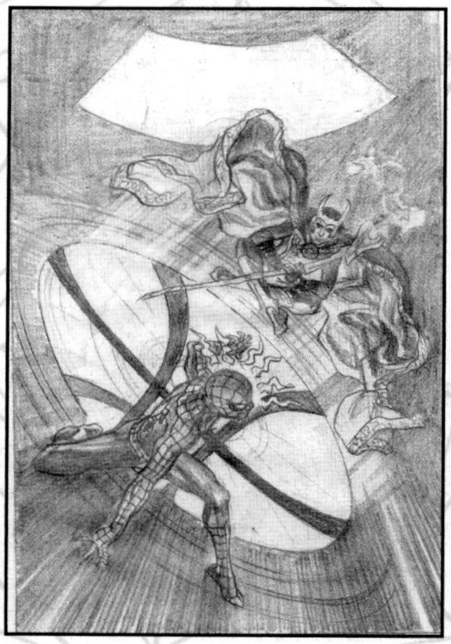
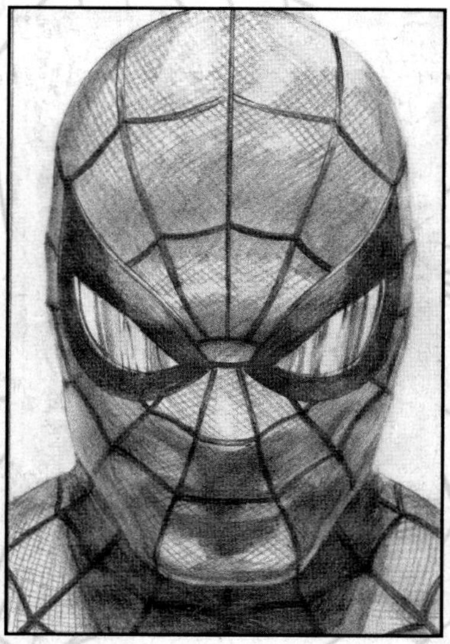
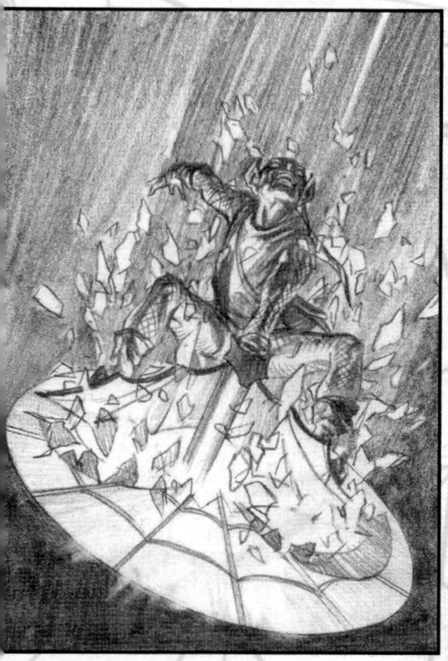
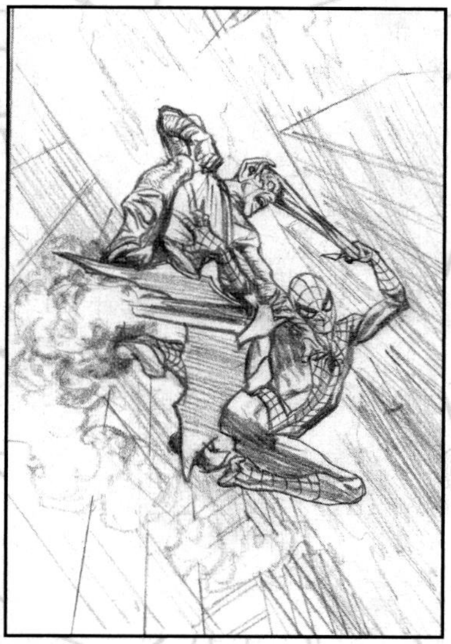
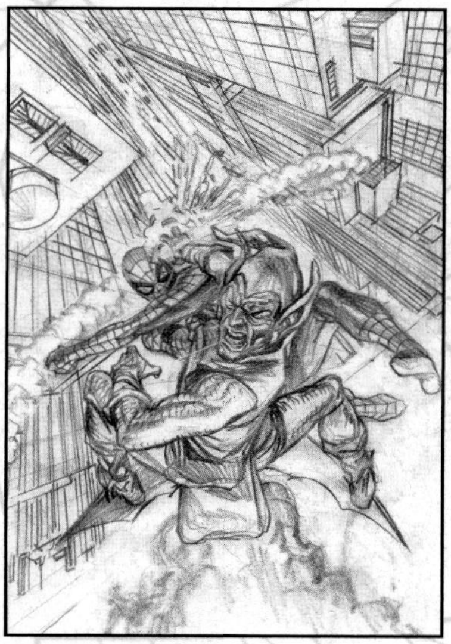
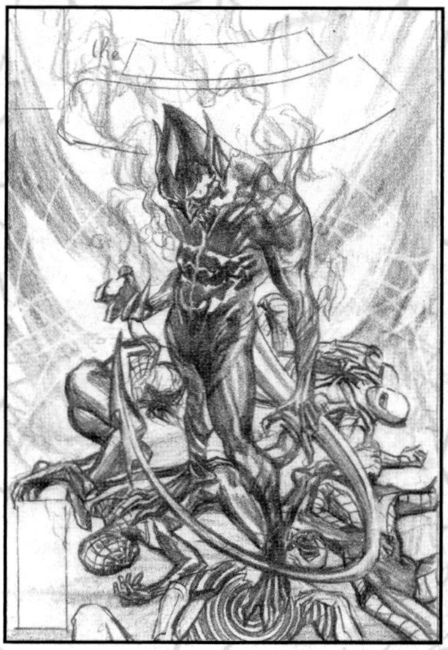
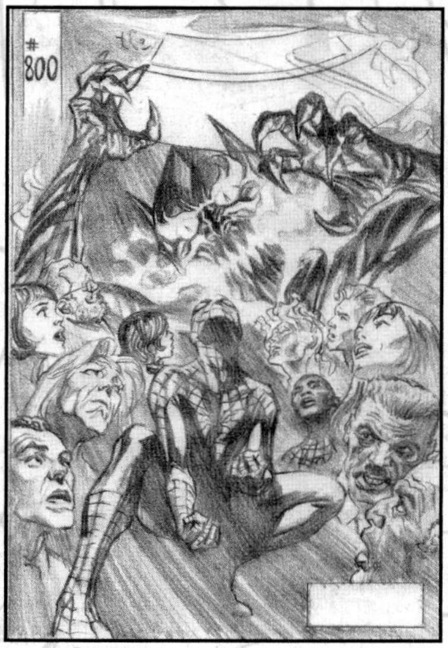
#800

#794-800 COVER SKETCHES BY **ALEX ROSS**

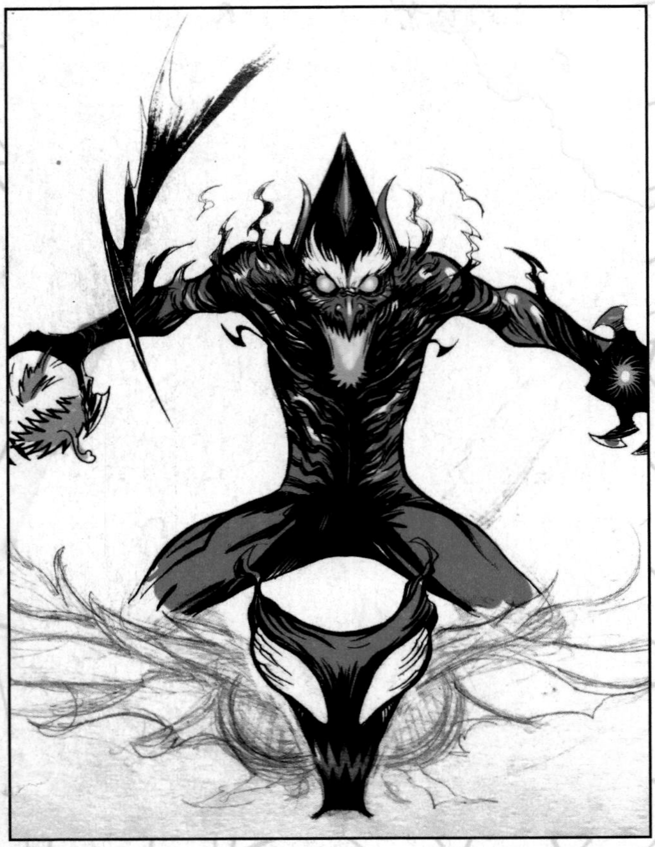

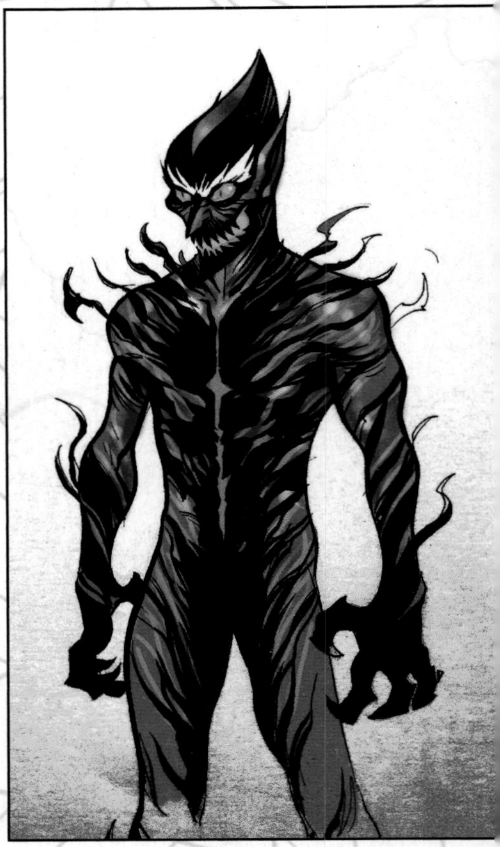

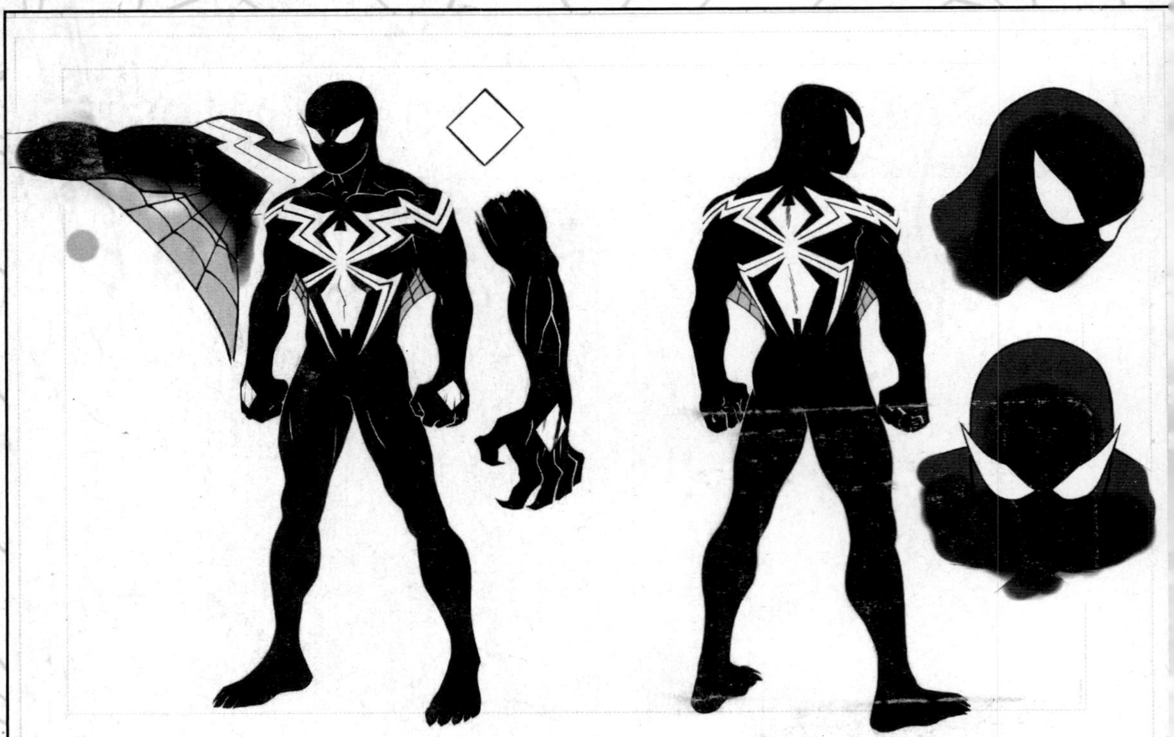

CHARACTER SKETCHES BY **ED McGUINNESS**